# The Aisle is Full of Noises

# THE AISLE is FULL of NOISES

A vivisection of the
live theatre

## MICHAEL COVENEY

NICK HERN
BOOKS
London

A Nick Hern Book

*The Aisle is Full of Noises* first published in 1994 by
Nick Hern Books Limited, 14 Larden Road, London W3 7ST

Copyright © 1994 by Michael Coveney

Michael Coveney has asserted his right to be identified as
the author of this work

Cover drawing of Michael Coveney © Antony Sher 1994

A CIP catalogue record for this book is available from
the British Library

ISBN 1 85459 231 9

Typeset by Country Setting, Woodchurch, Kent TN26 3TB
Printed and bound in Great Britain by
Biddles Ltd, Guildford and King's Lynn

*For Pamela Harris*
*in Stratford-upon-Avon*
*and Jovan Ćirilov*
*in Belgrade*

*Be not afeard; the isle is full of noises,*
*Sounds and sweet airs, that give delight, and hurt not.*

Caliban, *The Tempest*, Act 3, Scene 2

# CONTENTS

*Introduction*                                                          ix

## *January*
Cameron Mackintosh throws a party on the Titanic                          1
How I became a critic: the true story                                    7

## *February*
Critical awards and postcards from John Osborne                         15
French windows open on O'Neill: contemporary
    meaning in classics                             21
Black actors and the *Carousel* controversy                            26

## *March*
Fairy tales in New York                                                 31
From Antwerp and Sarajevo on Richard Eyre's birthday                   41

## *April*
Talking several shops with Andrew Lloyd Webber                         49
Radio waves, radio times                                               58
The observed of all Observers                                          62

## *May*
Violence, art and the new republicans                                  67
Festival fun from Glasgow to Montreal                                  75

## June

Bard and bar-room stories in Stratford-upon-Avon     85
Just another not very boring week                     93

## July

Running gags: to be fit, or not to be fat            111
Publicity angles and the hard sell                   118

## August

Not getting away from it all on holiday              123
Edinburgh strikes new blows for Europe               128

## September

Dashing to Dartington                                139
New home and new look for the Observer               144

## October

A day at the National with David Hare                149
Regional variations, Cardiff celebrations            156
Prince Charles cheers up at the Buck House buffet    164

## November

Standards high and low                               171
Meetings with famous directors, Part 1: Peter Brook  175
Meetings with famous directors, Part 2: Max Stafford-Clark  180

## December

Curtain calls and seasonal salvoes                   185
Ring out the old, ring in the new                    194

## Index                                             201

# INTRODUCTION

'TO TRAVEL hopefully is a better thing than to arrive', said Robert Louis Stevenson. I wanted to give an impression of the hopeful travelling, the nimbus of activity, endemic to a life of professional theatre-going, and also to develop some of the themes and issues, political, social and indeed autobiographical, that one never has room to write about in a review of the week's performances.

The idea was hatched during a chance encounter with Nick Hern on a train to Leeds, en route to see the West Yorkshire Playhouse's revival of Eugene O'Neill's *All God's Chillun' Got Wings*. Why not try and reflect the contemporary theatre through the working rhythms of a theatre critic in the form of a polemical calendar?

So this book is not a collection of reviews, nor is it strictly a diary. An anecdotal journal, perhaps. I aim to sink my dipstick in the oil of theatrical hurlyburly and take a reading. And, like an inquisitive geologist delving into a broken landscape, I hope to produce a miniature, but informative, version of the stratification.

I was following no exact precedents, though readers of James Agate's entertaining *Ego* volumes might accuse me of offering a less urbane (and hopefully less grandiose) modern equivalent. I enjoy reading Agate's criticisms enormously, and I hope it goes without saying that I relish and admire Kenneth Tynan above almost everyone else.

But I live a very different sort of life to Agate's, which was bound by the Café Royal, the Savage Club and the London concert halls; and also to Tynan's, which was rather high-flown, sybaritic, party-throwing, star-fucking. Like the character in a Jacobean tragedy, I was drawn arsy-versy into this business, from an unexpectant background, and if I am at all able to assess my own critical personality, I would say that I have never really grown out of my surprise and delight in discovering the theatre in my middle teens. The child was father to another child.

A capacity for enjoyment is as essential in a critic as a capacity for anger. 'Show me a critic without prejudices and I'll show you an arrested cretin', said George Jean Nathan, one of the American critics I most admire. The anger, I have learned, is the easy part. Without the enjoyment, the job is meaningless.

When my son Thomas was very small, he was asked what his father did for a living. 'He's a theatre cricket', he said. I like the mixed imagery of a lively, buzzing insect rubbing his hind legs together and of a batsman at the crease ducking and blocking and occasionally sweeping a ball to the boundary with the imperious confidence of getting something absolutely right, if only for a couple of seconds.

A few passages of this book appeared in a different form in the Observer during 1993. I am grateful to successive editors at the Observer, Donald Trelford and Jonathan Fenby, and to successive arts editors, Gillian Widdicombe and Lucy Tuck, for their encouragement in what has been a dramatic, and traumatic, year of change at the newspaper. Ownership moved from Lonrho to the Guardian, our offices from Battersea to Farringdon Road.

I am also grateful to Nick Hern for his editorial acumen and skilled interventions, and to the Theatrical Management Association for prompting me in the first place to crystallize my thoughts about our regional theatre in the year of the TMA's centenary. This anniversary coincided (cruel irony) with the most dangerous economic period its member theatres, and indeed all theatres, have endured since the subsidised repertory and fringe network was established a mere thirty years ago. If this volume does nothing else, I hope it indicates in some way the value of a cultural phenomenon that is being scandalously threatened by casual political incompetence and neglect.

*Michael Coveney*
*London, January 1994*

*The Aisle is Full of Noises*

# JANUARY

## *Cameron Mackintosh throws a party on the Titanic*

THERE IS no season to the British commercial theatre, but business is slowest in January and not even the pantomimes are up to much. The West End, as usual, is on the point of collapse, and the closure of several musicals in the first two weeks of the month fuels talk of wipe out. At the same time, Sir Andrew Lloyd Webber announces his new musical, *Sunset Boulevard*, for June, and Cameron Mackintosh and Sir Bernard Delfont throw open the doors of the refurbished Prince Edward Theatre in Soho, where the Gershwin musical *Crazy for You* will open in March.

So musicals go, and more musicals come. The launch party to celebrate the Prince Edward's refurbishment is an unusual occasion, especially during a recession. Mackintosh and Sir Bernard invite the journalists and producers in the auditorium to come up on to the stage; from here, the view of the reconstructed red plush interior and deco lighting is breathtaking. But nobody can applaud with a glass of champagne in one hand, so the response is rather peculiar and muted, like a small and creepy exhalation. As the gathering disperses through the auditorium, strewn through the stalls and scattered through the wonderful new bar, the drink flows and the canapés are passed around – large prawns with spicy sauces, little cheese pancakes, raw vegetables and tasty dips, sausages and devils on horseback. It becomes clear that Mackintosh is doing what he does almost as often and just as well as putting on a musical: throwing a party.

The last one of these I attended was at his house in Regent's Park, to celebrate his twenty-five years in showbusiness. Mackintosh has come a long way since managing the provincial tour of *Hair* and presenting a doomed stage version of *The Archers*. The touching thing about him is his loyalty to all the people who have known and helped him along the way over the years. In this, and in his capacity to enjoy his wealth with his friends and colleagues, he is quite different from his tortured contemporary in fame and fortune, Andrew Lloyd Webber. In his London garden on this 25th anniversary, dinner was served in the conservatory and an abutting marquee. Guests were seated at tables, and they ranged from his earliest collaborators such as the songwriters Tony Hatch and Jackie Trent right through to Christopher Biggins, Trevor Nunn and Nicholas Hytner. The food was magnificent. Several of us – Sheridan Morley, Ned Sherrin, Jack Tinker and I – had wound our separate ways from a revival of *The Sound of Music* at Sadler's Wells. I joined my wife at our allotted table. The other incumbents were Toby Rowland, the veteran producer and former sidekick of Binkie Beaumont in the post-War heyday of H M Tennent, and his elegant wife Millie; Eleanor Savaroni, the popular maîtresse of L'Escargot in Soho, who remembers feeding Cameron when he could hardly afford a meal, and her husband; and, alas, John Gale, the actor turned producer who made his fortune by presenting *No Sex, Please, We're British*. Gale was in a bad mood the minute he saw me. (He always puts me in mind of an old newspaper hoarding the day after a violent storm: 'Seven Die As Gale Rages'.) He loses no opportunity to tell critics how little they know and was soon laying in to me, presumably fired up by my bad notice of Christopher Fry's *Venus Observed* at Chichester, where he had resumed control that season after the unsavoury dismissal of Michael Rudman. I fought my corner but tried to neutralise the vulgarity of the noise he was now generating. Basically, Gale said critics know nothing about acting. He was an actor himself, once. I said that may well be so, but their job in the first place is to try and describe what the actor does, not understand how he does it. My reason for disliking Donald Sinden's Duke of Altair (the Olivier role in the Fry play) was that he came across as a dirty old man rather than, as would have been more appropriate, a moonstruck romancer. The situation became almost irredeemable when Gale's charming wife,

Listel, seated on my left, tried to calm him down with the result that he turned on her, too. There was nothing for it but to investigate the dessert situation and talk to Christopher Biggins. I didn't mind Gale wishing to have a punch-up. But he should have better manners than to start one at an occasion at which, for once, we were all equal guests in somebody else's house. The evening was badly marred.

Usually such encounters are not so unpleasant. A critic's victims have a perfect right to hit back and I am only surprised that they do not do so more often. Health-threatening physical encounters are curiously rare. Michael Billington was once cuffed around the head in the circle bar of the Royal Court by an aggrieved David Storey, and Steven Berkoff once issued a death threat to Nicholas de Jongh. I have received vile, hysterical letters from many eminent directors (interestingly, Peter Hall never once complains to a critic, nor thanks him; much the best policy, I always feel) and Michael Bogdanov has suggested I should never bother reviewing his work again after I said that his production of *The Tempest* was the worst show of the year. Juliet Stevenson once pinned me to the wall in the lion's den of the Dirty Duck, Stratford-upon-Avon, to protest, vehemently but rationally, against what I had said about her Cressida. The experience was chastening and informative. It did not change my mind completely about the interpretation, but the seriousness of her argument impressed me deeply.

Apropos of the foul Chichester notice that so upset John Gale, Ned Sherrin had hailed me with a cheery sneer earlier on that very same evening of the Mackintosh dinner party: 'Wrong again at Chichester, I see, young Coveney!'; feeling unjustifiably confident, I tossed back, 'I'm not paid to be right. I'm paid to be interesting'; I should have known better than to mess with Ned in the wit shop. He instantly replied, with a cackling bark, 'Oh dear, a failure on two counts, then.'

At the Prince Edward, for a bunch of has-beens and no-hopers, the leading lights of the Society of West End Theatre Managers are looking in surprisingly good order. Michael Codron, inscrutable and suave, is as impeccably turned out as ever. Michael White, who is producing *Crazy for You* in London, is sun-tanned and unexpectedly copper-coiffed after skiing in Colorado. The first of these near-legendary Michaels was instrumental in encouraging my career as a fledgling critic. The second, always pleasant up to a point, tried to have me sacked when I disliked one of his shows (the tiresomely jaunty, rocked-up *Pirates of Penzance*). John Gale sweeps imperiously around the stalls and any journalist talks to him at his or her peril. Old-timers Louis Benjamin, who used to run Stoll Moss before the group was bought out by Robert Holmes à Court, and Toby Rowland, gossip quietly while imbibing freely at the bar. Robert Fox, who is about to present Maggie Smith in *The Importance of Being Earnest*, tells me that his wife, Natasha Richardson, has enjoyed an unprecedented triumph in New York as O'Neill's Anna Christie. Equally sensational, says Fox, is Liam Neeson, the sexy hulk of an actor who is playing opposite her. I later discover that Neeson is also playing around opposite her, much to Robert's understandable dismay. David Land, who discovered Lloyd Webber and Tim Rice when he was working for Robert Stigwood, and who now owns and manages the delightful Theatre Royal in Brighton, greets me warmly, much to the disgust of Robert Fox: 'How can you hug a critic?' Fox snorts. David Land explodes in mirth and says 'It's all right, he's almost Jewish.' I say that it doesn't matter as I never review any of Land's shows these days, and I never feel I owe anything to someone who was, as Land was, a property speculator in Goodmayes, the grim neck of the East London woods where I spent my childhood. Harold Fielding, master of the charabanc trade and tireless admirer of Tommy Steele, appears to have stumbled on an inexhaustible elixir which makes him speak faster and funnier the older he becomes. Roger Filer, the bald accountant who likes magic tricks and now runs the Maybox consortium of theatres – the chief group of West End houses after Stoll Moss, which sacked Filer a few months ago – chats conspiratorially with a slim-line version of Duncan Weldon, the most touchingly star-struck of all West End producers. Filer tells me that *Crazy for You* will probably run for four years; Weldon invites me to lunch.

All of these agreeable fellows, with the single exception of Cameron Mackintosh himself, are helplessly presiding over the galloping demise of the West End as we know it. More than ever, the West End, if it is to survive at all, must turn to the subsidised sector for its 'product'. Its brand-name dramatists have decamped to the more cooperative and congenial climes of the fringe and the state houses: Harold Pinter has been reborn at the Almeida Theatre in Islington, Tom Stoppard relaunched at the National after an eight-year hiatus, David Hare ensconced at the same place, Peter Shaffer at the RSC; even Alan Ayckbourn now seems to shuttle exclusively between home base in Scarborough and the RNT's smaller venue, the Cottesloe. The writing was on the wall, of course, many years ago. These things do not just happen overnight. The current trough of creativity in the West End was inevitably predicated in the increasing costs of a labour intensive industry and the decline in the great tradition of patriarchal, commissioning producers (Beaumont, Henry Sherek, Stephen Mitchell, Jack Hylton and their final offspring, Peter Bridge and the Michaels Codron and White). The crunch came, I reckon, about 1973, ten years, according to Philip Larkin, after they invented sexual intercourse. Binkie Beaumont and Noël Coward died within a few weeks of each other, and Helen Montagu, the abrasive general manager of the Royal Court, was brought in by H M Tennent to see if the new wave of theatre writers could be turned into commercial successes. They could not; David Hare's *Knuckle,* a bizarre Chandleresque thriller, directed by Michael Blakemore and starring Edward Fox, was championed week in, week out by Harold Hobson in 1974 after it opened to otherwise lukewarm reviews. It flopped all the same. The problem – the unbridgeable chasm between intelligent new theatre writing on the fringe and the West End audience – was disguised for ten years or so by the continuing West End success, bolstered by the last generation of West End stars – Penelope Keith, Tom Courtenay, Alan Bates, Diana Rigg – of such superior boulevardiers as Alan Ayckbourn, Alan Bennett, Michael Frayn and Simon Gray. Finally, in 1992, Alec Guinness – who had graced the plays of Bennett and Gray – declared that he would no longer play for audiences of uncomprehending Japanese tourists on Shaftesbury Avenue.

Perhaps the answer might lie with the alternative comedians? The West End greedily invited the contributions of Ben Elton, Rik

Mayall, Sandi Toksvig and Stephen Fry. The latter made a huge amount of money by sharpening up the libretto of *Me and My Girl*, the 'Lambeth Walk' musical starring, in the first place, Robert Lindsay and Emma Thompson, which ran for seven years and is still touring. Elton's scrappy comedies were popular but aberrant. Sandi Toksvig's *Pocket Dream*, a lively overhaul of Shakespeare's comedy which made no claims to theatrical seriousness, failed to pull in the Channel Four 'Whose Life Is It Anyway?' audience. And Rik Mayall made a creditable stab at a Shaftesbury Avenue *Waiting for Godot* which pleased a few enthusiasts (myself included) but which confused his fans and did not set box office bells ringing for too long. It seemed unlikely that this cynical tactic of attempted popularity transference from small screen to large stage would save the producers' bacon.

At a time of creative impasse, some producers have taken to ringing up critics at home the moment they return from a visit to the regions. Will that latest production in Manchester or Glasgow fit the bill in London? They are oblivious, it seems, to the great attraction of reviewing shows out of town, indeed of reviewing anything: the question of whether or not there are any commercial legs in this or that performance is simply not my problem. A critic's duty is to create some coherent commentary on the work itself, not to assess its impact at the box office. Milton Shulman, the self-confessed tipster in the wide-brimmed fedora – am I the only person to have noted the physical similarity between Milton in his later years on the beat and the compact, streetwise and bruising film persona of Danny de Vito? – always wanted to back winners. To his credit, he backed the wrong horse more often at the bookmakers than he did in the West End. But he signally failed to differentiate between what might be popular and what might be of lasting merit, setting out his stall in no uncertain terms against the claims on his serious attention of every major post-War theatrical talent from Brecht and Beckett to Pinter, Osborne, Wesker, Orton, Brenton, Hare, Barker and Edward Bond.

## *How I became a critic: the true story*

NEWS THIS MONTH that Kevin Henriques, longstanding arts page sub-editor on the Financial Times, is retiring, prompts thoughts of how I arrived in this business in the first place. My first professional notice was delivered for the FT in February 1972. Freddie Young, the arts editor, had rung me at home to ask if I could trot along to the Round House in Chalk Farm to see a show called *Lila, the Divine Game* featuring the Bauls of Bengal. I could. Had I ever written an overnight notice? No. Had I ever written straight on to a typewriter? No. Never mind, said Freddie, I was to report to the side entrance of Bracken House, the FT's office in the shadow of St Paul's Cathedral, after the show. If I ascended to the second floor and sought out a chap called Kevin Henriques, who normally lurked in a mauve cardigan behind a pillar, I would be given some paper, shown to a typewriter and told what to do. Five or six short paragraphs, each one on a separate sheet of self-triplicating paper: one copy for Kevin to edit and give to the printers in the basement, who would set my pearls of wisdom in hot metal and run them off in a made-up page for the last London editions the next morning, one for his emergency use, one more for me to keep, file and fret over into the small hours. The notice appeared, miraculously I thought, if rather torrid in its expressions of enthusiasm, and my reviewing career was launched. I would have to get out of that ghastly teaching job in Canning Town.

How had all this happened? On a family holiday to the Netherlands in the early 1960s, our suitcases had been left out in a torrential downpour at Rotterdam. Our clothes were soaked. We were damp for the whole holiday, as it never stopped raining. One thing led to another and the upshot of it all was that, by the time we returned to England after an uncomfortable crossing from the Hook of Holland to Harwich, my younger brother, Martin, currently Philip Hedley's press officer at the Theatre Royal, Stratford East, had contracted pneumonia and had become delirious. He proceeded to remain very ill indeed for several weeks. As part of his recuperation, a doctor suggested to my parents that his days in bed might be relieved if he developed a concentrated reading habit. A pile of books and magazines was provided by my father, a clerical officer in the shipping firm which had in part subsidised our fateful holiday to Holland; it contained a couple of theatrical magazines, Plays and Players and the now defunct Theatre World. To these, and their monthly progeny, Martin became addicted. At this stage I was only interested in playing football. When he recovered, his Pauline conversion demanded satiation at source, so theatre outings to Stratford-upon-Avon and the West End became part of our domestic routine. Soon, Martin and I were travelling up to town on the Liverpool Street line from Essex and charging around the London theatres, collecting handbills, sometimes autographs, and seeing, if possible, three plays on a single Saturday. As brothers, we were virtually inseparable; together, we became hooked on theatre.

We joined a local amateur theatre company, the Renegades; we acted, painted scenery, tore tickets and even wrote reviews. The company was run from the rehearsal-cum-living room of James Cooper, a former South Coast dancer and War-time stage manager for Noël Coward who had modelled his entire persona on an imitative amalgam of the three theatrical figures he most admired: Coward, Olivier and Danny Kaye. This was years before anyone, least of all Donald Spoto, had dreamed of imputing any sexual camaraderie between two of those three titans, though troilist imaginings do not now seem too far fetched; in some curious way, Jimmie Cooper, whose father was a brush salesman from Barking, could be said to have been a suburban reincarnation by osmosis of all three. He used to sail up and down the Cranbrook Road in grey flannels, blue barathea blazer and silk cravat like some superannuated chinless wonder who had been magically preserved in a pair of French windows in a 1950s Loamshire comedy ('Act Two. The following Sunday; the sunlit drawing room before luncheon').

He chain-smoked Perfectos cigarettes, was riddled with stomach ulcers and died after a rapid decline in his stage authority, and powers of memory, which necessitated the posting or glueing of various textual guidelines and aides-memoire around the set, on his cuffs, in cupboards and wardrobes. Thus insured, Jimmie could produce the missing line like a trump card, as a piece of 'business', with the effect, so polished was his technique, of making any other actor on the stage look like an idiot while he sailed on to the next crisis of amnesia.

The Renegades met each Monday night in Jimmie's head-quarters, 'The Stables', in a mews alley next to the rear entrance of Ilford train station. It was obligatory, once a month, for any Renegade who had not appeared in the last production to provide a written review and read it out there and then. Friendships turned instantly to dust. The most robust critic was the company's front of house manager, a milkman glorying in the name of Blagdon Mansfield, who was transformed once a month into an unlikely combination of Phineas T Barnum and James Agate. He would man the auditorium in his black tuxedo to discharge his 'Roll up, roll up' duties, cheerfully consigning the Ilford faithful to another dollop of Philip King, Rattigan or Agatha Christie, as a masochistic prelude to demolishing the whole exercise in front of its perpet-rators the following Monday in a series of brutally frank and unflattering assessments: 'Margo Kenrick did not quite get to grips with the housekeeper; Lila Myra needed to speak up more in the graveyard scene.' But his biggest blows were reserved for James Cooper himself: 'Jimmie Cooper's characterisation as the old grandfather was a bit corny.' 'Jimmie Cooper laid it on a bit thick as the vicar in the last act.' Or 'Jimmie Cooper may have been a year or two too old for a lover boy, but there was no need to reveal himself quite so brazenly in those black tights.' Jimmie would lie back on his chaise longue, clutching at his ulcer-ridden stomach and sipping his milky coffee, and disdainfully remind Blagdon Mansfield that he knew not of what he spoke and that he was, anyway, a relative newcomer to the theatre business, with no pro-fessional qualifications whatsoever. Cooper, after all, had been des-cribed by the Ilford Recorder as 'the powerhouse and inspiration of

Ilford's theatre,' and his performance as Hamlet at the Town Hall in 1948, in the same year as Paul Scofield's and Robert Helpmann's alternating princes at Stratford-upon-Avon, had been thus noticed in the News Chronicle by Alan 'Jock' Dent, Agate's amanuensis and friend: 'By no means the worst Hamlet I have seen this year: a worthy pioneer!'

I learnt in the best possible way to say what I thought to the faces of those I was reviewing, though I have obliterated from my memory every word I wrote and uttered at that stage of my fledgling career. Attacks on my own Renegades performances were negligible because the impact I made as a performer was exactly that, though I remember being reasonably proud of a quivering interpretation of the youngest soldier, Private Whitaker, in *The Long and the Short and the Tall.* Martin was always cast as the young schoolboy whenever one was needed, and I chugged along happily enough in his wake, quietly helping out, playing the piano for Jimmie's music hall programmes, and increasingly concentrating on my school work. Jimmie's pantomimes were always first class. Martin and I played footmen in the ballroom scene of *Cinderella* which was graced by a bevy of young girls from the local Betty Finch Stage School. One of them, Liz Robertson, a policeman's daughter from Grove Road, Chadwell Heath, was an undoubted star even then, and it was an intense adolescent pleasure to watch her from the back of the stage each night for three weeks, thrice on Saturdays. She later burst through the Ilford bubble to join Dougie Squires's Young Generation on the first steps to a distinguished solo career and marriage to Alan Jay Lerner.

Then at Oxford, I continued to review in the university papers while spending most of my mornings in the Oxford Playhouse coffee bar and most of my afternoons rehearsing with the college and university dramatic societies. I choreographed Victorian pantomime. I produced the unfunniest revue ever seen in Oxford, with melodic music by Nigel Osborne (this was before the now Professor of Music at Edinburgh University fell under the baleful influence, and indeed tuition, of Penderecki and Lutoslawksi), witty lyrics by Chris Stuart, now the Radio Two 'easy listening' disc jockey, and a title, 'Trip no further,' chosen in ironic honour of the Playhouse administrator and licensee, Elizabeth Sweeting ('Trip no further, pretty sweeting'), who had severely disapproved of the Experimental Theatre Club's previous annual revue, a brilliant, savage and gory narrative concoction by my revered senior contemporary, Nigel Williams.

Finally, buoyed by the brilliantly perceptive (ie, generally favourable) notices in The Times (by the late Jeremy Rundall) and the university magazine Isis (by Anthony Holden) of my OUDS production of Arthur Miller's *A View from the Bridge*, I applied, along with a thousand other budding Peter Brooks and Trevor Nunns, for the trainee director scheme sponsored by Thames Television. The field of applicants had been narrowed to six, three of whom were to be attached to regional theatres in Glasgow (where Giles Havergal and Philip Prowse were just starting up at the Citizens), Birmingham (the Rep under Michael Simpson), and Leatherhead (the Thorndike, where Hazel Vincent Wallace and her redoubtable chairman, Greville Poke, reigned supreme), and a fourth to Toby Robertson's touring Prospect Theatre Company. The judging panel comprised the artistic directors – Havergal, Simpson, Vincent Wallace and Robertson – along with a Thames Television representative, the producer Michael Codron and the critic B A ('Freddie') Young of the Financial Times. They interviewed each of us in turn after considering our written applications, which were bolstered with two reviews of plays we had lately seen. My chosen targets – and I wrote with noisy, destructive passion about both of them – were the nude revue *Oh! Calcutta!*, which I had seen on a visit to New York as a fairy (Cobweb, actually) in the Oxford and Cambridge Shakespeare Company's production of *A Midsummer Night's Dream*; and Edward Albee's *Tiny Alice*, directed with Gothic splendour and a crack cast (David Warner, Irene Worth, Ray McAnally) by Peter Hall for the RSC at the Aldwych. After I left the room, it is alleged that Havergal and Codron turned to Freddie Young and said, 'We don't want him; you do!'

The other finalists were Keith Hack, brilliant and erudite, with experience even then of working at the Berliner Ensemble, who went to Glasgow; Dusty Hughes, the playwright and director, appointed to Birmingham; Patrick Lau, to Leatherheard; Kenny MacBain, who joined Prospect (and died tragically young a few years ago after making his name as a gifted television director of the *Grange Hill* classroom series and *Inspector Morse*) . . . and Mike Bradwell. Bradwell and I were the quality rejects. He went off to found Hull Truck. I graduated from Oxford in 1970 and took a teaching job supplemented with bits of piano playing in restaurants, script reading and stage-management at the Royal Court, and the occasional contribution to Plays and Players.

Some time in early 1971 I was unpaid musical director on a 'Sunday night without decor' production at the Royal Court of a trenchant office satire *The Backroom Boys* by the Australian playwright, Alexander Buzo. Nigel Osborne, whom I had persuaded to write a score, and another Oxford musician friend, the percussionist John Toll, joined me in the pit; in the interval, Freddie Young popped his head over the rail to say hello and asked if I was still interested in writing theatre notices. I said yes. A further year elapsed before the call came to review the Bauls of Bengal.

In those days the FT had three theatre critics: Freddie (who had succeeded T C Worsley in 1964), the former theatre director Garry O'Connor, and a changeable third hand charged with reporting the newly burgeoning fringe and lunchtime scene in London. Freddie installed me in this latter capacity, and I was soon having trouble getting back to my teaching duties in Canning Town after having to attend a lunchtime premiere in the Almost Free in Rupert Street, or the Act Inn round the corner in Brewer Street (where I confidently predicted that an actor called Jeremy Irons had very little chance of achieving any success). I exchanged teaching for upping my contributions to Plays and Players, where I was eventually appointed assistant editor by Peter Ansorge (now commissioning editor of drama series at Channel Four) in the spring of 1973.

Kevin's early retirement from the FT, happily embraced for the greater good of concentrating on his cricket-watching and his jazz, marks the end of an era in more ways than one. For the informed and enthusiastic arts sub is an essential ally in the business of overnight reviewing. And overnight reviewing is rapidly, and regrettably, becoming a thing of the past owing to a combination of factors: earlier deadlines dictated by the new technology; the reluctance of editors to carry the cost of changing a page where it is thought to be not strictly necessary; and the refusal of arts editors and critics themselves to treat first nights as news.

They do treat them as news, of course, the moment they are confronted with an Andrew Lloyd Webber musical or a Tom Stoppard comedy. It was a great boost to the theatre – in terms of prestige and box office realities – when all first nights, from Shaftesbury Avenue and the National to the Bush, were reviewed as a matter of course in the next morning's London editions. But now those notices trickle through over several days, and are invariably downpaged, without illustration, beneath the rising tide of routine interviews and puffing previews. As a result, the amount of theatre work actually reviewed has diminished; in this way, the print media have, in my view, reneged on their responsibilities and thrown away a large part of their influence.

You are more likely to read in a daily broadsheet a full-length feature about backstage conditions in the Barbican, or an ego-massaging interview with a leading lady, than you are any piercing jeremiad about the Royal Shakespeare Company's lack of a new writing policy, let alone a full-length, fully illustrated descriptive account of last's night's opening. The work itself is disappearing in a welter of PR-led ballyhoo, and the prime cause is the abrogation of the daily newspaper critic's responsibility to deliver last night's news.

In the national daily Press, Jack Tinker of the Daily Mail alone maintains the old standard, which is why he is the most influential critic in what used to be known as Fleet Street. On the FT, we not only covered last night's London openings, but we made it our business to deliver, on a properly organised and systematic basis, reviews of the most important openings around the regions and in Europe. One of the saddest evolutions in my time at the FT was the betrayal of the objective, scholarly arts page standards set by the newspaper's remarkable chairman Lord Drogheda ('Here is young Coveney,' he used to say at the annual contributors' party in his house in Lord North Street, with an airy wave of his elegant right arm; 'he writes about the sort of plays nobody wants to go and see'). Although the authority of that newspaper's arts coverage has not been entirely undone in recent years, there is a pervasive feeling among the senior executives that certain areas of its coverage, certainly in the theatre, are best dealt with by non-specialists. The aim now is not to discuss the latest new work or innovation, but to wave the middle-brow flag in simple Janet and John language fully comprehensible to the mousey, middle-class wives of the editorial hierarchy.

# FEBRUARY

## *Critical awards*
## *and postcards from John Osborne*

THE FOURTH annual London Critics' Awards ceremony is held in the Theatre Museum, Covent Garden. All slightly embarrassing, really. People who give awards draw attention to themselves. In the case of a newspaper, like the Evening Standard, or an organisation in search of publicity, like the Prudential or the Society of West End Theatre, the harmless fun can be beneficial to all concerned and a reasonable excuse for a party. But the impoverished Critics' Circle is hardly an institution which the nation might want to respect, let alone support; and a few canapés washed down with cheap wine and orange juice hardly fuel or presage one of the great showbusiness gatherings of the year.

The business of awards has got out of hand. Nowadays they even give them to critics. And in New York, contrary to Sibelius's confident prediction that no-one would ever build a monument to a critic, they re-name theatres in our honour (the Walter Kerr, the Brooks Atkinson), which I find frankly creepy. It won't happen here. Can you imagine the Hobson Hippodrome, the Tinker Tivoli or the Morley Music Hall on Billington Boulevard?

The nation did, however, somewhat belatedly, pay tribute to Harold Hobson last November in the actors' church of St Paul's, Covent Garden. The Sunday Times, where Hobson worked from 1947 until 1976, had not exactly rushed to celebrate his memory. He died in a nursing home, alone and incapacitated, predeceased by his first wife, the devoted Elizabeth, and indeed also by his second. His old friend and regular first night companion, the actors' agent and producer Richard Jackson, organised the memorial.

Peter Hall recalled Hobson's enthusiasm and his perception. Harold Pinter frankly declared that Hobson's review of *The Birthday Party* in 1958, when all other critics had damned it, encouraged him to carry on writing. Paul Eddington read from Hobson's autobiography. Maria Friedman sang, superbly, from one of his favourite musicals, *Irma la Douce*. And Michael Billington astutely remarked that the best criticism was a form of autobiography, and that Hobson had supplied a new chapter each week for almost thirty years.

The characteristic sound of a Sunday morning was once said by Penelope Gilliatt to be that of Harold Hobson barking up the wrong tree. For every Beckett and Pinter there was an overpraised nonentity or Oxonian, most famously the St Peter's College don, Francis Warner, whose pretentious little plays, with nude women contorted on lavatory seats, Hobson invariably championed. But he stuck to his guns, and he never flinched from finding mystical significance and religious truth in the thrillers of Agatha Christie or the comedies of William Douglas Home.

Some years ago, when the Londoner Clive Barnes, who had become drama critic on the New York Times, was honoured with a CBE, Alan Bennett said that this was like giving Goebbels the DSO for his contribution to the war effort. And it was Christopher Hampton, on television, who memorably remarked, when asked what he thought about critics, that you may as well ask a lamp-post what it thought about dogs. Critics are best kept in their place, and the whole attraction of the job, surely, is that it carries no status or ticket to High Tables. Mavericks unite, you have no reputation to win, lose, or promulgate.

Critics should confine themselves to dishing out awards, not receiving them, and the most useful award a critic can give is a colourful, well-argued and enthusiastic notice. For many years the London Critics' Awards were collated and published by the theatrical monthly, Plays and Players, which I edited in the middle 1970s. Each January issue would appear before Christmas with a full list of how the critics had voted and a summarising article of the whys and wherefores, the haves, have-nots and near-missers. It was good for the small circulation, fun to read and unconfined to the metropolitan menu (though this condition did not, of course, deter most critics from nominating only London productions).

But the magazine went downhill, the feature became mismanaged and slow to appear, and certain members of the Circle, David Nathan prominent among them, felt we could arrange our own awards ourselves. Hence the ceremony in the Theatre Museum. For the first three years, the event was cheerily sponsored by de Courcey champagne in the Hyde Park Hotel. But this year we have to settle for a modest do in the Theatre Museum. Contrary to all expectation, it turns out to be a very jolly morning.

Benedict Nightingale, chairman of the drama section of the Circle, characterises 1992 as the year in which the critics went to war with Norway (the destructive notices of the Norwegian musical *Which Witch* at the Piccadilly nearly prompted a diplomatic incident) and made their peace with John Osborne, whose *Déjàvu* at the Comedy, a sequel to, and deconstruction of, *Look Back in Anger*, had received a generously whole-hearted response in most quarters. Benedict Nightingale is harbouring no illusions that the rapprochement with Osborne would be any more than merely temporary. By way of introducing the awards' compere, Sheridan Morley, Benedict recalls receiving a post-card from Osborne, sent on behalf of the Playwrights' Mafia, which advised him to stay clear of down-town Chichester, adding 'Fatso Morley's next.' He summons the 'svelte, sylph-like' figure of old Sherry to the stage, and Morley lumbers thither, dragging a broken foot behind him. The injury has been sustained by falling off a chair while changing a lightbulb, the kind of simple physical task that defeats even the astutest of critical brains. And, as he has undergone root canal surgery this morning, the merry Morley can justly lay claim to be suffering from foot and mouth disease.

As each critic is beckoned to the podium to announce an award, each has an Osborne post-card story to tell. Nicholas de Jongh had received one describing him, he says, as 'a second string pouf,' a strictly accurate description at the time, he hastens to add. John Peter squints through his spectacles to reveal that Osborne had sent him a card calling him 'a dim Hungarian,' a description that meets with redoubled laughter in the audience, not all of it coloured with protestation or dissent. Michael Billington expatiates on a letter he has received from Osborne this very day, but as the contents contain no insults to Billington's person or blood group, the audience shifts about a bit; Osborne, says Billington, had once asked Peggy Ashcroft what she thought about Hester Collyer in Rattigan's *The Deep Blue Sea*, a role in which she received acclaim almost as tumultuous as that accorded Penelope Wilton in the Almeida's 1993 revival: 'Stupid bitch,' was all Dame Peggy had had to say on the subject.

Morley promptly intervenes to say that his next book will be an edited collection of John Osborne post-cards. Jack Tinker feels honoured that, when Osborne wrote to him for the first time, he was addressed as Ms Jack Tinker, and informed that he had earned quick promotion on death row alongside Mr Nightingale and Mrs de Jongh. Charles Spencer of the Telegraph rather sadly confesses that he has never received a post-card from John Osborne, nor has Peter Hepple of The Stage, nor Jane Edwardes of Time Out, whose dress sense comes in for some muttered, rebarbative commentary from Ned Sherrin.

Sherrin is surveying the scene with his old chums David Nathan and Herbert Kretzmer, both of whom contributed to the satirical television show Sherrin produced in the 1960s, 'That Was the Week That Was'. Nathan has mixed his critical career on the Daily Herald, the (pre-Murdoch) Sun, and the Jewish Chronicle, with other work in television, radio and books. Kretzmer wrote lyrics for many shows before making his fortune on *Les Misérables*. He has forsworn the public prints, except when using them to plug his own work or to deliver trenchant assessments of his former colleagues: they would not, on the whole, he has recently opined, know a good show tune from an anchovy pizza. In his day, of course, Herbie did not know a good play from a slice of salami. And now he doesn't have to. But he was always very well dressed, and good company, even before he had all this silly money.

There is a great line in Oscar Wilde's *The Picture of Dorian Gray* about buying off critics; judging by their appearance, none of them would be very expensive. The same holds true today. Benedict Nightingale, loveliest of men in other respects, gives the impression of someone who has been dragged through a hedge backwards and hi-jacked by a second hand stallholder in Church Street market. Best chum Billington of the Upper Fifth hardly inspires confidence with his throwback hairstyle, grey flannels and dainty trainers. Jonathan Miller once asked after my colleagues 'porky Billington' and Irving Wardle: 'How is Irving, the jumpy old bastard, still twitching away in his anorak? A severe case of anoraksia nervosa, I always think.' Even the younger brethren, Charles Spencer and Paul Taylor, Balliol contemporaries and refreshing new voices on, respectively, the Daily Telegraph and The Independent (the one impatient with pretension, the other easily the most lucid and intelligent of all current practitioners) usually look as if they could forge a second career as models for Millet's, or as the Before Men in a new series of advertisements for what the fashionable thirty-somethings are wearing these days. The gap from Gap is enormous. Only little Jack Tinker in his floor-length John-Paul Gautier and slightly absurd pony-tail strikes a note of fashion-conscious metropolitanism. And even this is a comparatively recent transformation. For years, Jack looked as though he had been dressed by Mothercare and Miss Selfridge.

All a far cry from the peacock glamour of a figure like Kenneth Tynan, though critics like Shulman, Kretzmer and Bernard Levin, known collectively as the kosher butchers, were always well-suited on first nights. Perhaps the changing face of theatre itself discourages the sartorial instincts: the stuffing of hot bodies into small theatres like the Bush and the Pit, the brazen informality of nights at the Almeida in Islington, the Tramway in Glasgow or the Royal Exchange in Manchester, the downmarket, youth-oriented and highly popular policy of the new regime at the Nottingham Playhouse. Still, nothing wrong, I feel, with occasionally brushing your hair, polishing your shoes or changing your shirt.

In the Theatre Museum, John Peter has invoked Tynan by saying that, while he envied his great predecessor his dress sense, his unparalleled wit and his incontestable sexiness, he parted company with him on his injunction never to be grateful. Peter is moved and delighted by, and extremely grateful for, the performance of Paul Eddington, voted Best Actor in the Almeida's revival of Pinter's *No Man's Land*. Eddington, nut brown and smiling, though palpably ravaged by illness, accepts the award by saying that some people think of critics as myopic, indiscriminate, pathetic, foul-mouthed creatures who are smarting with failure, smitten with inadequacies and generally crawling beneath contempt. Rubbish! (Laughter all round, even among the critics.) He, too, is grateful: for the award, and the work of small theatres like the Almeida which, he feels, are gradually replacing the old repertory theatre system.

The critics' Best Actress is Eileen Atkins for her performance as Hannah Jelkes, the virgin spinster, in the RNT's revival of *The Night of the Iguana* by Tennessee Williams. She says that, unlike some of her colleagues in the profession, who claim they never read reviews, she reads everything she can lay her hands on, especially if it isn't about her, and even the Pigeon Fancier's Gazette if it is. This leads to a brief flurry of suggestions from the floor of great shows reviewed by the Pigeon Fancier's Gazette: *Seagulls Over Sorrento*, *Canaries Sometimes Sing*, *Bye-Bye Birdie*.

Years ago, Atkins says, she played Celia Coplestone in T S Eliot's *The Cocktail Party*. On the first night, she scored a triumph. The reviews the next morning were wonderful. On Sunday, they sang her praises even more fulsomely. That weekend, she went home to visit her family. They were a sour-faced lot, she implied, healthily unimpressed with young Eileen's career to date. Nothing was said on the subject over Sunday lunch until the dessert course was served. Toying with her trifle, Atkins tentatively asked the table if anyone had seen her reviews. 'Yes,' said her no-nonsense mother, 'you weren't exactly the Daily Mirror's idea of a martyr.'

## French windows open on O'Neill: contemporary meaning in classics

ON A Valentine's weekend trip to Paris, I go with a friend who teaches Elizabethan and Jacobean drama at Amiens University to see Eugene O'Neill's *Desire under the Elms* at Armandiers Nanterre on the outskirts of the city. In a mere twenty years, the French theatre has been abandoned by writers and overtaken by directors on a scale inconceivable to those in Britain who bemoan the onslaught of 'directors' theatre'.

The French theatre is dripping in money from the state, but starved of creative writing to such an extent that Michel Vinaver, a most distinguished French dramatist, feels more at home when abroad. The theatrical culture of Genet, Sartre, Anouilh, Giraudoux, Claudel, Cocteau and Duras is now the plaything of directors seeking contemporary frissons in the beautiful, technologically adroit deconstructions of the classics, of Beaumarchais, Marivaux, Corneille and de Musset.

In Britain, Max Stafford-Clark at the Royal Court has been an exemplary opponent of what he regards as an unhealthy obsession with the classics among the new generation of directors. Doing new work is obviously harder and riskier, in his view. And Britain's answer to Michel Vinaver, Arnold Wesker, has dubbed the Nicholas Hytner generation of thirty-something classicists 'the necrophiliacs'. When Stafford-Clark does get down to the classics, he treats them as working scripts to be subjected to the same kind of continuous overhaul he insists upon with his contemporary writers. New plays, as the old saying goes, are not written; they are re-written. With Stafford-Clark, old plays are not revived, they are reconsidered in the light of exactly the same critical criteria as would be applied to new work. They are therefore readjusted and indeed re-written accordingly. Thus, Stafford-Clark had Chekhov's *The Seagull* relocated by Thomas Kilroy in the West of Ireland; in his RSC debut last year, Stafford-Clark brought in playwright Stephen Jeffreys to re-write Richard Brome's lost Caroline comedy, *A Jovial Crew*, with spectacularly resonant results; and in his mainstage farewell to the Royal Court, where he has been artistic director since 1979 (the year Margaret Thatcher became Prime Minister), he set *King Lear* floating free from the Edwardian country house party through scenarios of political chaos culminating in the killing fields of Bosnia-Herzegovina. The main agent of historical transition, and the crux of the play, resided in the treatment of Lear's Fool, the biggest stumbling block for all modern-day interpreters. The Fool was first seen as a transvestite bottom-smacker in Lear's house. Deprived of a social function after the domestic upheavals, he becomes a political dissident, sustained by lines transposed from the earlier acts, and is finally strung up by the jackboot militia. In this way Stafford-Clark achieved the classic two-way effect of a great received text: he penetrated the carapace in search of revelatory meaning while throwing back an image of the day in the face of a contemporary audience.

The Parisian theatre has had its great classical productions in recent years from the likes of Roger Planchon, Patrice Chéreau and Giorgio Strehler. But the hold over them of a plugged-in, street-level sensibility has been on the wane since Planchon's Théâtre National Populaire company went into terminal decline. And that process has severed all links with the great French populist-intellectual tradition embodied at the TNP and in Louis Jouvet's Company of Four.

It is rare nowadays to find a Paris production that pays its dues and has something to say about the way we live now. But the city has been electrified this season by *Desire under the Elms*, O'Neill's first 'Greek' tragedy, as directed by the German, Matthias Langhoff. Langhoff describes his hyper-realist, essentially theatrical treatment as 'un film sur scène'. It deliberately mixes realism with artifice. Old Ephraim Cabot's New England farm of the 1850s is usually presented as a multiple setting on a proscenium stage; Langhoff's design is a fully inhabited hillocky warren sealed in a transparent cylindrical gauze, ploughed by a real horse, populated with two real cows and several chickens, serviced by a practical water pump under an audience-encircling sky flecked with blood red clouds.

O'Neill's stage directions, which describe everything from the 'sinister maternity' of the two large elms to the wall-melting sexual intensity between Cabot's youngest son, Eben, and Cabot's new wife, Abbie, are delivered on tape by the gravelly, authoritative voice of Alain Cuny. The cows are real, but their mooings are recorded. The third act party in honour of the new baby, heir to the land, is brilliantly staged in chiaroscuro and silhouette, but the baby itself is palpably a prop. The guests all know the father is Eben, not Cabot. The music of Olivier Dejours is portentous, filmic. The text of Françoise Morvan recasts O'Neill's stilted Irish American in a coarse, often impenetrable, Breton patois (the show is a co-production with the Théâtre National de Bretagne at Rennes).

The ecstasy of life in death, of procreation in infanticide, is pulverisingly expressed in the dream-fixated dolour of Clovis Cornillac as Eben and, especially, in the corrupting, joyous fleshiness of Evelyne Didi as Abbie. The lean and craggy veteran Jean-Marc Stehle (also responsible for the costumes) invests Cabot, the Walter Huston role, with dignity, desperation and tragic grief.

This play is always written about in terms of O'Neill's response to the myths of Oedipus, Medea and Hippolytus. But Langhoff seems to be saying something profound, and indeed disquieting, about the new territorial fanaticism that is sweeping Europe and threatening to engulf us in a frenzy of right-wing neo-Nazism. One of my other Parisian friends, Jacques Darras, the 1989 Reith lecturer on the future of Europe, flees from Nanterre at the interval, appalled at these pressing analogies, the decadence, as he sees it, of the production, and the fact that this is expressed in a provincial, unenlightened patois and orchestrated by a German director. All very sinister.

I see his point, but I think Darras underestimates an audience's powers of intelligence. If Langhoff is identifying a new mood in

Europe through this play, then he does so with deliberate irony and critical distancing. The play is presented almost objectively through the narrator's voice, and cinema usherettes move among the audience in a scene-break. He could hardly be said to be endorsing the situation he highlights. The tone is artificial throughout, though the passions expressed are anything but. The baby is killed by his own mother so that she will not disinherit her lover, the baby's father. Eben and Abbie embrace death with ecstasy rather than forfeit a patch of land.

In September 1991, I went to Belgrade for the 25th anniversary of the Belgrade International Theatre Festival, BITEF. As I arrived, a twenty-mile convoy of Serbian army tanks left the city for Croatia. Like Hamlet, I saw the imminent death of twenty thousand men 'that, for a fantasy and trick of fame, go to their graves like beds, fight for a plot whereon the numbers cannot try the cause.' During the tragedy that has unfolded since, I have never forgotten this sight. For anyone who knows the country once known as Yugoslavia, for anyone anyway, the disaster that has overtaken the people there is almost too unbearable to contemplate. I callously wonder at it having taken so long to erupt since the death of Tito, whose hold over the ethnic factions and different cultures was so strong yet without lasting guarantees. Shortly after Tito's death, I was in Belgrade and saw Ljubisa Ristić's production of *Hamlet*; I have never seen a version that reminded me so forcefully that the play is primarily about a succession. The old king, clearly corresponding to Tito, was accorded a ceremonial burial that signalled the end of an historical era. So it has proved.

That Ristić production was another example of how the present pushes up through the classics. Sometimes new writing is unable to express the mood of a nation because the mood itself, busy being created, cannot be pinned down so quickly. In Britain at least our playwrights try, but it is difficult to gain a quick purchase on slippery, depressing and recession-led times. As David Edgar points out in his talk this month to the Royal Society of Arts, all great periods of British playwrighting occurred in the wake of national triumph: Shakespeare after the Armada, Farquhar after the Restoration, Shaw after the great industrial and imperial achievements of Victorian England. And the post-War British boom in playwriting, signalled by John Osborne's *Look Back in Anger* in 1956, began as a way of coming to terms with victory in Europe; our contemporary playwrights are, to a certain extent, still confronting the present in the consequent issues of meritocratisation, feminism, youth revolt, national identity and the tensions in a Welfare State society, not to mention the question of Europe itself.

This seems not to happen in France. One theory, put forward by Michel Vinaver, is that a Frenchman has no doubts about his identity and therefore no need to discuss it in the theatre. The same is not true in Germany or in Britain, and the result has been a rich and persistent new play culture in both countries. Hence the unexpected impact of Langhoff's O'Neill production, which adopts all the external characteristics of the decadent technological French theatre but releases a depth charge of poetic passion on the very subject which liberal-minded Frenchmen take for granted and which they find unpalatably embodied in the right-wing political fanatics in their own country and across Europe.

# Black actors and the 'Carousel' controversy

In the Royal National Theatre's joyous revival of Rodgers and Hammerstein's *Carousel*, the New England fisherman, Mr Enoch Snow, is impersonated by a black actor, Clive Rowe. Richard Ingrams, the satirical writer, who plays the organ in his local country church, has got in a state over this and reactivated a debate that has rumbled on the edge of theatrical discussion for several years. The effect, says Ingrams, is absurd and insults the author, although there is no record of the Rodgers and Hammerstein estates, notoriously protective of their material, lodging any protest. His objections are based on the assumption that there were no black men in New England around 1873 and that the RNT, just as you would expect in the subsidised theatre ('subsidised' being a pejorative term in the Ingrams handbook), is pandering to a wishy-washy liberal, politically correct sense of fair (and dark) play when it comes to casting.

As a nominal joke, Enoch Snow at the RNT takes some beating. The night I went, the audience gasped with pleasure at Rowe's appearance; 'Enoch' in our collective memory immediately conjures another snow-white Enoch, the politician Enoch Powell (although Mr Powell's complexion is of a strangely pallid, greenish hue), and his 'rivers of blood' anti-immigration speech in 1968. Subsequently, we responded warmly to the striving sub-plot of domestic bliss among the Snows and their toddling brood of mixed-colour offspring. Here, at once, is the unpalatable reality for Ingrams: the theatre does not exist as an instrument of historical representation (nor does the cinema, but it is more suited to that function); it exists in the violently alterable present, even when its stories are apparently set in the past, or indeed the unknowable future. In the second act of *Carousel* we ascend to heaven. I trust that Bob Crowley's bleak cerulean box, populated by Puritan panjandrums in Ku Klux Klan pointy hats, lived up to Ingrams's confident expectations of the place.

Nothing can ever be pure or simple, let alone black or white, in such a messy medium. Today's *Carousel* is a complete hybrid: played over a fifteen-year period starting in 1873, based on a 1921 Hungarian play by Molnar, written in the conventions of the Broadway musical of the 1940s and sifted through the contemporary skills, sensibilities and theatre technology of the 1990s. As *Carousel*'s director Nicholas Hytner has observed, the average 19th century New Englander tended not to spin horizontally down his garden path in a piece of Kenneth MacMillan choreography.

But what if he did, and what if *Carousel* is, after all, as Ingrams wants it to be, a social document? Is it not conceivable, if not probable, that some of that mixed-race whaling community vividly reported by Herman Melville in 1851 (the year of *Moby Dick*'s publication) had worked its way the short distance inland from Nantucket? And rather than insulting the author, does not a black Mr Snow, quietly operating as an industrious adjunct to the whirling, seafaring community so prodigiously evoked in the staging of the sailors' chorus of 'Blow High, Blow Low', take us to the edge of Walt Whitman's inclusive spirit of 'athletic democracy' in America, a mid-19th-century vision on the beach where 'a vast similitude interlocks all: all nations, colours, barbarisms, civilisations and languages, all lives and deaths, all of the past, present, future'? That is the true American spirit behind *Carousel*, not the diminishing prattle which seeks to defend an idea of English culture circumscribed by Trollope and Elgar. Even on those terms, the Ingrams argument is exposed when you consider one of the best English symphonic choral works of the century, Vaughan Williams's 'Sea Symphony,' a splendid and triumphant setting of the Whitman oceanic poems quoted above.

But Ingrams's irritation is really caused by the allegedly incongruous appearance of black actors in the classics. Why does this upset him so much? He quotes the case of Charles Osborne, an Australian, who objects to black men playing Hamlet on the grounds that they do not look 'Danish.' (It is always the immigrant colonials among the critics who make the loudest protest about multi-cultural casting; Milton Shulman, a Canadian, used to go bonkers about what 'the Bard' may or may not have intended. Policing the heritage is one of the most unattractive traits in a critic; genuine scholarship is preferable, an open mind even more so.) Shakespeare never visited Norway. He wrote a play, not a travelogue. The 'Danishness' of Hamlet is the least important thing about him. *Hamlet*, like *Carousel*, does not exist as a finished entity upon which a theatrical interpretation impertinently paints a gloss. As a text, *Hamlet* exists undisturbed on the library shelf. You can have whatever *Hamlet* you care to imagine in your head. But as a play, it exists merely as an outline for performance, a prompt and a challenge for a theatrical combustion between actors and an audience. I suspect that, deep down, it is the dangerous mutability and volatility of theatre that worries Ingrams and his heritage-sensitive ilk. He cannot control this unruly medium, or make it fit his tweedy, reductive world view, or indeed persuade audiences themselves that he is right. Audiences in the theatre tend to accept what is presented to them and reserve their deepest reactions for the emotional and physical twists of the plot, and the overall dynamic of the production. And they do not demand watertight realism. The whole beauty of the theatre is that it can function on many levels simultaneously and, much though it may peeve the cultural police, an audience has a limitless capacity for juggling present realities with factual information, historical reference, musical diversion, scenic elaboration, discordant person-alities, anachronism and every other device which reminds them that they are, in fact, sitting at a performance and participating directly in its formulation.

A few weeks ago Sir John Gielgud spoke informally at a gathering of drama students on television. At least half of these RADA hopefuls, all British, were either black or Asian. They are the future of the theatre in Britain, just as Clive Rowe was a few years back when he first crossed my bows as an electrifying musical comedy prospect at the Guildhall School. Apart from being black, Mr Rowe is a mighty fine actor and singer, one of the brightest hopes of our stage, which he has so far graced in many musicals, regional theatre productions and the RNT's *Fuente Ovejuna*.

The great Paul Robeson, who did so much for the dignity and influence of black performers in white-dominated entertainment media, would be astonished to learn that this debate is still going on. The evidence will soon settle it. Black theatre is on the march in Britain. But as far as conscious casting by the host culture goes, leading white directors of the classics such as Peter Brook and Jonathan Miller have been innovative for many years. Admittedly Brook had to create his Centre for International Theatre Research in Paris, but his determination to cast actors of all colours and creeds in Chekhov, Shakespeare, Jarry and other classic European writers goes hand in hand with a policy of post-Third World theatre which embraces, in exactly that Whitmanesque spirit, the full majesty of all cultures, not segregated pockets of faith and literature. Brook's theatre of the past twenty years has created a series of pan-cultural masterpieces — *Orghast at Persepolis*, *Conference of the Birds*, *The Ik*, and *The Mahabharata* — which strive to explore languages and identities in the corporate experimentalism of theatre underpinned by an attempt to find the best way of expressing the spiritualism of mankind.

There is no reason why the creed of multiculturalism, which can be expressed in many different ways, should be the only philosphy of theatre. Palpably it is not. But theatre's prime responsibility is towards its audience, not towards its own inheritance. And of course, the more you think about it, the more the two aspects coalesce. Some critics would draw the line at, say, casting black actors in Oscar Wilde. But their objections have already been anticipated by a Temba Theatre production of *The Importance of Being Earnest* in which the experiment of casting black actors was widely considered to be justified. I see no reason why Wilde's effete dandies should not be tested by the contradictory cultural appraisal of a West Indian actor, providing he met all the technical requirements of the role. And last year the Birmingham Rep presented a version of *Hobson's Choice* in which Hobson's three daughters were all black. The audience found this totally acceptable, not on logical narrative grounds, but in the wider, more profound, sense of participating in the performance of a classic play in a community and city where issues of race and shared cultures inform every kind of civic and artistic activity.

One brilliant black actress, Josette Simon, has already played Isabella in *Measure for Measure* for the Royal Shakespeare Company (directed, as it happens, by Nicholas Hytner); the Marilyn Monroe role in Arthur Miller's *After the Fall* at the National; and, also at the RNT, Vittoria Corombona in *The White Devil*. And in award-winning touring companies like Cheek By Jowl and in radical regional theatres such as the Glasgow Citizens, the fundamental traditions of classical theatre have been stretched and refreshed by countless instances of the black casting Ingrams and his ilk so dislike. This process goes further, deeper and wider than mere tokenism. It signals a changing theatre as much as it heralds a changing world. Neither Trollope nor Elgar, not even 'the Bard', nor yet the distant double diapasons of every country church organ in the land, will be sufficient to the dawn of a new day.

# MARCH

## *Fairy tales in New York*

MY HABITUAL SHOCK of excitement at landing in New York is more of a shock than usual when I see the weather we land in. Swirling snow and nil visibility at Newark Airport on the first weekend in March. You have to remind yourself you really have crossed the big pond these days. The television service on Virgin Atlantic is hosted by the egregious Jonathan Ross, whom I'd cheerfully cross oceans to avoid. The first theatre posters you see coming off the plane are for *Cats*. And the first big hoarding discernible through the flurry of snowflakes as we enter the Lincoln Tunnel echoes the British occupation of Broadway: *Miss Saigon*, *The Phantom of the Opera* and *Les Misérables*.

Something new since my last visit two years ago. Begging is completely upfront. People sidle past you quite casually on the sidewalk, openly requesting a few cents. I'm always happy to oblige when threats and knives aren't involved. But even more remarkable are the new standards of performance in begging. On the subway uptown from 42nd Street, I witness the extraordinary, but evidently commonplace, sight of a supplicating woman, possibly Eurasian or Ethiopian, in a Helene Weigel headscarf, holding out a crumpled brown paper bag and directing her stream of sorrowful beggary to one particular but massively unimpressed seated lady passenger. The Weigel surrogate leaves the compartment after a couple of stops without a dime, still keening and droning on about her pitiful condition. This is Tony Award-winning stuff. And, sure enough, I later learn that there is an unofficial advice bureau in the East Village where paupers are trained in how to make the most of their plight, how to hit the potential donor hardest.

I first came to New York when I was a fairy. Let me explain. In 1968, a group of students in Oxford and Cambridge Universities had a brilliant wheeze: by forming something called the Oxford and Cambridge Shakespeare Company, and printing headed note-paper with Sir Ralph Richardson's name at the top as a patron, they could wangle some reasonably well-paid bookings on the East Coast college circuit and thereby take a party of British students on a six-week tour of America. The architects of this grand plan were two Cambridge undergraduates, Stephen Wright (now a leading music agent) and Jonathan James-Moore (head of light entertainment at BBC Radio). I helped out on the Oxford end of the administration. The cost to each student for the entire trip was £50. Two weeks of the six-week period were spent in New York, playing at Columbia University and Hunter College. We had plenty of time to discover the museums, the jazz clubs, the record stores, the Blue Bar in the Algonquin, Sardi's, the theatres (I saw Joel Grey as George M Cohan, Tammy Grimes and Brian Bedford in *Private Lives*, and Dustin Hoffman, who had just become a big star with *The Graduate*, in a Murray Schisgal comedy) and, most of all, the exhilarating, noisy excitement of the place.

And we were a hit, something you cannot afford not to be in New York. The New York Times gave us a rave review and we played to enthusiastic houses. The production was *A Midsummer Night's Dream*. James-Moore was Peter Quince, Diana Quick was a wonderful Helena, Michael Wood (the television historian) an Ian Richardson-influenced Oberon, Russell Davies (the humorous columnist) an amusingly decrepit Starveling, Jeremy Treglown (the writer and editor) an energetic Bottom, Hermione Lee (the critic and literary biographer) a slightly stilted Hippolyta, Mark Wing-Davey (the actor and director) a brilliant Flute, Martin Young (the news reporter) a demonic Puck, Stephen Wyatt (the playwright) a stout little Snout. Various fairies were played by Julie Covington (the actress and singer), Rob Buckman (the doctor and humorist), Nicola Gurry (I wonder what happened to her?) and myself. The director was the professional Richard Cottrell, who had drilled us mercilessly in the draughty old ADC Theatre in Cambridge, and the production was fast, well-spoken, beautifully costumed (by Hugh Durrant) and great fun to play. I think I was an unconvincing fairy, in spite of my dark Egyptian body make-up, skin-tight spangled costume and detachable, plastic pointy ears. Julie Covington used to hit me on the head with a tuning fork in order to get the note for our fairy song in Titania's bower; and she would hit me on the head with it afterwards, as I never succeeded, in the entire six-week period, in sustaining the simple melodic line. I was always a flat little fairy. We travelled with a Cambridge Footlights late-night revue written by Clive James, Russell Davies and Rob Buckman. The latter two were joined onstage by Jonathan James-Moore, Pete Atkin (who had written the music) and Julie Covington, and we Oxonians used to watch their witty and highly professional efforts with drooling pleasure not unmixed with envy almost every night; an attempt to mix the Footlights style with the harsher, more political and thematic Oxford revue of that time being written by Nigel Williams and Michael Rosen had ended in bitter failure and a major rumpus.

It is strange how experience is always coloured by memory. Whenever I return to New York, the present reality is invaded by an accumulation, if not a remembrance, of things past. I always try and do something brand new on each trip: this time, I switch my temporary allegiance from Sam Goody's Record Store near Radio City to Tower Records and the great HMV store at 72nd Street, and I eat two sensational meals, one Ukrainian and one Chinese, with my friend Rivka Nachoma. I love finding out new places for breakfast. And I try and learn more about the subway and bus services, a much more exciting way of getting about than being stuck in the back of a yellow cab. On that first trip with the OCSC, I stayed in an apartment somewhere along Riverside Drive on the Upper West side of the city. This time, in deference to the Observer's budgetary constraints, I am staying in a strange, predominantly residential, hotel in the same district. On Saturday morning, bright and cold with a thin film of snow lending the Riverside Park a crisp and crunchy aspect, I go looking for nothing in particular. People jog, people say, 'Good morning'. At about

90th Street, I come across a film crew shooting on location by one of the many beautiful Beaux Arts houses hereabouts. Actors are wearing costumes of the 1930s and a vintage car is significantly parked on the corner. I stop and stare with two other passers-by. We form a small crowd. We discover that the film is of Arthur Miller's *The American Clock*, a kaleidoscopic play of the Depression which is almost unadaptable, I feel, from stage to screen. The other guys are delighted to see a film being shot in New York, 'and a film with words, not all that LA metal flash.' I agree, and on my revealing that I saw the Miller play performed at the National Theatre in London, an impromptu tribute is delivered by one of my new friends to the seriousness, vigour and respect for words of the British theatre. I reply that the Americans have nothing to be shy about on this score in their own theatre, citing not just Miller and Tennessee Williams, but their contemporary successors Sam Shepard, David Mamet, Wendy Wasserstein and David Greenspan, diligent and brilliant wordsmiths all. It turns out that the Miller film will star John Malkovich, an actor who has haunted all my New York theatre visits of the last ten years, since he first made waves in the Big Apple in a sensational production of Shepard's *True West* from his hometown theatre, the Steppenwolf in Chicago. That whirlwind display was followed in 1983 by his charismatic, powerfully muted Biff to Dustin Hoffman's Willy Loman in *Death of a Salesman*. And now Malkovich is everywhere. On the Virgin crossing, one of the films I watched was the re-make of *Of Mice and Men*, in which he plays the homicidal giant with a great baffled dignity opposite his old Chicago colleague, Gary Sinese; and my first play last night was Mamet's *Oleanna*, the controversial sock in the jaw about a college professor ruined by his politically correct student's allegation of attempted rape, in which Malkovich is slated for London. (Malkovich dropped out, to be replaced by David Suchet.)

I walk up to the Gothic monumentalism of St John the Evangelist on 110th Street then back along Columbus Avenue, preparing for a hectic New York weekend. Lunch in Sardi's confirms that the much-needed improvements heralded by Vincent Sardi's return to the restaurant have been maintained, and I am in a benign mood for the undemanding banalities of a new musical in the hideous Marquis Theater. *The Goodbye Girl* has been adapted by Neil Simon from his own 1977 screenplay with a mediocre score by Marvin Hamlisch. Only the stars, Bernadette Peters, looking more like a Rastafarian poodle than ever, and a Canadian zany making his Broadway debut, Martin Short, rescue the proceedings from total disaster. The Marquis is a featureless new theatre housed inside the repellent Marriott Hotel, the so-called soul of one of those shameful mid-town property developments blasphemously constructed on the site of the old Helen Hayes Theater. It is distinguished only by the whizzing, headache-inducing speed of its glass elevators and the myriad constellation of naked light bulbs that assault the intruder at every turn. The sign-posting is non-existent (the theatre's Box Office is at ground level straight off Times Square, but the entrance to the auditorium is somewhere between the second and third floors), so that crowds of blazered and polyester-clad middlebrow theatregoers from upstate New York and Milwaukee (*The Goodbye Girl* has opened to damning reviews but also to a ten million dollar box office advance) wander lost and disconsolate among hotel guests and conference wallahs. The whole thing is like a nightmare devised by a sadistic cultural supremo whose warped sense of humour has even egged him on to plaster the public rooms and suites with theatrical monikers. The Gilbert and the Brecht Rooms are forbidding enclaves presumably designed to keep witty paradox and shapely antitheses in a separate compartment from social realism and the alienation theory.

Sanity is restored at the Ethel Barrymore in the evening, where I see Wendy Wasserstein's new play, *The Sisters Rosensweig*, which has moved onto Broadway from the Lincoln Center with a record three million dollar advance. The comedy is a smart contemporary reworking of Chekhov's *Three Sisters*, without the gloom, the military occupation and any longing for Moscow. You'd hardly expect one of Wasserstein's worldly-wise women (the play is set in London) to long for Yonkers or White Plains. Any seat in the stalls, front or back, costs $50. Such is the demand that I can only secure two singles for the Saturday evening performance. My companion, Rivka Nachoma, sits at the far left of the second row near the stage and is told by the usherette to restrain herself from joining in the performance. My seat is at the far right of the fifth row from the back. As I wend my way there, feeling at least presentable in my new red jacket, an imperious lady swathed in furs hands me her tickets, assuming that I am there to tear them. Suitably deflated I settle down to enjoy the play, especially those lines which reflect badly on the characters' sartorial judgement. The delightful Madeline Kahn plays the daffiest sister, stepping ever so lightly through the emotional turmoil as if mincing on eggshells. In the last scene she unwraps a gift of a pink Chanel suit and drapes it about herself, asking 'Do I look like Catherine Denoove?'

The weather remains perfect on Sunday. I am invited to brunch by Michael Redington, the London-based producer who is in town to support Hugh Whitemore's *The Best of Friends*, which he presented in the West End with Sir John Gielgud and Rosemary Harris. The stars here, and opening tonight, are Roy Dotrice and Michael Douglas's mother, Donna Douglas. Michael gives me what sound like reasonably precise instructions on how to find his apartment and I plan a long walk through Central Park, down to 54th Street on the East Side, where I indulge in a hot bagel smeared with cream cheese and pick up an Opera Cake (chocolate sponge, meringue, fresh cream, praline butter, chocolate icing and hazelnuts) for Michael's table before heading directly across town to my appointment at 420 West 54th Street. There is no 420 West 54th Street. I find a telephone and dial Michael in disarray. 'East, east,' he squeals intemperately down the line, and I hop in a cab to return whence I came on foot. The apartment is on the top floor of the Rivertower. It belongs to Gillian Lynne, the choreographer of *Cats* and a very old friend of Michael's. Gillian and her husband are currently staying in another of her properties in the Caribbean. Michael is here with his wife, Ann, and the other brunch guests are a fellow New York producer and his pretty blonde actress wife. The view of the East River from a great window running the length of the apartment is breathtaking. It sweeps right around over the whole of Manhattan and you feel that the city has come on parade for your own personal inspection. We drink Buck's Fizz and

Sancerre, and we eat salmon cakes, salads, nutty brown bread, ice-cream, a fresh fruit compote and the Opera Cake. Life, for the moment, is very sweet. There are days and days in New York like this.

Time passes too quickly and I must dash away by cab to Greenwich Village for a matinée. I am immediately reminded of the really big change in the New York theatre community: as in London, this has been wrought by the AIDS epidemic. Almost everyone in the Village wears a red ribbon, and the Larry Kramer play, *The Destiny of Me*, playing here on Christopher Street, has the most gut-wrenching third act of any play I've seen for years. The chief character, Ned Weeks, whom we first met in Kramer's *The Normal Heart* in the mid-1980s, nursing his own stricken lover, ends the play by raging against the well-meaning doctors and nurses, pulling out his drips and splattering the Washington hospital's tiled walls, and the audience, with the blood bags collected to try and save him: 'Why do I never stop believing that this fucking plague can be cured?' The havoc wreaked on the artistic community is felt everywhere in its expressions. Thus the curtain calls at the end of the Kramer play become a rallying point, and the fine actor who plays Ned Weeks, Jonathan Hadary, makes a short and dignified speech which is as essential to the meaning of the play as any other part of it; money is collected on the door, and more red ribbons disseminated.

I stagger back to the hotel, severely shaken, to prepare for the chief purpose of my visit, dinner with the comedian Jackie Mason. Four years ago, when the 58 year-old ex-rabbi (Jacob Maza) from the Lower East Side scored a hit at the Playhouse near Charing Cross in London, he posted me a stale bagel. Inside the bagel was an invitation to lunch: 'You said what you thought about me; now come hear what I think about you.'

Having missed that treat, it would have been churlish to reject a second bidding. We have fixed a date in a fine French restaurant on Third Avenue. His friend Raol Velder arrives first, a sort of sweet-talking warm-up man. Velder's a hot divorce lawyer, who acted for Robin Givens against Mike Tyson and is known in court as 'the piranha'. He tells me what a great guy Mason is. Mason is thinking of running for President of the New York City council this year, a post second to the Mayor. His discussion show on Channel Nine last year was, Velder says, a phenomenal success. Last night, however, he was only on Cable TV, soft-soaping Michael York. Mason is accustomed to the highs and the lows. His three elder brothers are rabbis, and he only quit the rabbinate for fulltime showbiz when his father died. He was an immediate hit, but spent twenty years in the comparative wilderness after allegedly giving the all-powerful Ed Sullivan the finger on a live show in 1964. His films have been catastrophes. 'Chicken Soup', a recent television sitcom series with Lynn Redgrave, was ditched after nine episodes. But no-one is funnier than this man on top form, delivering devastating, rapid-fire volleys in the guise of casual dissertations. No wonder his best friends are lawyers. In Britain, his best friends are Bruce Forsyth and Ted Rogers. But his true performance peers are Jack Benny, Mel Brooks, Lenny Bruce and Milton Berle. His comedy is driven by social observation and anger at politicians. Uniquely for a Jewish comic, he talks a lot about Jews.

Mason, stocky and blazered, no tie, arrives in the restaurant with Jyll Rosenfeld, a bright blonde businesswoman twenty years his junior whom he picked up outside a coffee shop in 1974. At that point, Mason was in one of his periodic troughs. Within a few months Rosenfeld was running his career. Two years ago they married, but they keep separate apartments. She orders his food: onion soup, a plate of peppers and mozzarella cheese, a side order of roast potatoes and corn, soufflé, no dessert, tea. 'I can feel too tired for sex, but I'm always in the mood for a pastrami sandwich,' is a familiar Mason line. He glows and dodges like a boxer in the pink. His fragile hair is strangely reddened.

Onstage, he ambles around like a fractious stuffed frog. At table, he answers questions by asking his own. 'You married? To a Jewish girl? If you're not Jewish how come you couldn't find a gentile yenta? Did her mother resist the marriage? Yes? But not because you weren't Jewish? Because you weren't wealthy and also not tall? Hey, this is better than my act!'

I ask who is conducting the interview around here and why does he go on about Jews and gentiles so much. 'I pick on Italians as much as Jews, Puerto Ricans or anybody else. Anyone who says I'm a racist should be shot in the street like a horse. The basic differences in lifestyle are the same today as they were fifty years ago. Jewish kids don't become athletes. Jews don't fix cars or television sets. They never become farmers or coalminers. How often do you see a Jewish drunkard? The only time you see a Jew in a bar is because it's a singles bar; he's looking for goils.' ('Or he owns the bar,' adds Velder, stealthily).

Velder slips away to the movies and is replaced by another friend, a young criminal lawyer called Mel Sacks, who is defending a guy who saved a girl by killing her assailant. The hero had no licence for the gun, so is facing a murder charge on a technicality. Sacks is confident of winning the case. He tells me what a great guy Jackie Mason is and what a phenomenal success his TV show was. He also laughs a lot. The warm-down man.

Speaking quickly, gutturally and seriously, Mason says he is running for office because of his despair at the mounting violence and hypocrisy in New York. 'People are intimidated. They have forgotten they're supposed to be living in a democracy.' If elected, he will take a big loss; 'money to me is not such a green god in my life.' But he will continue speaking wherever the price is right. 'I'll even go to Philadelphia for sixty thousand bucks; I found myself at a birthday there in a restaurant. It was so small I had to stand on the staircase. They had four guys with tuxedos on sitting there, and I'm standing at the top of the stairs telling them jokes.'

Unlike Ken Dodd, he re-works his material constantly. And like Dame Edna Everage, he can do this in interviews. 'I never thought I'd live long enough to miss Dan Quayle. This guy Gore should be called Bore. He is the most boring man left on oith. Clinton? I never saw a guy running so much and gaining weight at the same time. He's running because Hilary Clinton is following him. He runs round a few trees, stops for a McDonald's, and starts running again. Clinton looks like his whole life was his haircut. He's sharp, he knows how to charm people to death. And he's already broken every promise he ever made in an hour and a half. Bush told one big lie, read my lips; this guy tells a big lie every five minutes.' Mason reveres his brothers, the rabbinate representing to him the last bastion of decent people. 'No society based on competition has a right to preach love. You call it a civilised world when there are twenty wars going on for reasons nobody can even figure out?' I agree with him. The lawyer nods and laughs loudly. Jyll picks up the tab.

My last morning is blessedly crisp and sunny. Just as the airport bus swings out to New Jersey affording a spectacular view of the Manhattan skyline, another bus roars past with the destination Allentown, PA, showing on the front. An image of Ruby Keeler, who has just died, flashes across my mind's eye: in the movie *42nd Street*, she plays the little chorus girl from Allentown who gets her big chance when the leading lady of a Broadway show falls unaccountably sick; the producer, Warner Baxter, tells Ruby Keeler to go out on the stage and come back a star. Which is precisely what she does. The lullabies and mythologies of Broadway are notoriously trite and sentimental; but they are also tenacious and beguiling, and, however hard you try to deny them, they bounce back to hit you on the nose when you least expect them. New York, like many great cities, always justifies its fictional reputation. Not even another sight of Jonathan Ross on my personalised Virgin television screen can douse my high spirits.

## From Antwerp and Sarajevo on
## Richard Eyre's birthday

ON THE LAST WEEKEND of March I had to be in two places almost at once: Antwerp for the opening weekend of that city's inauguration as the European Capital of Culture, 1993; and Hammersmith in West London for Richard Eyre's fiftieth birthday party. I had long fretted over what gift would be appropriate for the director of the Royal National Theatre, a man who may not have everything but certainly could do without a collection of unfavourable reviews or a box of melting Belgian chocolates. My wife, Sue, had hit on the brilliant idea of fifty pansies. If Eyre's house was going to be a scene of wall-to-wall luvvies, he might very well feel like putting a few pansies in pots and leaving them out to get soaked in the rain by the end of the day.

Early start at Heathrow on Saturday morning. Find I am on the same tiny plane — what is known as a little Fokker, no doubt — as my old mucker Michael Kustow (the only man known to go jogging on Hampstead Heath while listening to Harrison Birtwistle on his personal stereo), and film producer Derek Bailey and his adorable wife, Gill. Kustow and Bailey are thinking of making a programme about *Sarajevo*, the main dramatic event of the opening festivities in Antwerp. On landing, we are met by Erica Bolton, the best publicist we have for avant-garde dance and drama, a civilised chum and all-round good egg, who is simultaneously seeing off John Russell Brown back to London fully gorged on the Jacob Jordaens exhibition which is the main attraction at the city's Museum of Fine Art; it is also the four hundredth anniversary of Jordaens' birth. Even after years of travelling around Europe and Britain, I still find there is simply no pleasure greater than arriving for the first time in a new place with the sun shining, a good map and a couple of hours to spare. I push my way round the Rubens-huis, incredulous that so much polished wood and fine furniture is unprotected from the crush of tourists; in Stratford-upon-Avon, they would have the rooms roped off and policed by scowling elderly members of the National Trust. The city is clean, lively and welcoming. There are parades and bands of pipers and trumpeters on bicycles. For lunch, there is no missing the fresh shrimps and mussels and chips. I head out towards the Jordaens exhibition, savouring the clean grey streets of art nouveau buildings, the close-ness of the river and a covered market with a stall where you can stand and consume, for a few bob, a platter of oysters and a glass of white wine. This is the life. Satiety is fully achieved at the museum, where room after room of great big boring Jordaens paintings, heaving with rolls of pink flesh and minor mythological scenes, lull you into a rather unpleasant sense of over-gorged well-being. There is nothing for it but to beat a hasty retreat to the centre, purchasing a few chocolates for Easter presents back home.

In a sudden kink to the schedule, Erica whisks Gill, Derek and myself out to the Turkish quarter to witness the raising of a branch-and-twiggy monument on the engineering principles of Cleopatra's needle and the pyramids. We stand around watching fellows winch up bits of trees to form an impractical wigwam. They do not even have the glamour of well-oiled, oven-ready Nubian slaves. It is all anoraks and scrofulous endeavour, community culture with no-one watching apart from a few stray media types. Oh dear. We do not dally. The small but perfectly formed British contingent has arr-anged to meet in the hotel bar for a drink before the evening's exer-tions. Kustow breezes in and Derek and I attempt to convince him that, in skipping the twigs, he has missed the cultural heartbeat of Antwerp 93. Michael looks briefly forlorn, but our giggles give us away and we call up the barman. Gill and Derek scoot off to their theatre. Michael wants to watch a Harrison Birtwistle concert, or something like it, on television, and insists that Erica and I join him in his bedroom with our drinks. I had never thought to be so sed-uced. The concert is not on yet, but the addictive tellyman sits on the end of his bed, punching the remote control and sampling every single worthwhile European channel in a space of ten minutes.

We go to see the main festival offering, a dramatic tapestry woven around the fate of this year's saddest city, Sarajevo. I once went to Sarajevo for a wonderful festival of 'small fringe theatre'. The city is, or was, magical, not just because of its historic and architectural qualities, which are, were, considerable; but also because of its significant European location, at the crossroads of the old medieval caravan routes. Like Trieste, a whole history of Europe passes through this place. How tragic, and ironic, that in the very year when, in theory, the European borders are dissolved, in the wake of the dismantling of the Berlin Wall and the forging of the common European market, this magical place has been systematically destroyed by sectarian warfare. The whole ideal of European unity, a dream of post-war rehabilitation, has been mocked, traduced and shattered in a conflict that is as gratuitous and obscene as any in our genocidal twentieth century. What price progress, what price civilisation?

Such are the questions lurking behind *Sarajevo*, a performance that was, in fact, more significant than wholly successful. As we gather in the square behind the beautifully restored Bourla Theatre, an impromptu demonstration by torchlight is under way. On a video screen, a cellist plays a Bach partita in a devastated room in Sarajevo. There follows a speech, in Serbo Croat, denouncing the the trivialisation of the slaughter-strewn crisis in a theatrical presentation at a cultural festival. The same argument I had heard in last year's BITEF festival in Belgrade. The best possible rebuttal would have been a searing performance. Instead, *Sarajevo* is a limply contrived dream play of a wounded girl through whose memory flits images of Sarajevo's past. Muslims, Serbs, Croats and Jews have all contributed to this richness that now explodes in the country's face. There is no attempt to represent the horrors or violence of the current conflict. Instead, in a walled, partially tiled corrida not all that dissimilar to the setting of Ariane Mnouchkine's great Greek tragedy tetralogy, *Les Atrides*, in Paris, an architectural student searches for the silver soul of Sarajevo. She meets Sufi clowns, Turkish outlaws, anarchists, priests of four religions, Winter Olympians from 1984, and a cross-section of contemporary professionals: a fireman, a postman, a taxi-driver, a soldier, a journalist. The airport (and the sky) is closed for lovers wanting to escape. A Bosnian casserole recipe ends in tears. A cellist is raped by her neighbour, but only in reported form (the nearest we get to the verismo of the documented horror now flooding the European media). The great excuse of the twentieth century is reiterated: we did know, and we did nothing. For all its failures — dramaturgical banality, low temperature stage action, a pervasive piousness — *Sarajevo* at least acknowledges the crucial link between life and art. Nothing matters more at the moment, or indeed for the rest of the year, than a solution, however brutal, to the obscenity of what is happening in Bosnia-Herzegovina. As a critic reporting this event, however disappointing, I feel that my job this weekend has some meaning.

I wish this sentiment was more enthusiastically shared by my newspaper; the Observer, of all organs, makes nothing much of my visit and restricts me to a few meagre paragraphs, with an injunction from my arts editor to cut out 'all the political crap'. Yet another instance of that political isolationism and cultural namby-pambiness that may explain, in part, why the paper is going down-hill; though I do recall, in my time as editor of Plays and Players in the early 1970s, that Kenneth Tynan had to bring to me an important update piece on the Berliner Ensemble because his masters in St Andrews Hill had deemed it too local and political an offering. I remember he told me that I could have the piece for £50, an unprecedented fee in those days on the tiny specialist maga-zines. The beneficial upshot of Tynan's reasonable materialism was that the publisher, having agreed to this demand, established a precedent and every other contributor became better paid as a result. (A few days after returning from Antwerp, I note that Michael Kustow has placed his superb account, running to well over twice my length, and illustrated, in the Independent. He was probably fixing the deal, and having something decent to eat, while I was wasting my time at twig city with Gill and Derek.)

In Howard Barker's mis-titled play *The Europeans*, which opened in London this month, a character asks 'How do we escape from history?' and answers his own question with: 'We reproduce its mayhem in our lives.' This trite and terrible aphorism sums up for me the entire fallacy of so-called serious left-wing drama in Britain in the 1990s. You cannot escape from history, and to imagine that you can either endure or absorb its horrors in some domestic equalisation is almost the biggest obscenity of all.

After *Sarajevo*, there is a party where I meet my old friend Dragan Klaić, the moving spirit behind the show. He looks glum, as well he might. Dragan is a rare bird, a Serbian Jew, who was a theatre editor and professor of drama in Belgrade until last summer when he fled with his family to Amsterdam. He could bear the situation no longer and is now head of the theatrical institute in the city of Rembrandt, canals and hard porn. *Sarajevo* may be a way of trying to make sense of his depression at what is going on but, without saying anything to each other, we know that it hasn't worked. We exchange social pleasantries and I go for dinner with Erica, Kustow and the Baileys.

Three hours' sleep later (it's the weekend where the clocks go forward for British Summer Time), I am on a very early plane to London and Richard Eyre's fiftieth. It is disconcerting to walk into his Hammersmith house and see Salman Rushdie talking to Neil Kinnock. The first is fatter than he'd like, the second shorter than we'd expect. I last saw Rushdie cresting the wave of the initial *Satanic Verses* hype in the lounge of the Shelbourne Hotel in Dublin and laying down the law to some hapless journalist on the day of its Irish launch, as though people there needed to be told very much about the evils and advantages of ritual affiliations. I was taking tea with one of my closest friends, an Australian former diplomat, writer and castle-restorer in County Offaly, Peter Bartlett, who has since died of AIDS. We could hardly hear ourselves speak because of the avalanche of self-promotion at the next table. This abominable experience has always slightly undermined my orthodox liberal responses to Rushdie's subsequent vile dilemma. But the writer has surely endured something even crueller than death by sexually transmitted disease; living in the shadow of execution, he inhabits death row with all the spurious privileges of access and the unsettling terrors of uncertainty. Here in Hammersmith, I simply do not know what to say to him, apart from muttering something vaguely fraternal, and I shuffle away from his beseeching gaze like a coward, inordinately helped by Kinnock's general profusion of empty friendliness towards someone he mistakenly assumes to be a fellow spirit. Ho-ho-ho, he must be in the media, therefore he supports Labour and is sympathetic to my condition of abject failure and defeat. I am indeed forlorn that Labour lost last year's election, but not at all forlorn that Neil Kinnock is not Prime Minister. For all his deficiencies, John Major is more appealingly and transparently dull than Kinnock, who disguises his dullness in a series of ghastly, vaudevillian, media-conscious poses. I think that Major, at the end of the day, would listen more seriously to your objections to what is happening in Sarajevo, or to our own public transport, public health and the education system than would Kinnock. Much later on, I bump into Glenys Kinnock on the stairs, handling young children with considerable aplomb; by this time we have established that the actor Bill Paterson, a very old friend of mine, is an even older friend of the Kinnocks, so I can grin across his small talk with easy equanimity. This does not help on the stairs. Stuck yet again for something to say, I offer that she looks as though she has found herself a real job at last. I do not mean to say this and regret it immediately. I regret it even more when I see the look on Glenys's face. Tact, tact; thank God I'm only a critic and not a politician.

I turn with only a modicum of relief to spy the novelist Nigel Williams, with whom I've lately had a correspondence. In a book of fringe theatre interviews by the director Roland Rees, Nigel, one of my Oxford heroes, has deplored the fact that journalists 'like Michael Coveney earn more than most of the people whom they review in plays.' How does he know? Shocking, he calls it. But what, I ask Nigel in a letter, gives him immunity against the same parasitic charge, as a middle-class BBC trainee and shadow-Bragg media opportunist who has written about working-class schoolkids and teachers (in *Class Enemy*) and supervised countless arts and books programmes on television, as well as writing, most recently, a television film about two Cambridge academics and critics, F R Leavis and his wife Queenie. I bet Nigel's earned much more over the years than the Leavises ever did, and I know for certain who's made the greater contribution. Nigel has written back saying point taken but 'it's still shocking'; next time, he says, he'll attack Benedict Nightingale.

In *Class Enemy*, his most successful play, Williams placed the action in a dead-end classroom, 5K, 'K for cunts' as one of the boys said. I reported this detail in my Financial Times notice. My copy was edited, then sub-edited, and passed down to the printers for what was still in those days setting in hot metal. There was a furore. 'What the fuck's this!' the dreadful Ron, the foul-mouthed head printer, exclaimed: '5K, K for cunts; we're not having that fucking language in this fucking paper, tell 'im to fuck off.' So I did just that and let them have their wicked way with my parasitic copy. I thus failed to make a breakthrough comparable to that of Freddie Young, some years earlier, who had proudly declared that he had at last got 'a bugger' onto the arts page; this triumph was coolly received by the sub-editor, the estimable Kevin Henriques, who was mindful of an arts page history embracing the careers of Derek Grainger, T C Worsley, Andrew Porter, Clement Crisp, Nigel Andrews, Alastair Macaulay, Max Loppert, Dominic Gill and diverse fey and incorruptible musical reporters, a veritable stream of queens down three decades: 'What on earth do you mean, Freddie? We've had buggers on the arts pages for years!'

Bill Paterson shuffles his small children around the Eyres' kitchen and talks glowingly to Neil Kinnock. 'Hello, Neil,' sounds a peculiar form of greeting in the Glaswegian accent. I am impressed that Richard is still in contact with all his closest friends from his days at the Nottingham Playhouse in the mid 1970s. When he went there, the Royal Court had unwisely closed its doors against the fringe graduate generation of Griffiths, Hare and Brenton. Richard took them all to Nottingham and reaped the benefit: *Comedians*, *Brassneck*, *The Churchill Play*, all modern classics. This was the real root of his success and aspiration to the top of the National Theatre tree. Peter Hall spotted his successor. Hall is an absentee guest at this feast, but there are countless connections. Ian Holm was the archetypal RSC actor, straddling Pinter and Shakespeare in his definitive performances as Lenny in *The Homecoming* and as the Duke of Gloucester (Richard III) in *The Wars of the Roses*; he is here with Penelope Wilton, to whom he is married. Also present: Christopher Morahan, an old stalwart of the Hall era, and his wife Anna Carteret; Eileen Atkins; Julie Christie; Brian Glover, the former wrestler and Yorkshire actor, and his longterm partner Tara Prem, an inventive television producer; and others and no doubt countless others who will arrive after I have left in order to avoid any further embarrassments and arguments. Richard later writes to say that he is potting out his fifty pansies. And, I think to myself, he doesn't even have to pay them the Equity minimum.

# APRIL

## *Talking several shops with Andrew Lloyd Webber*

ON APRIL FOOL'S DAY, on the eve of rehearsals for his new musical version of Billy Wilder's great movie, *Sunset Boulevard*, I am interviewing Sir Andrew Lloyd Webber in his house in Eaton Square. He is a strange, obsessive creature, not nearly as humourless and self-important as he's cracked up to be. When he produced *Daisy Pulls It Off*, an Angela Brazil-style gymslip jamboree, in the West End, he wrote a rousing school hymn under the anagrammatised moniker of Beryl Waddle-Browne.

Taxi cab-drivers, and millions of theatregoers, think that Lloyd Webber is a genius. Not even Ivor Novello in his heyday, nor Noël Coward in his prime, commanded such universal admiration and respect. On the other hand, no-one in today's theatre arouses such knee-jerk, automatic passionate hatred. Why? Because snobbish 'music-lovers' (how often have you heard someone say 'I love music, but I hate musicals'?) feel that he plagiarises Puccini (whom they don't much like anyway), debases the currency of rock music (which they know nothing about) and frightens the spirit of informal adventurism in theatre. He is also sinfully successful, *and* he votes Conservative.

He is suspended between the Scylla of those who think he has nothing to do with main line modern music and the Charybdis of those who think ditto in his relationship to modern theatre. For a synthesizing populist with an undoubted melodic gift, he will simply have to make do with his personal fortune, enduring fame and the idea of being taramasalata, if not caviar, to the general.

Everything he writes comes ready-mixed with an instant feel of familiarity, even though you can't always quite pin down the reference. This is quite a gift. You could say he was a cultural opportunist with the proclivities of a thieving magpie; you could also award him points for exemplifying post-modernism. One of his biographers, the Time music critic, Michael Walsh, says that his overall style is 'a semi-conscious agglutination of rock, show music and classical influences'. *Jesus Christ Superstar*, says Lloyd Webber, was a mixture of Bill Haley and Stravinsky. But in that musical's atonal setting of the Seven Last Words, you can also detect traces of Ligeti and Penderecki.

His younger brother Julian, the cellist, for whom Lloyd Webber wrote the Variations on a theme of Paganini that is the signature tune for Melvyn Bragg's 'South Bank Show', says that the piece contains the best writing for the cello since Britten. Most serious music critics recognised the honesty and fleeting charm of his *Requiem*, but withheld full-hearted approval of its patchwork quality: 'Ravel, Fauré, Orff and Prokofiev parade past in graceful salute,' said the New York Times. The *Requiem*'s beautiful 'Pie Jesu', which became a chart-topping hit, combined a boy treble with Sarah Brightman's bell-like soprano in rising thirds, just as Mozart combined the two sisters in *Cosi fan tutte*.

What triggers the modish intellectual distaste for Lloyd Webber is not just the churchy, conservative elements in his background, training and cultural predilections, but also the apparently contra-dictory, but unquenchable, appetite for publicity. He simultan-eously announced the end of his first marriage and made public his affair with the singer Sarah Brightman the morning after the first night of *Daisy Pulls It Off* and managed to marry her just in time to meet the Queen at a royal gala of *Starlight Express*.

He maintains a professional liaison and friendship with Bright-man, whom he divorced, while enthusiastically embracing his third wife's interest in clothes' design and equestrianism. He has written two election campaign anthems for the Conservative Party as well as a sixtieth birthday mini-musical for the Queen, *Cricket*, with Tim Rice, directed by Trevor Nunn and fortuitously produced by Edward Windsor; he has saved a large, bland Canaletto 'for the nation' at a personal cost of £10m (only after he had acquired the 1749 'Old Horse Guards,' did he notice two tiny chaps relieving themselves against a wall in the middle-ground); has supported various charities, including research into diabetes (his first wife is a diabetic); and has duly received the inevitable knighthood.

*Sunset Boulevard*, which is his first big show since *Aspects of Love*, has book and lyrics by Christopher Hampton and Don Black, and is directed by Trevor Nunn. Patti LuPone, who played Evita on Broadway, stars in the Gloria Swanson role, and the electrifying young film actor Kevin Anderson is the ensnared writer, Joe Gillis, played in the movie by William Holden. The Adelphi Theatre in the Strand, half-owned by Lloyd Webber, has been completely refurbished. Billy Wilder's script has been honoured in the structure and no attempt made to put music to such legendary lines as 'I am big; it's the pictures that got small;' or 'I'm ready for my close-up now, Mr de Mille.'

'It's the start of the sleepless nights,' says the richest and most powerful figure in the London and New York theatre, sitting back in his drawing room, where a fire crackles beneath one of his more mundane Millais paintings (all the best ones are in his extensive Victorian and Pre-Raphaelite art collection in Sydmonton Court, his Hampshire home).'The one thing I know *Sunset* needs is a director like Trevor who can really work with actors. As long as I can keep him from over-elaborating, which I think I can because he knows what is needed . . . '

*Sunset* has long been a cherished project. 'It was a possibility at the time of *Evita*. Hal Prince had acquired the rights and Stephen Sondheim was interested in doing it; I think he wanted to push the story forward in time. I didn't, and I started thinking about it again at the time of *Phantom*. The car chase is the difficult bit: without it, the writer does not arrive at Norma Desmond's house and there is no story. For all its gothic romanticism, the piece is really about the relationships of four people. We need a chorus for certain scenes, but I was worried that there would be too little to justify having them. But you have to stay true to what you've written; and anyway, in *La Bohème*, the chorus only appears in the second act . . . '

The musical was 'tried out' at last summer's annual Sydmonton Festival, where Lloyd Webber presides over a weekend of japes and junketing, performances in his converted chapel, demonstrations of napkin-folding, balloon modelling or Scottish dancing, and the Saturday night black-tie dinner with a debate which is blithely chaired by one of his staunchest friends, the Minister for Agriculture, John Selwyn Gummer.

At past Sydmonton debates, scriptwriter Richard Curtis has upstaged his own Black Adder star, Rowan Atkinson; Derek Jameson has won all hearts; the disgraced, drowned entrepreneur Robert Maxwell has loomed ferociously over Sunday Times editor Andrew Neil. And last year, Jack Tinker locked horns with Stephen Fry, who delivered a sort of preppy Young Conservative speech against critics, knockers and second-raters who dared to deride success stories like Sir Andrew and his own hallowed mate Kenneth Branagh. He very nearly got the bread roll treatment he deserved from Cameron Mackintosh's table.

Meryl Streep flew in to join the invited audience of producers, record company executives, friends and neighbours. She witnessed a performance by Patti LuPone as Norma Desmond which moved her to tears — of sympathetic emotion, or blind envy, we shall never know. La Streep still holds out fading hopes of *Evita* on film and Norma Desmond on Broadway (Glenn Close has been announced for the Los Angeles opening later this year). For it was clear to everyone present that Patti LuPone had simply resolved all arguments over who should have the *Sunset* lead in the London premiere. This was not a 'try-out'; it was a flabbergasting, full-scale assault whose impact was as unexpected as that of Olivier performing Othello with all the stops out at his famous first rehearsal at the National. There was talk of a Los Angeles opening before London, but Lloyd Webber still regards London as his creative home base, 'partly because of the enormous turnaround in the range of musical skills and abilities', a situation for which he is largely responsible.

Lloyd Webber has almost total control over his destiny these days, a situation he relishes. He is not a back seat driver. When he floated the Really Useful Group on the stock market he made a personal fortune of £9m. Over four years, the share price increased three-fold, but outside speculators, notably the Australian tycoon Robert Holmes à Court, and Robert Maxwell, were building up large stakes. In 1990, Lloyd Webber put a stop to the uncertainty: he bought back the company for £77m and sold thirty per cent to Polygram (for £78m!), who deal with his music publishing and recordings. In the following year, the annual turnover was £54m. This year it will be £70m.

He fills his day to the brim with his work, his children, his paintings. Only Charles Saatchi is comparable in Britain as a private collector of such dedication and thoroughness. One of his oldest friends, David Crewe-Read, was his companion and adviser around the salerooms for years until they fell out after a dispute over the price of a Leighton sculpture (a law-suit is pending); Lloyd Webber's associate in the markets these days is David Mason, a former 'Antiques Road Show' host and sponsor of the Gatcombe Horse Trials. Ironically, Lloyd Webber's third wife, brigadier's daughter Madeleine Gurdon, was introduced to him by Crewe-Read, and Mason came to Lloyd Webber through Madeleine.

None of this deflects Lloyd Webber from his consuming passion for the Pre-Raphaelites. Everything flows from Millais' 'Design for a Gothic Window' in the Sydmonton entrance hall, and the house is crammed with Victorian furniture and ceramics, and a vast, inexhaustibly interesting display of pictures by Millais, Burne-Jones and Rossetti (no great Holman Hunts, as yet) as well as such popular masterpieces as Leighton's 'Dante In Exile', Luke Fildes' 'The Village Wedding', Arthur Hughes's 'Silver and Gold'. One of his latest acquisitions (£1.6m at Christie's last year), soon to be hung in the Tate, is Richard Dadd's crowded, brilliant and peculiar study of Titania and Oberon, painted in Bethlem Hospital where the artist was committed for killing his father.

One day, all of these pictures will be placed on permanent public view by the foundation Lloyd Webber is establishing. He has never, until recently, bought an Alma-Tadema, whom he does not much like, but he thought he'd better have one. It stands propped up in the hall in Eaton Square, a stilted mythological scene ludicrously composed in front of the Roman Coliseum.

The London house itself, bought on a whim of Sarah Brightman, for £10.5m, is much less to Lloyd Webber's taste than either Sydmonton or his retreat on Cap Ferrat in the South of France. It is ornately furnished, bearing the pretentious hallmarks of oil-rich ownership (Soraya Khashoggi, ex-wife of the arms dealer, leased the premises to a Nigerian chief, his two wives and their twenty children, all of whom were unceremoniously evicted in 1985 after non-payment of serious bills). The six-storey, higgledy-piggledy mansion is linked by a spectacular conservatory to a pair of knocked-through mews houses where three cheerful Sloaney girls man the office.

This house, like the apartment in the Trump Tower in New York, was Sarah Brightman's idea of the high life. Lloyd Webber's favourite possessions, apart from his paintings, are the eight volumes of Dugdale's *Monasticum Anglicanum*. He is addicted to the ideas propounded by Pevsner in *The Englishness of English Art*. Hence his liking for the Tudor unpretentiousness of Sydmonton Court, with all its odd architectural accretions, and the surrounding six thousand acres, including Watership Down, about which he is fanatical.

'Sydmonton is quintessentially English, architecturally indifferent, sitting in the middle of very ordinary English countryside. I have all that land partly because I want to keep it that way, which is why we've planted so many trees – 30,000, I think, over the past five years.'

Where did all this start? 'My interest started at Westminster School. The abbey is a medieval building, but I was always very intrigued by some of the glass there, a lot of it Victorian. The best glass was designed by a chap named Bodley who was also a church architect. Then – and John Betjeman was a great influence on me – I became interested in Victorian churches, and they in turn had a lot of windows by William Morris and company.

'From there it was a short step to Rossetti and Burne-Jones and the Tate Gallery. It was great fun because, in the late 1960s, it was blindingly obvious (to me, at any rate) that the Pre-Raphaelites were ludicrously underestimated. I remember Lord Leighton's 'Flaming June' being bought in a junk shop in Fulham for £50. It now lives in an art gallery in Puerto Rica in an art gallery where nobody goes, and the current evaluation would be between three and four million.'

Anyone with talent and ambition in the British theatre would want to work with him. He keeps the finest interpretative artists of the day on permanent tenterhooks – Trevor Nunn, Hal Prince, Steven Pimlott, and a legion of choreographers, stage and lighting designers, orchestrators and costumiers. These are not necessarily sycophantic dependants (though they may, sometimes, be made to feel like that), but the cream of our theatre talent.

The hype and publicity, all part of the act, all part of the desire to reach millions while making them, provoke strong reactions to this fidgety, intense, conspicuously unrelaxed 45-year-old whom Sarah Brightman affectionately described as 'a slug in flared trousers'. Julian Lloyd Webber gets fed up with the constant barrage of attention: 'If I go somewhere to play the Shostakovich or Honneger concertos, the last thing I want to hear is some cretin banging on about whether or not I like *Starlight Express*'.

When that rollerskating spectacular of rock, blues and hot gospel opened nine years ago, Gerald Scarfe provided the Sunday Times with a cartoon of Lloyd Webber's face distorted into a diesel engine on the 'No Story Line', appending the couplet 'This is the Webber train crossing the border/ Bringing the cheque and the postal order'. And last year, Malcolm Williamson, the more or less anonymous Master of the Queen's Music, described Lloyd Webber's music as 'absolutely fatuous'. It was, he admitted, everywhere (which is more than you can say of his stuff), adding with a taste-lessness that demolished his own argument, 'But then so is AIDS.'

Lloyd Webber has become inured against such knockabout over the years, but he does seem to have one serious problem, one he shares with his admired Puccini: finding compatible collaborators. Richard Rodgers, whom Lloyd Webber met as a stage-struck schoolboy, and who remains his idol, worked with Lorenz Hart for twenty-five years and with Oscar Hammerstein for eighteen. Lloyd Webber may or may not work again with Tim Rice, his collaborator on *Joseph and the Amazing Technicolor Dreamcoat*, *Jesus Christ Superstar* and *Evita*, but their partnership now appears to be channelled towards recovering and protecting their rights in that early work.

Don Black, an adept, workmanlike lyricist with a fine ear for idiom and musical phrase, has long been a loyal, but fitfully employed, colleague. There was more than mere promise to Charles Hart's work on *Phantom*, but precious little since. How long will Christopher Hampton last? 'I do feel the introduction of Chris Hampton into my life has been rather useful, to put it mildly; it's the first time, other than on *Jeeves*, that I've worked with a first-class serious dramatist.'

The critic Mark Steyn thinks that Lloyd Webber is like Sigmund Romberg, a fine melodist with no appreciation of words. The evidence does not entirely support this: although tunes tend to come before the lyrics (and after the 'phone-call), Lloyd Webber is at his most skilful and compelling when a song demands energetic or complex rhythmical setting, such as in 'Everything's All Right' with its bright tonality and bouncy 5/4 time signature in *Superstar*; 'Take That Look off Your Face', a pounding conversational item in *Tell Me On a Sunday* with a zingy, mobile beat; or 'Another Suitcase in Another Hall', a satisfying, wistful ballad in *Evita*. The entire score of *Evita*, in which Rice's lyrics, although sometimes banal, are vigorous and racy, is a vivid compilation of abruptly shifting metres, Latin rhythms and parodistic dance numbers.

The clean break from Rice, after a series of disagreements, was achieved when *Cats* suggested itself as a dance musical derived from the poems of T S Eliot. The hit song 'Memory' is widely held to be a clever subversion of 'One Fine Day' from *Madam Butterfly* (Lloyd Webber certainly hauled in the tune from a long-stagnant Puccini project), just as 'I Don't Know How To Love Him,' Mary Magdalene's lament in *Superstar* is, as Lloyd Webber is the first to acknowledge, a flattened out transcript of the triple-time slow movement theme in Mendelssohn's *Violin Concerto*. But creative borrowing, like creative miserliness, is nothing unusual among composers. And, like Beethoven and Rossini, Lloyd Webber steals most often from himself.

*The Phantom of the Opera* was lush, in the same way as *Sunset Boulevard* will be lush. *Aspects of Love* was really a chamber piece over-blown in production for economic reasons. It may be that Lloyd Webber, in order to pacify cynical objections to his onward march, may have to pare right down to the basics not only in presentation but also in compositional style. Unlike Stephen Sondheim, who shares the same birthday, he is reluctant to submit to workshops or out-of-town try-outs as a way of redefining his talent.

Duke Ellington once said that there are only two kinds of music: good and bad. It is one of Lloyd Webber's favourite aphorisms, and he refuses to draw demarcation lines between pop and rock and classical and jazz. It would be wrong to conclude that he is a creature of the Classic FM era merely because he seems to suit it so well. He came first.

I ask Lloyd Webber about the alleged displacement of good new plays in the West End theatre by his sort of musical. 'That's rubbish. We are hardly occupying theatres that might otherwise be homes to new plays. In fact, the reverse is true. Musicals always used to play in houses like the Albery – *Oliver!* for instance did – but now have to play in big barns because of the technical requirements. The New London was a death zone before *Cats*. And you'd hardly say the Apollo Victoria, home of *Starlight Express*, was a great place for a play. The Lyric on Shaftesbury Avenue, where *Five Guys Named Moe* is playing, was always a musical house. And so was the Adelphi; it had things like Rodgers and Hart's *Evergreen*, which re-opened the theatre more or less as we know it under Charles Cochran's management in 1930. Oh no, that really is a lot of rubbish. There is lots of room for new plays. But who is writing them? And the more big musicals there are, the better. The more people will come to London. It's like restaurants. If you suddenly find there are four good restaurants in a village in Devon, you say let's go and stay in that village and try all four, don't you?'

## Radio waves, radio times

A NEW PLAY by Tom Stoppard, *Arcadia*, brings me for the first time in some weeks into a BBC radio studio. The play is virtually incomprehensible in the theatre, but I arrive at Broadcasting House with my colleague Sarah Hemming of the Independent to encounter a more or less unqualified deluge of support for Trevor Nunn's National Theatre production. 'Night Waves', the arts programme which goes out live nightly to a very small audience, is one of Nicholas Kenyon's innovations as director of Radio 3. There are others, such as entrusting the news headlines to barely competent arts programme presenters, that are downright insulting and suicidal. But 'Nightwaves', though I hardly ever listen to it, is a decent, civilising programme struggling somewhat to compete convincingly with the ever resourceful 'Kaleidoscope' on Radio 4.

It is merrily presided over this evening by a chap called Roy Porter, who apparently writes books about madness. The more he enthuses, however, the less enthusiastic I feel about the play and suddenly find myself, partly against my will, cast in the role of devil's advocate. I feel slightly jumpy to start with, as I possess a son called Thomas Coveney and a colleague called Benedict Nightingale, and the two chief activating characters in the play are named Thomasina Coverly and Bernard Nightingale. In *The Real Inspector Hound*, Stoppard has already written the nightmare of a critic turning up in a play he has innocently gone along to review ; and if there is one predominant theme in *Arcadia*'s firework display of coincidence and collision in a nineteenth-century Derbyshire country house, it is that if you really exist, and sometimes even if you don't, you will, one day, finally appear in a Tom Stoppard play.

There is no-one like Stoppard for making you feel both spoilt and inadequate as an audience. There has been an erotic encounter in the gazebo and Ezra Chater, a poet whom Byron excoriated in his *English Bards and Scotch Reviewers*, has been shot. Chater never existed; the reference has been divined by Nightingale in a pencilled superscription on a contemporary edition. But this fictional Chater may also have been a botanist who discovered a dwarf dahlia in Martinique in 1810 and died there of a monkey bite. The genius of the place is described as a hermit with a tortoise, and that explains, or at least contributes to an understanding of, the scientific investigation running parallel to the literary speculations. The combustion Stoppard seeks is in telling a murder mystery with intellectual acrobatics.

In *Jumpers*, we witnessed love among the logical positivists. In *Hapgood*, Stoppard's last stage play, a plot of mystery and espionage jostled alongside quantum physics and the atomic theory of particles. Once you get round to reviewing these plays, you can delight in their ingenuity and fizz. Sitting through them in the theatre is, I invariably find, a bit more of a problem. Roy Porter and Sarah Hemming have had no such difficulty. They blaze away while I feebly try and suggest that what they are doing is extrapolating an experience from something that never really caught fire. Trevor Nunn's production does everything possible to ignite the proceedings and the acting all round is superb, and the play, I concede, finally bursts its bounds in the sensual submission to the strains of the waltz, which invades the past and the present. A discussion about carnal embrace was the play's starting point.

It is interesting how inexact and unrewarding the discussion of books, films and plays on the radio can be. I slink home from 'Nightwaves' feeling that scant justice has been served on Stoppard, whatever one's view of the play. The same used to be true on 'Critics' Forum', but at least the discussion was properly structured by the producer, Philip French, and there was ample opportunity, in a 50-minute programme, to both fly some kites and nail a few colours to the mast. Controlled descriptive analysis is the commodity that escapes all radio discussions. Speakers become either fixated on irrelevant detail or trapped in a variation on a theme that has not been properly expounded in the first place. You do not, as a contributor, have any real control over what the discussion is saying about an artefact or event, and one is invariably content to drift along in a miasma of self-congratulatory babble that has more to do with filling up air time without coming a cropper than with actually fulfilling any serious critical commitment. There is one really wonderful moment in my 'Nightwaves' contribution that must have been a nightmare for the producer: I completely freeze, in mid-sentence, while searching for the title of another Tom Stoppard play. The night waves hum with nothing more than silent static for several seconds until the redoubtable, irrepressible Mr Porter comes to my rescue. The irony is that the play I was seeking, *In the Native State*, was written by Stoppard for radio and may very well be his most accomplished and most brilliant piece of work to date. I certainly think it is superior to *Arcadia*, and it does not surprise me at all to learn later in the month that the Royal National Theatre has plans to produce it on the stage.

As chance would have it, I am back in another BBC radio studio within several days, this time for the programme that replaced 'Critics' Forum', 'Third Opinion'. To my absolute horror, this, too, goes out live and pretty well untended. In the old days, Philip French would have scripted the introduction and linking passages with his chairman. Each contributor would have been in contact with the 'Critics' Forum' office during the week, collecting information, making appointments, feeling part of the whole process. Then on the Thursday afternoon, we would assemble for lunch, a ferociously competitive salon presided over by Philip, at which various soups and salads, cheeses and desserts would be consumed with a certain amount of wine, mineral water and coffee. Over the coffee, Philip would ascertain where each of the four critics stood on the five topics, usually a book, a film, a play, an exhibition and a broadcast play or documentary. The ritual was both highly enjoyable and totally nerve-wracking. The show would be recorded in two segments, and Philip would edit the proceedings on the following day for broadcast on Saturday afternoon. This, at least, was the procedure in the latter years of the programme, before it was unceremoniously axed by the outgoing head of Radio 3, John Drummond.

No particular disrepect to Christopher Cook, who now presents 'Third Opinion', but this substitute neither corrects the alleged weaknesses of 'Critics' Forum' (its chummy metropolitanism, its stiffness and formality, its air of intellectual do-gooding) nor seeks a more populist path. The subject this week is new plays in London, with an interpolated interview about a National Theatre studio season. None of the contributors is properly briefed or prepared. Christopher Cook, a fine broadcaster, appears in the studio just ten minutes before we go on the air. Nicholas Wright, the National Theatre associate director, has no idea what plays are under discussion by myself and the other two panellists (the poet and playwright Michelene Wandor and the festival director Lucy Neal), nor whether he is supposed to join in a discussion of plays he has not seen. Even as we talk, I know, because I have heard the programme many times at home, that nothing of what we say makes any real sense to the listening public for the simple reason that it has not been properly prepared, described or contextualised. The physical detail of each play has been airily entrusted to each of the panellists in turn, but no script has been agreed or even outlined. The resulting broadcast, lively enough in its extremely limited way, is simply inadequate, hectic and uncontrolled. The time is up, Mr Cook thanks us all for coming, no refreshment is offered and we are bundled out of the studio and back onto the streets. Later that evening, my mother-in-law in Halifax, West Yorkshire, telephones to say that it all sounded very good but that she did not know what on earth we were talking about.

## The observed of all observers

I LEFT A SECURE JOB on the Financial Times for a considerably less secure one on the Observer at the start of 1990. Just how insecure would not be apparent until the middle of this month when it finally emerges that the Observer is about to be sold. The chief bidders were the Independent, who certainly planned to close the paper in order to improve the mediocre performance of the Independent on Sunday; and the Guardian, spiritual bedfellow but unlikely, it is thought, to be in a position to pay off the debts and invest in an effective re-launch.

I had not really planned to move papers, but when the opportunity arose I had no qualms about taking a weekly column. Not because I was tired of writing overnight notices, as has sometimes been suggested; but because any change is as good as a rest and, for all its travails and imperfections, the Observer placed the coverage of arts and books at the very heart of its editorial operation. I felt I could thrive in such an environment and this, after all, was the home of all the critics I had most admired as a boy: not just Tynan, but the film critic C A Lejeune, her current successor Philip French, and almost everyone else from Ronald Bryden and Paul Ferris to Clive James and John Naughton. William Feaver, the art critic, and Jann Parry, the dance critic, were already good friends and valued colleagues.

The invitation was first mooted, I recall, in October 1989 at the first night of Peter O'Toole in *Jeffrey Bernard is Unwell*. The then Observer drama critic, Michael Ratcliffe, said he would like a word in the interval. I found him in his fauteuil. He said that, after six years in the hot seat, he was moving across to take charge of the Observer's books pages. Could the editor, Donald Trelford, write me a letter? I said that he could, but I did not really envisage moving from my jealously guarded perch in the pink pages. The technological revolution had suited me very well, though some of my more epicene, other-worldly colleagues were resisting the advance of the Tandy and the word processor with all the doomed fatuity of King Canute confronting the waves. After the *Jeffrey Bernard* performance, I drove home, poured a glass of wine and happily tapped my notice into my machine which, thanks to the magical modem and a touch of British Telecom in the night, whizzed the copy straight into the FT computer system. The downside of the computer revolution is that one is deprived of the companionship and subliminal input of office colleagues, especially that of the sub-editor, the irreplaceable Henriques; Kevin is audibly unhappy on the phone about my conspicuous lack of presence in the office these days, not because he craves my company, but because newspapers, in his view, work best when journalists are talking to each other in between, and even concurrent to, doing the job. There is a lot to be said for this. On the other hand, I will have filed my copy and be free of my obligations a full one hour earlier than was usually the case in the old days.

Donald Trelford's letter duly arrives and I later discover that not only Ratcliffe, but also my old FT colleague, Gillian Widdicombe, now the Observer's arts editor, have urged my appointment upon him. I report to Chelsea Bridge House and Trelford explains that Lonrho, the Observer's owners, are investing afresh in their loss-making newspaper to counteract the launch of the Independent on Sunday, itself a spiteful invention aimed at destroying the promising new Sunday Correspondent and exploiting a wavering Observer reputation among the chattering classes, at least in the south of England. He is still visibly wincing at the defection of his literary editor, Blake Morrison, to the new Sunday paper, and of Neil Ascherson to its opinion columns. Morrison, a gifted Yorkshire poet and fine newspaperman, is one of the youngest and most brilliant protégés of the Observer's legendary literary editor, Terence Kilmartin. He will perform wonders on the Independent on Sunday, whereas Ascherson will mysteriously shrivel in authority in the way that commentators unaccountably sometimes do when they change their bath water.

I say that the Observer will not have really lost its way until Hugh McIlvanney, the distinguished sports writer, leaves. Trelford is a well known sports freak, most affectionately renowned among his colleagues in the latter years of his editorial tenure for departing the office for lunch at the Garrick Club with his snooker cue tucked under his arm. He hails from Coventry and supports that city's football team. While chatting, I impertinently deplore the fact the Observer is no longer listing next week's soccer fixtures in the sports pages. I also say that I cannot join the Observer without maintaining my FT salary, joining the staff and taking charge of a Tandy computer. That's that, I feel, as I hightail it out of Battersea.

Within a week, I receive a letter offering me the staff job. And next week's soccer fixtures have been immediately reinstated. The following three years, while enjoyable, and fraught with friendship, see a steady decline in circulation which culminates in this month's crisis. The internal changes at Lonrho, where hard-headed Germans have bought into the company, means that losses of nearly £9m a year on the Observer can no longer be justified. The end of April is characterised in London by rail strikes and a new spate of IRA bombings. The city is under siege, and on Shakespeare's birthday, April 23, the rumour spreads through the Observer offices like wildfire that the Independent is indeed on the verge of buying the Observer. The impact of this news is immediate: a public campaign is launched to save the title, Members of Parliament, as well as Guardian executives, are heavily canvassed, we all raise the battle cry on our respective fields of operation, and the response is quite fantastic. People who no longer read the Observer regard it as an affront to their lifestyle that it may soon be subsumed in the Independent on Sunday. Letters are written, telephone calls made, the wires hum. What are we trying to preserve, beyond our own jobs? Michael Frayn, who worked on the paper in the sixties as a humorous columnist in succession to Paul Jennings, writes a wonderful article in the Sunday Telegraph. He says that for him, in the fifties, the Observer was not just a reflection of the world; it *was* the world. He cites some of the great reporters of the past, and declares that something of the Observer's old self has always remained, through all its travails and transformations.

The problem has always been adjusting to the present and if there's one thing I have not really liked about my time on the newspaper it is the insistent dirge about the Observer's status, past editors and writers, its over-readiness to claim a reputation for distinction and independence while not keeping an open mind, and focused eye, on the real issues; that reputation was slightly undermined by the Harrods issue, in which a special mid-week Observer questioned the suitability of the Fayed Brothers as prospective owners of the Knightsbridge store when their chief rival was the Observer's own proprietor, Lonrho chairman Tiny Rowland. And far too much attention has been paid to reader surveys – always a sure sign of editorial dithering – instead of getting on with discovering what it was the paper really believed in. Also, its political heart seems to have stopped beating at the very moment in our nation's history – stuck in a trough of indecisive Tory leadership under John Major, with an anonymous Labour opposition under John Smith and an electorate totally bemused by whether or not we should be approving the Maastricht Treaty – when it needed to be pumping away more violently than ever.

Just when all seemed lost, it is announced a few days after the Independent rumour that the Guardian has bought the title. Jubilation, perhaps premature, is the order of the day in the offices. But when the new editor, Jonathan Fenby, and his Guardian colleague Peter Preston, address the staff, they make it perfectly clear that nobody's job is guaranteed and that savings and cuts are to be made in a draconian style. The Guardian has agreed to shoulder the debts, and Lonrho will take care of the redundancy payments. This means that the new editorial team can literally hire whom they like and start what is virtually a brand new paper within the Guardian's premises on Farringdon Road. In theory, we assume that many of the staff journalists will be retained on the paper. But in practice, there is no reason why that should necessarily be so. It is going to be a very tense summer for all of us. We shall not know the best or the worst until the autumn, in my case as I am packing my bags for the Edinburgh Festival. One of the buzz words at the Fenby/Preston conference is synergy, which I take to mean the merging of facilities, the exploitation of shared means of production. I can see that, when this takes place in the respective advertising, marketing and indeed managerial operations, the savings could be as much as £5m a year. I hope the line is drawn, though, at encouraging me and Michael Billington to share a bedroom at Edinburgh. Meanwhile, all one can do is audition for one's job on a weekly basis by writing a decent column. Personally, I've never thought of myself as doing anything but that in all of my journalistic career.

The great thing about the Observer is that, even in retreat, one is working for a newspaper whose readers claim extraordinary rights of ownership and intervention. Since moving from the more sedate world of the FT, I have had more letters in a week than I would usually receive in a year. I have missed reading my own overnight notices, if you can understand that subtle regret, and I have occasionally felt frustrated at the Observer with the need to cramp my descriptions of productions – what actors actually *did*, what designs actually *looked* like – into the pint pot of about 1,000 words for four or even five productions. But I have felt curiously liberated, too, not from the overnight scramble, which I always relished anyway, but by the task of taking brutal decisions within the wide range of British theatrical activity. We could do with more reviewing space, but the current editorial wisdom prefers features and arts news to the luxury of an additional four or five hundred words of critical writing. This is a battle I hope not to have lost for ever. Just as I hope, one day, a resurgent Observer will renew its faith in its Scottish and Irish readers by providing more coverage of their communities in the overall political coverage; the Scottish edition was cut as an economy in my early days, and has cost the paper dear in its standing north of the border and indeed north of Watford.

# MAY

## *Violence, art and the new Republicans*

I AM ALL FOR VIOLENCE in the theatre and in the cinema. Up there, beyond us, to gawp at, is where it belongs. This is the principle behind much of Jacobean drama and, I would submit, the controversial film *Reservoir Dogs*, which I take to be one of the most brilliantly acted films of recent years, classical in many ways, with an impressive control of narrative structure in flashback by the new writer/director Quentin Tarantino.

In one crucial sequence, in the warehouse where the gang is fitfully congregating after a misfired heist, a policeman who has been taken hostage has his ear sliced off by the most chillingly masochistic of the crooks. Many people I know, including my wife, had to leave the cinema at this point. I sat there squirming, telling myself loudly under my breath that I was only watching an incident enacted and pre-recorded on film. Reality can be unwatchable on celluloid. So can pretence, but with fiction you have the intellectual safety-net.

The scene is exactly comparable to the blinding of Gloucester in *King Lear* without the comforting transparency of theatrical artifice (prop jelly eyes, fake blood, obvious physical sleight of hand). Another way of playing this scene, as Jonathan Miller cleverly demonstrated at the Old Vic a few years ago, is for the violence to be implied by being enacted offstage. As Gloucester's eyes were skewered out in the wings, Frances de la Tour as Regan stood alone, looking off, shuddering with banal pleasure, confused by the sensations running through her. Brilliant.

There is one sequence in this year's new *King Lear* starring Robert Stephens at Stratford-upon-Avon which is even more violent than the 'out, vile jelly' bits. Simon Russell Beale as Edgar, disguised as Poor Tom, a madman, finally crosses the insolent servant Oswald and instead of merely killing him with his dagger, stoves in his face with a pike staff. Again and again and again. Until the body lies limp, and we flop weakly in our stalls.

This was alarmingly, but theatrically, realistic, and people in the audience can apply that essential brake on their sensibilities in knowing they are watching actors pretending because they, the customers, are sitting there. Film inevitably evokes intenser reactions because the effects of violence can be so much more realistically, and mercilessly, deployed. Pundits therefore assume that its influence is for real. The media as scapegoat for reality has become a familiar refrain in the newspapers. The Sunday Times has published long extracts from Michael Medved's book in which Hollywood's sordid preoccupations with sex and violence are excoriated. Trouble is, the Sunday Times is owned by Rupert Murdoch, who is actively invading the lower end of the media market with satellite slush and extending his ownership and control of those very same Hollywood studios that pump out the supposedly detrimental violence-without-morality and sex-without-love movies that Medved so deplores.

So who is kidding whom about the responsibility for violence in the media? The situation is analogous to that which now surrounds the monarchy. The sex lives of the royals are common property thanks to the relentless campaign of exposure in the Murdoch press, in the name of 'the people's right to know'. What is so great, exemplary or moral about the lives led by these prosecuting journalists? Would we really rather take the club-haunting, opinionated, rather sinister editor of the Sunday Times as a national role model in preference to Prince Charles? Both men are about the same age. One seeks to change the world for profit; the other is trying to justify a role he never asked to play by being as useful as he can.

The other great 'Times', The Times itself, is holding a full day's seminar on the issues of royalty. It is chaired by a chap called Peter Stothard, the new editor of The Times, who was Murdoch's second choice after he failed to sign up Paul Dacre of the Daily Mail. Stothard has an above-average intellect wedded to an even more

above-average survival instinct. His moral and philosophical view
of the world, instinctively formed in a humble background, found a
back-up system in the emergent intellectual right-wing meritocracy
of the Thatcher era, embodied in Roger Scruton's Salisbury
Review group. He is no rabid monarchist, but nor is he a
committed republican. I would imagine he shares the Murdoch
view that the monarchy does a job of public importance and should
therefore be subject to rigorous scrutiny. I would be prepared to bet
a large sum that not many ordinary people think likewise. Stothard
is now fully implicated in a campaign that would have landed him
in the Tower and on the scaffold three hundred years ago.

Stothard came arsy-versy into this business of journalism and is
now one of the most influential people in Britain. His wife, Sally
Emerson, the novelist, was an esteemed and delightful colleague of
mine in the middle 1970s. She was my assistant and office chum
for a while on Plays and Players (where I worked from 1973 to
1978) before moving sideways to edit the sister publication of
Books and Bookmen and finally taking the plunge into both
motherhood and fiction. We worked for a one-man publication band
owned and ruled with a terrifying single-mindedness by a strange
closet homosexual called Philip Dossé, who eventually killed
himself when his debts became too dispiriting to live with. We
were lodged in a cramped but atmospheric basement sweatshop in
Artillery Mansions in Victoria Street (oh, happy days, hard by the
Army and Navy Stores, so near St James's Park). The other titles in
this strange little consortium included Films and Filming, Music
and Musicians and Dance and Dancers. The playwright Snoo
Wilson once suggested we should start another title for gay butchers called Mince and Mincing. In a way, we had. The company was
called Hansom Books ('handsome is as handsome does,' one of the
queens who worked there used to say) and we had an effervescent
telephonist-cum-advertising manager called Roy who used to man
(sic) the switchboard and greet each incoming call with a cheery
welcome: 'Hansom Books, the pretty pages, can I help you?'

One day we were stuck for someone to review some Greek
tragedy at Greenwich. Sally suggested that Pete was our man (he
was always Pete, not Peter, in those days), not unreasonably as

Pete had read classics at Oxford and was a palpably bright and intelligent fellow whenever he talked books, theatre or movies. He was working for Shell or some such oil company. He wrote about the plays brilliantly. It was his first writing job. Sally's best friend from Oxford was Tina Brown, who was at this time trying, with only moderate success, to hack out a reputation as a promising playwright. Thanks to Sally's Tina-connection, Stothard took a neat side-step from industry into journalism when Tina's husband Harry Evans assumed the editorship of The Times. He was appointed assistant features editor to Anthony Holden. When Murdoch took over The Times and Evans left, Holden resigned in solidarity with Evans. Stothard cleverly stayed put until, after a stint in Washington, he carefully made his way along the corridor to the editor's office himself. So we can safely conclude that the way to become an expert on the future of the monarchy is to review a Greek tragedy for a small theatre magazine. Anthony Holden, too, Stothard's first boss in journalism, himself an inveterate royal commentator and biographer of Prince Charles, was initially renowned for his translations from Greek poetry and indeed his dramatic criticism on Isis, the Oxford university magazine which he also edited. Q.E.D.

Arts, politics, royalty and violence in the media are also enmeshed in the public pronouncements of William Rees-Mogg. Nothing amuses me more than the creepy spectre of Lord Rees-Mogg, a former Times editor and Establishment figurehead, quondam moralising panjandrum of the influential, grant-dispensing Arts Council, collecting his monthly cheque from Murdoch in order to pontificate in The Times while employed as some sort of watchdog arbiter of TV standards which themselves have been placed under threat by the man signing those very same cheques. Where does the ultimate responsibility lie? Rees-Mogg has allowed himself, with no discernible sense of irony, to become the voice of a morally self-justifying, but simultaneously venal, worldwide media network.

Commentators talk about 'quality drama' when they mean 'Inspector Morse', or costumed classics. If there is any attempt, however risible, to take a new look at the sexuality in D H Lawrence's

*Lady Chatterley's Lover*, as there is to be this summer on television by Ken Russell, the press has a field day in both pruriently exploiting the sexual content while suggesting that the television companies, especially the BBC – 'which we pay for, as licence-holders' – should not be threatening the fabric of the nation's moral standards. A classic row has erupted over *Lipstick on Your Collar*, Dennis Potter's six-part series for Channel Four. The Daily Telegraph published a letter attacking the sex and violence in the show and described a scene showing 'the pretty heroine's face being beaten to a swollen, violet pulp by her boyfriend before he dragged her into bed for a session of triumphant sex.' As the pro-grammes' producer Peter Ansorge quietly replied in the Guardian: 'No such scene appeared.' Like a forest fire, the adverse commen-tary spread not through the review columns, but through the editorial punditry sections. There are more people giving opinions in newspapers these days than actually reviewing what happens on our stages and screens. It is all part of the rush to the pulpits that have been vacated by the clergy. Journalism once used to consist of writers reporting what they saw, places they had visited, adventures they had undertaken. Nowadays journalists like Julie Burchill merely shout their opinions and proudly boast – without any fear of contradiction – of not going anywhere, not doing anything, not knowing much.

Lord Rees-Mogg, the King Canute of his day, has now dropped the fight against pornography in favour of the fight against Europe by challenging the Government's enthusiasm for the Maastricht Treaty in the High Court. But not even he flinched from cruelty in Shakespeare. Anthony Burgess did: 'One play of his we are un-likely ever to see on the stage again, and are totally certain never to see adapted to television, is the tragedy of *Titus Andronicus*.'

Wrong! The play has become a crucial text in recent European theatre, a flashpoint of how we might begin to deal with violence, absorb its cathartic effect by transferring our worst nightmares to a piece of enacted fiction. In the past few years, there have been stage productions by Deborah Warner at the Royal Shakespeare Company, Peter Stein in Milan, Daniel Mesguisch in Paris, and the National Theatre of Craiova in Romania. This latter version summoned a fantastic, sinister parable of casual state terrorism; the others, in different degrees, and on various personal levels, addressed the 'performance' problem of how actors convey to audiences a notion of the capacity for grief, and how best we might express it.

What this proves is that there is a cultural life beyond Hollywood and what might be dictated in the newspapers. A play like *Titus*, with all its adolescent imperfections, has wormed its way into the repertoire and consciousness of a broadly based, intellectually inquisitive European audience.

Why is this? The play shows one barbaric regime replacing another. It reduces political conflict to personal revenge. It offers a Senecan anaesthetic to pain by showing how the moment of conflict is encapsulated in the moment of dismemberment. It is brutal. It is unpretentious in its poetry, even basic and childish. It is terribly direct, and it does not really sound like Shakespeare. Above all, the play challenges its main characters to express their grief in the face of barbaric indifference.

At every turn it seems to have become a play for today, and every single performance I have seen in the past two or three years utterly refutes Burgess's thesis. People are not incited to riot or to dismember each other at productions of *Titus*. Nor are they thus affected at most screenings of *A Clockwork Orange*, the Stanley Kubrick film of his novel that Burgess now renounces, years after reports that quartets of boys, fantastically dressed in the style of the film, raped nuns in Ploughkeepsie and beat up senior citizens in Indianapolis. It was not the aggression itself the youths learned from the film, says Burgess, but the *style* of aggression.

These instances which changed Burgess's mind are indeed alarming. It is at those rare, isolated moments when real-life violence imitates cinematic violence that one begins to get nervous. The old debate is back about the alleged media glorification of violence leading directly to violent crime. Any number of rapists and murderers appear in the courts admitting that the idea for some disgusting debauchery was fired by a film about serial killers. But where does the line have to be drawn? The evidence linking crimes to violence on screen is by no means conclusive. And it is fairly easy to argue that people who commit dastardly crimes of violence are as likely to be influenced by films as they are by any other media outlet of newsprint, television and pornography. We could only negate all possibility of criminal violence by destroying all forms of artistic, and indeed inartistic, expression. And then how would you account for the same, or similar, crimes when they continued to be committed?

Some people would certainly approve draconian action. Burgess himself cited the opinion, without endorsing it, of the novelist Pamela Hansford Johnson at the time of the Moors Murder, when the child killer Brady admitted that he might have been influenced by reading the Marquis de Sade's novel *Justine*: she said that if the burning of all the books in the world were necessary to save one child's death, we should not hesitate to light the faggots. You could take a national referendum on that proposition and probably return a majority in its favour.

I would almost certainly vote against. As Robert Hughes says in his magisterial polemic, *Culture of Complaint*, 'literature isn't a nice normalizing course of treatment whose purpose is to guide and cuff us into becoming better citizens of whatever republic we are reading in.' The arts are dangerous, and the imaginative life is often poisoned with imperfections. If one child dies as a result, or one mind is warped, or even several thousand, are we to close down the workshops and banish the artists? Brady could read de Sade. Many more Bradys might nowadays see violent pornography on satellite television. The agency of this new possibility of destruction is the irreversible expansion of the media and satellite communications, the global imperialist empire of communication masterminded by impresarios like Rupert Murdoch and tacitly supported by editors like Peter Stothard and pundits like Lord Rees-Mogg. We are all implicated.

As a result of the latest flare up, Sir Anthony Hopkins has stated categorically that he will not appear in any sequel to *The Silence of the Lambs*; but he has not offered to return the knighthood which this performance largely inspired (you could hardly have knighted him, Your Majesty, for his other film work to date, or for his bland performances as Antony and King Lear at the National). Hopkins's best stage performance of recent years was as Lambert le Roux, an unscrupulous colonial newspaper tycoon in *Pravda*, by David Hare and Howard Brenton. Le Roux was a recognisable Murdoch clone, tearing through the moribund British Establishment, and its newspaper industry, to gain control. This media revenge is inextricably bound up with the republican agenda Murdoch has set on the British monarchy. In every sense of the word, the Empire is striking back.

As for art, it must be dangerous and it must be disrespectful. You cannot make money out of promulgating trash and then turn around and complain about cultural standards. And there is a distinction to be made between rubbish and art. The difficulty is that good art, such as *Reservoir Dogs* or *King Lear*, does itself quite often exhibit the characteristics of pornography.

And that difficulty has never been expressed better than by Jean-Paul Sartre, writing apropos of de Sade and the artists he termed the true Surrealists: 'Art, of its essence, is opposed to that which exists; its task is neither to glorify nor to explain; its value is one of terrorism; it is a weapon against traditional values and morality; it is aggressive, challenging, destructive; it leads established society to deny itself through the medium of the culture it demands.'

# Festival fun from Glasgow to Montreal

FESTIVAL-GOING generally broadens the mind and, if you don't take enough exercise, the bottom. I love the serendipity of festivals, the sense of common purpose, the discovery of the unexpected and previously unknown, the camaraderie, the concentration. Looking back over the years, I realise that most of my first-time encounters with great new forces in world theatre were at festivals. And quite often unscheduled. When editing Plays and Players, I would be invited as a matter of course to BITEF in Belgrade. Here I saw Yuri Lyubimov's radical Taganka company on their first trip abroad, whose doomed leading actor, the poet Visotsky, the Bob Dylan of undergound Moscow, with a voice that sounded as if he had swallowed broken glass, croaked out his Hamlet while the moving walls listened; here there were workshops with Grotowski and his most brilliant disciple, Eugenio Barba, each challenging the theatre's social conventions and traditional differentiations between actor and audience; here came Peter Brook, and Ellen Stewart's La Mama from New York with the first productions of Andrei Serban, the D H Lawrence trilogy from the Royal Court, directed by Peter Gill. The point was that the ferment of a festival indicates a shared interest in humanity and politics that is all too readily lost in a diet of domestic cultural consumption. New countries, new people, new audiences, new languages, even new critics: the attempts at some sort of internationalist discourse are of use and value to all who participate. And invariably, one's appetite is renewed.

One totally unexpected invitation, in my Plays and Players days, arrived from Mexico City in 1976: would I care to attend an international festival in the old colonial town of Guanajuato? I would, but (I am afraid I had sniffed an air of careless generosity in the letter), it was essential that I travelled to Mexico with my secretary in order to fulfil the vast range of my theatrical obligations. Her name was Sue Hyman, my future wife. When we returned to Mexico the following year on the same jaunt, we were indeed married and Sue was pregnant. Being pregnant in Mexico is not recommended for tourists. One night, Sue fainted on the steps of the opera house and we found ourselves in the back of an ambulance fighting off people who wanted to stick needles in her arm. More happily, it was in Guanajuato that we discovered, quite by chance, the Rustaveli Theatre of Tbilisi performing Brecht's *Caucasian Chalk Circle* and a Georgian folk comedy. Had I not reported on this chance discovery, John Drummond may never have flown to Tbilisi to book them for his first Edinburgh Festival as director in 1979. The fact that in Guanajuato we also made friends with Dolores del Rio, honorary president of the festival, and magnificent even in old age, was something of a bonus. And here, too, we first met our friend Peter Bartlett, a professional diplomat with the Australian Embassy in Mexico City who retired from the service to settle in Ireland, where he acquired the ruined, haunted Leap Castle in County Offaly before sadly succumbing to AIDS. Bartlett, whose family was wealthy from running hotels in his native Perth, was a truly civilised companion who rarely travelled with more than a toothbrush and who invariably met me at Dublin Airport whenever I touched down in the Irish Republic.

Festival cities I have known and continue to love include Adelaide, Amsterdam, Paris, Barcelona, Berlin, Belgrade, Edinburgh, and Budapest. This month I am visiting one of the cities I know and like best in Britain, Glasgow, and one that is new to me, Montreal. There is a link between them in the work of Robert Lepage: Lepage is based in his home city of Quebec, but his work was first given international focus in the Festival of Americas in Montreal. And Lepage has been a welcome visitor to Glasgow's Tramway through the support and advocacy of two young British impresarios, Neil Wallace of the Tramway, and Michael Morris, who enthusiastically represents Lepage's company in Britain. Wallace and Morris are part of a circuit of internationally minded young British producers – the others include John Ashford of The Place, and Lucy Neal and Rose de Wend Fenton, admirable directors of the biennial London International Festival of Theatre – who are gradually changing the face of our theatre by exposing it to new European and American companies and artists in both theatre and dance. Such people often feel more at home in Glasgow than they do in London, where the theatrical climate remains resistant to foreign influences. And Glasgow, like Barcelona and Montreal, is a melting-pot city with robust traditions of socialist drama, music hall-variety and artistic hospitality.

This year's Glasgow Mayfest has a production worthy of any great international festival: *Macbeth* at the Tron, starring Iain Glen, directed by Michael Boyd. The stone and Tudorish atmosphere of the 1793 Tron Kirk is superbly exploited, the walls covered in brown panelling, candles fixed to the pillars and the havoc wrought by 'Bellona's bridegroom' indicated in a prologue by the piling of sacks of bodies in the below-stage hatches. The agents of avenging evil are not witches, but three weird children who rise from the carnage to hasten Macbeth's perdition. They return to be killed as Lady Macduff's little ones. The offstage banquet – music, shadows, laughter – leaves the scene clear for a thunderous eruption by Banquo's ghost, breaking down the door and heading furiously for the dining table. Fleance is allowed to flee by the Third Murderer, one of the various roles subsumed in Jimmy Chisholm's genuinely funny Porter, the demon doorman. The blind King Duncan, who finds the mind's construction in the face by feeling features, joins the march of ghosts on Dunsinane, and the church shutters are finally thrown open: the stained glass windows are illuminated by redemptive sunlight. I much admired Alan Howard's musicality in the role at the National earlier this year, but the Scottish play does go marvellously into Scottish accents, as Alec Guinness proved at the Royal Court in the mid 1960s. Local hero Iain Glen completes an outstanding quartet of muscular Shakespearean performances – in the past three years he has been an exciting Hamlet at Bristol, a powerful Aufidius at Chichester, and a superb Edgar at the Royal Court – with his handsome, driven thane. He unveils a pleasant, false face to the world but all his dark misgivings to the audience.

Mayfest has not been so lively in some years. This may be a delusion reinforced by the fact that I am staying not in a hotel, but in Babbity Bowsters, a lively hostelry in the refurbished merchant area of the city near the Trongate. Babbity's has six bedrooms, each of them clean and pleasant, without telephone or television, and I've inveigled myself onto their preferred list of clients thanks to the good offices of my friend on the Herald, Jackie McGlone (I do rather object to the Glasgow Herald re-naming itself thus, as many people objected years ago to the re-naming of the Manchester Guardian). The experience of staying there is infinitely preferable to staying in one of the city's over-priced hotels, although in recent years I have come to enjoy occupying a front room in the Copthorne on George Square. Babbity's is much cheaper than any hotel, but what you save on the room you are in danger of spending at the bar. The food is excellent and the company always worth keeping. The Herald's colourful columnist Jack MacLean holds court here, lawyers and trades unionists mingle over their pints of heavy and malt whiskies, writers and actors mingle rumbustiously, the whole place buzzes with people performing and drinking for each others' benefit as much as for their own. Just round the corner, in the Glasgow Print Studio, I have been beguiled by an exhibition of orchid prints by Elizabeth Blackadder and my vacillation over whether or not I should buy one is resoundingly resolved by Jack MacLean's powerful advocacy at the bar; I buy one.

The general air of jollity is reinforced at *Sabotage* in the Tramway, which might be subtitled 'The Body Show'. A series of installations is arranged as in a fairground. We enter a muslin maze, a hempen helix, brushing our bodies against coarse fibres and other bodies. At a peep show, we witness a couple perform stilted pornographic poses and then make gentle love. We, the audience, are standing on a platform and peering down through a canvas drum at the uninhibited couple. There is, for the first time in my theatre-going experience, hard and indisputable evidence of onstage sexual arousal; you never saw a chap standing to attention in *Oh! Calcutta!*, *Carte Blanche*, *Let My People Come* and other such limp festivities. I must confess I do not know quite where to look, though such hesitations do not seem to be afflicting my companions on either side of me at the peep show, Jackie McGlone and Anna Stapleton (the Scottish Arts Council's director of dance and drama). Moving right along, we come to a doctor telling us about our heart conditions, with a spurious volunteer (one of the actors of the NVA troupe) seated in a gyroscopic steel chair, wired up to monitoring apparatus. Then, a hall of hieroglyphs and mirrors with much brushing up against fake fur and polythene before entering the disorientation chamber of pounding music and kaleidoscopic amoebas in a slide show. If I had been high to start with, I might have gone through the roof at this point. Instead, I take in a rock concert played by unmanned instruments and visited by mini-Daleks. I watch two nude chaps climb up a fibreglass mountain. I listen to a real-life sufferer of chronic rheumatoid arthritis kick out his pain after drifting sensuously to ground in an acrobat's harness. Then, either side of a vertiginous journey along the raised scaffolding of all the installations, two little theatre pieces: Ken Currie's charcoal portraits of physical burn-out and decay; and a rather funny playlet about Elvis Presley's after-life performed by his dead twin visiting Graceland and performing an Elvis megamix. Life, death, the whole damned thing. *Sabotage* is all a bit 'sixties' and takes you back to the days of Liquid Theatre, some of the People Shows and Pip Simmons's wonderful version of Zamyatin's *We* (the audience, despatched through the hinterland in groups of forty, is ordered about by impersonal guides in white boiler suits, wielding torches). I spend most of the time wondering how the chap in the peepshow is going to keep it up all night. The alternative installation to *Sabotage*, if you wander into the outer arena of the emporium, is a decelerated, utterly silenced 24-hour version of Hitchcock's *Psycho*. When I go in to *Sabotage*, Vera Miles is opening a door. When I come out, she is still opening it.

The Tramway has become synonymous with the best of international theatre, its imprimatur stamped by Peter Brook who, when he brings his work from Paris to Britain, brings it here. For two reasons: the space is ideal; Neil Wallace invites him. Robert Lepage's *Tectonic Plates* and his masterpiece *The Dragon's Trilogy* were seen at the Tramway. At the other end of this month, I track Lepage almost to home base by accepting an invitation to the Festival of Americas in Montreal. Lepage has directed a Shakespearean trilogy – *Coriolanus*, *Macbeth* and *The Tempest* – for his

Quebecois Theatre Répère company. My schedule allows me to see the first two, and I relish the adventure of a) finding my way round a new city, not only getting my bearings, but also finding the best route for my daily run, and checking out the museums, bookshops and cinemas; and b) cracking the public transport system instead of cocooning myself in a convenient taxi. The metro system is excellent, the streets arranged on an easily comprehensible grid system. The place feels like New York without the scale, the noise and the danger. The red light district is quite louche; around the corner from my hotel is a strip of transvestite bars and clubs which takes me completely by surprise. The festival reception area is dotted with useful literature, friendly personnel and a large bowl of strawberry-flavoured prophylactics for general consumption. One sweet-toothed visiting festival director from Sao Paulo reaches for a preventive rubber to pop in his mouth, as though it were some fruit-flavoured chocolate. A colleague discreetly points out that in order to obtain maximum benefit, he should not pop it in, but pull it on.

Lepage is presenting his performances in a remote and rather dispiriting gymnasium. I wend my way there on the metro with Robert Robson, the chain-smoking director of Mayfest who hopes to find something suitable for Glasgow next year both at the Lepage events and elsewhere in the festival. We try and find somewhere to eat. We succeed, but only in a minimal sense. In the theatre, we are separated. I am minding my own business before the show starts when my row is interrupted by the arrival of a small, hunched man in black and a couple of people who are seemingly protecting him from the public gaze. Instantly, for I am trained in these matters, I recognise Al Pacino. I last saw him in the flesh in David Mamet's *American Buffalo*, very good, fucking and blinding and fucking and swearing. Tough guy, huh. I snare him for an extremely terse, but exclusive, interview as he pushes rudely past me to his seat. Such prime dope: 'Er, pardon me, huh, thanks, yeh'. He's in town to support a John Cassevetes film festival and to interview Robert Lepage for his, Pacino's, long marinating documentary film about performing Shakespeare (he has already bagged Sir John Gielgud and Kenneth Branagh). He exudes a twitchy, fascinated interest in *Coriolanus* throughout the performance; and he finally unbuttons, I learn later, backstage, locked in a session with Lepage that is reportedly artistic love at first sight, a *coup de foudre*. Director and actor agreed on the spot to work with each other soon in Quebec. Of such unlikely conjunctions are festivals sometimes made.

Like Al, who was reliably reported to have seen 'nothing like it, ever, period, huh, sure, yeh', I was completely beguiled by Lepage's beautiful, original and funny (yes, funny) production of *Coriolanus*. Lepage transcends international barriers, and not just because he is inventing a new theatre. His work is everywhere these days – apart from the Peter Gabriel concert he staged in Britain last month, he is about to open a new piece, *Map of Dreams*, in Munich, and he is bringing an operatic double-bill (Bartok's *Bluebeard's Castle* and Schoenberg's *Ewartung*) to this year's Edinburgh Festival. Because we tolerate so much sloppiness and dross in our own Shakespearean tradition, it is worth stating that Lepage matches an unrivalled technical sophistication with a wonderful aesthetic intelligence. *Coriolanus* has always posed problems in the British theatre. I cannot recall a totally satisfactory staging, for all the histrionic splendours of Ian Richardson (at the RSC) and Ian McKellen (at the RNT). Lepage delivers the goods and deals a decisive death blow to all that banner-waving naffness and smoke-infested triumphalism.

The performance is shot, almost cinematically, through a rect-angular slit, a frieze-framed Roman gallery of domestic and political skulduggery, brilliantly pointed and polished in the style of Fellini. The world elsewhere ('Il y a un monde . . . ailleurs'), the hero's site of battle, is also the emotional and erotic alternative to the Roman frippery.

We thus see Coriolanus and Aufidius, stark naked, wrestling in a ferocious love battle, reflected up through the stage on a huge tilted mirror. And the final betrayal of Aufidius by his new general earns Coriolanus not a stab in the back, but a sharp stab in the neck by a loyal catamite. There is nothing precious in all this. Men will be men. In Rome, the public speeches are made in a recording studio (where Virgilia is the producer!), transmitted by television to the local bar, where the characters disport themselves in sculptural splendour. Each scene is prefaced with a Roman numeral and location directive. The Roman camp is a locker room. The battles are represented by some fine, visibly manipulated puppets; Coriolanus sweeps these figures away as he crumbles before Volumnia's entreaty not to march on his native city.

There is none of the imbalance between visual representation and language that marred Lepage's 'Mud-summer' *Night's Dream* at the National last year; Lepage also failed to make parts of the *Dream*, notably the Pyramus and Thisbe interlude, work at all. No such problem here. The notions of political loyalty, the birth of democracy and emotional blackmail are perfectly projected in Michel Garneau's supple and idiomatic translation. The symbiotic relationship of Jules Philip's Coriolanus and Gerald Gagnon's Aufidius is not a simpering public schoolboy affair but a rash of violent fraternity across a deep cultural divide. The street sounds of Rome are incorporated in a brilliant score (by Guy Laramée) of claxons, bells, traffic and horns. And the domestic screws are tightened by the elegant and tartarish Anne-Marie Cadieux in a swish of haute couture. She makes Volumnia unforgettably funny for the first time ever. I'd never before thought of the old bat as a close relation of Coral Browne or Bette Davis, let alone Monica Vitti.

In *Macbeth*, the second part of the trilogy, in a translation more suitably barbaric, reinforcing the timeless medievalism of the split-level stage atmosphere, Gerald Gagnon's brutalist Macbeth is shown the apparitions climbing above: his crown springs from his head like a coil of fluttering golden birds. The banquet scene is a thrilling shadow play, and there is another important first in world theatre: the onstage flight to her death by Lady Macbeth. This is done by the slow motion descent of a ladder, to which the naked Marie Brassard is secured by an ankle rope. She flies slowly downwards and folds gently in two like a resting leaf. Brassard – who played a key role in *The Dragon's Trilogy* – prowls the ramparts in the buff, touching herself and sucking in Macbeth through his letter. When Gagnon arrives, she duly absorbs his literally ravishing entrance as she summons the evil demons. The dynamics of sexual disaffection are as carefully choreographed as in the current National production, but with added freshness. It is always said of Lepage that he is inventive, but his inventiveness is seldom gratuitous. Total fluidity and homogeneity of stage composition is a rare virtue. And in these two productions Lepage achieves it. The movement around and across the set is continuously hypnotic – the platform descends to provide a slatted screen behind which characters flit like the photographic models of Eadweard Muybridge caught in a new strobe. Macbeth and Banquo first appear suspended on horse-back in mid air like Samurai warriors. The witches swing buzzing thuribles above their heads, which become the whirring crossbows of the final avenging battle. There is also a genuinely funny Porter, which cannot be said of the National's version. He is caught hilariously short, which is why he cannot answer the door.

There is no 'new' way to do Shakespeare, but I come away from Montreal feeling that there are endless possibilities in the language in which he is spoken. The Glasgow Mayfest had reanimated the text in a fine setting with superb native actors; but Lepage has investigated the poetic super-text of the play, run a little with its meaning, dared to go beyond. Theatre is an interpretative art, as well as a creative one, and in his Shakespeare productions Lepage very interestingly blurs these distinctions. His use of stage space, of lighting and of sound, is beyond compare among contemporary directors. When he loses touch with the acting process – as in the RNT's *Dream* – the results can be lopsided. But with his own actors, and on his own terms, the synthesis of effect between intelligent performance, contemporary concern and adventurous, creative technicality, represents the highest point in my experience of theatre in the 1990s so far.

I spend time in Montreal with Ruth Mackenzie, the executive director of the Nottingham Playhouse, who is hoping to bring Lepage's *Coriolanus* to her theatre to celebrate – in a quirky, unexpected fashion – its 30th anniversary and opening production of the same play (starring John Neville). Ruth, a former Arts Council bureaucrat and South Bank wallah, smokes a lot and keeps her personal effects in a strange metal mini-briefcase. We decide to spend Sunday together. It is Free Museum Day. We look at lots of paintings, and she is revealed to be an expert. We enter a large room and she knows immediately which one or two pictures are worth looking at. We decide to penetrate the Ritz-Carlton for lunch or a drink. Lunch is a five-course brunch and we are seated in a bad corner, so we leave and improvise. Montreal offers specially-priced Sunday lunch all over the place. We alight on La Lutèce, one of the city's greatest French restaurants, with Second Empire decor and furniture, which proposes a superb five-course lunch for about £10 per head. We have a famous afternoon.

Before I leave Montreal, I spend another lunchtime with Ruth and Michael Morris, the busy impresario from north London. The pair of them are like the artistic facilitators in Martin Crimp's acid Royal Court play about New York, *The Treatment*. The main difference is that, in the play, the woman, played by Sheila Gish, practises fellatio on her colleague (who happens to be her husband) during office hours. Otherwise, Mackenzie and Morris are joined in all decency at the hip, on the hip. They like Lepage, Wilson, Brook, the same sort of thrusting chic avant-garde that is devised in stark opposition to the prevalent, spotty concerns of most British theatre and television writers. I usually respond to their enthusiams, though I reserve the right to be seduced once more by spottier and less obviously ambitious aesthetic undertakings. But in Montreal, over lunch, and in the heady environment of internationalist cultural conspiracies, I am happier in their company, and in their conversation, than I have been anywhere else all year. As James Agate said when he lunched the equally verbose Hermiones, Gingold and Baddeley: 'I did some of my very best listening.'

# JUNE

## *Bard and bar-room stories in Stratford-upon-Avon*

MY FIRST STOP-OVER TRIP of the year to Stratford-upon-Avon in 'Shakespeare's County', as the roadsigns now describe Warwickshire, is much later in the year than usual. The RSC season opened before Easter with the double-whammy of Kenneth Branagh's Hamlet and Simon Russell Beale's Richard III, both seen by the critics last season, the first in London, the second in The Other Place, Stratford. Robert Stephens's slightly delayed King Lear followed in May. I had scooted up and down by car with Michael Billington. In spite of the rewards of his careful driving and stimulating company, this is no way to 'do' Stratford. We had left the re-launch party of the publishers of this very book in the middle of the afternoon, eaten rapidly in the Dirty Duck in Stratford at six, sat through nearly four hours of *King Lear*, dabbed our eyes a bit at Stephens's decline, and sped back to London straight afterwards. I woke up the following morning totally exhausted.

The next opening, of *The Merchant of Venice*, I have missed by being in Montreal. So the plan is to catch up with that main stage production on a Wednesday, and to see the Thursday matinée in the Swan of Goldoni's *The Venetian Twins* followed by the opening of Ibsen's *Ghosts* in The Other Place. The RSC now has three fully functioning Stratford theatres, and in order to maintain an overall opinion of the company's form it is essential to visit all three several times a season. The RSC does not help by refusing to schedule all that many back-to-back openings. The demands they make on a serious newspaper's arts budget are most unreasonable. I have been enjoined by my managing editor to travel as cheaply as possible. To be strictly accurate, I have volunteered these economies after an outbreak of muttering about travel costs on the paper. It would be absurd for the Observer not to cover the regional theatre. But in order to offset the remote possibility that some executive might pull the plug entirely on out-of-town travel, I have decided to make all my own arrangements and claim back the expenses.

There is no direct train service between London and Stratford, presumably because British Rail has never heard of William Shakespeare. Anyone wishing to visit the shrine of our greatest poet without a car must either endure the torture of the RSC shuttle bus or set off by train with a compass and a spirit level: from Marylebone Station you change at Leamington Spa; from Euston, you change at Coventry, switching to a bus, or laying out life savings on a taxi. If the Observer travel department, through its booking agents, American Express, orders a return ticket from London to Coventry, I am issued with a three-month Standard ticket costing about £37. If I buy the ticket myself at the station, the price is £24. The necessary taxi link costs about £40 return for the 20 mile journey between Coventry and Stratford. The man to call on in these circumstances is Larry Adler, not the mouth organist, but the ace local limo driver. Larry's rates are about the same as a regular taxi's, but you can halve the cost by sharing with another client Larry has invariably booked and you always have an interesting journey. Larry is one of the best sources of RSC gossip, although he exudes an air of dignity and discretion. He is a former German prisoner-of-War, domiciled and married in Stratford. He is a brilliant road hog whose idea of a restful holiday is to drive through France and Germany tasting fine wines. He is amusingly intolerant of litter, bad manners, late train arrivals, sudden changes of plan, 'bloody foreigners' (the inconsistency of this attitude has never struck him), and, I suspect, most of the RSC's productions. Artistic directors of the RSC never drive themselves anywhere, so Larry has spent an aggregate of several years, if not decades, on the road with Trevor Nunn, John Barton, Terry Hands and Adrian Noble. Terry Hands's annual bill with Larry was once said to have been sufficient to subsidise a major regional theatre company for an entire year. Larry chats and drops hints when engaged in conversation on RSC matters but I have never gleaned anything really juicy from him. He is fond of all his charges and intensely loyal to them. In the new penny-pinching climate, however, I see less of Larry than I would like.

I have decided to turn this current escapade into an adventure. I shall take the newly introduced RSC shuttle bus from Victoria Station to Stratford (£39 return) and stay for the first time at Caterham House, a superior bed and breakfast establishment run by my friends Olive and Dominic Maury. After *Ghosts*, I shall take the return bus to Victoria. I have booked a second seat for Caroline Maude, the enterprising manager of the Gate Theatre, Notting Hill, who has a special interest in *Ghosts* – its director, Katie Mitchell, is a Gate colleague. I have mixed feelings about the bus. There was a Press outing last year to launch the service. Ominously, it coincided with the opening of the season on April Fool's Day. The experience was utterly exhausting, but I am prepared to give it another try. Also, I want to see what happens outside of the special circumstances. Who's on it, for instance? In the event, disaster. I never see the bus. The pick-up point is the Scandic Crown Hotel at Victoria Station. I report one hour early and wait. Having been chained to my desk all morning, I am unaware that, in the summer heat, due to melting tarmac on the city's outer roads, the centre has ground to a halt and the bus is snared in a terrible jam around Hyde Park. Gridlock. Quarter of an hour beyond the appointed time, I despair of the bus and, swearing heartily and not all that much under my breath, I run to the tube station and travel to Euston. Before boarding the train to Coventry, I ring Larry Adler and ask him to meet me. He can't. He has another appointment. At Coventry by about 3.30 pm, I try and find a bus. British Rail staff are monosyllabically unhelpful. When I do find the right bus stop on the Warwick Road, the timetable tells me that there is no bus to Stratford for another fifty minutes. Feebly, I resort to the taxi rank.

Caterham House is in Rother Street, next door to the very bed-and-breakfast I stayed in several years running with my father and brother when we paid our first visits to Stratford in the early 1960s. I am consumed in a wave of Proustian nostalgia. Our hostess was the splendid Mrs Richardson, who has long since died of drink. 'Been anywhere nice today?' she would ask as we toddled back from Ann Hathaway's Cottage and a cream tea in Shottery, her face caked in powder and her mouth haphazardly smeared in the brightest of red lipsticks. Her breakfasts were remarkable both for their size and their greasiness. The eggs swam around in a lake of molten lard, while the bacon and tomatoes struggled for survival in the deadly shallows. We stuffed ourselves regardless, usually because my brother and I had returned from the early morning queue at the box office. Students and tourists used to bed down outside the theatre to await the opening of the box office for the sale of that day's allocation of tickets, and we sloped along to join them at about six a.m. in order to supplement our stock of pre-booked tickets.

We saw David Warner's disaffected, red-muffled Hamlet, with Glenda Jackson as Ophelia, Elizabeth Spriggs as Gertrude (she vomited after drinking from the poisoned cup) and Brewster Mason, in a bright blond wig, as Claudius. I was upset by discovering in later life the sniffy reviews this production received; for us, it was probably the most exciting event of our lives to date, so much so that my brother and I returned two or three times on matinée days and entered the theatre illegally with the interval throng to watch the second half, in the words of my father, 'free, gratis and for nothing'. On our official, paid-for visit, the second scene was slightly stymied when the great table in the Danish court, which was evidently supposed to glide towards the audience, presumably with all the dignitaries seated around it, resolutely refused to budge. Instead, Mr Mason harrumphed authoritatively and the actors stood up and rearranged themselves sheepishly downstage. We had never met anyone like David Warner before, on stage or in life, and he seemed to us the ideal embodiment of the glamorous, rebellious youth to which one day we might aspire. J C Trewin thought he spoke without nobility, but our world, and our theatre, were untainted by professional criticism at this stage. We saw the complete cycle of history plays, *The Wars of the Roses*, mostly from standing places at the back of the stalls. At one matinée, an American couple seated in the very front row had had enough and told my brother and I, as they passed us at the standing rail at the back of the stalls, which seats they were vacating during this interval. We delightedly took them. When Warwick, the king-maker, met his end, the massive Brewster Mason (without a blond wig this time) crashed to the floor and, as we could see from our ringside vantage point in the side-stalls, Row AA, fumbled with a sachet of Kensington Gore before rolling over – bloodily – onto his back. The clash of steel, the smell of leather: it was all so close, and all so real, even though we were *so* close we could see the actors standing in the wings, preparing their various stratagems and deceptions.

Returning to Stratford since those early visits has always been a pleasure, and I never tire of the country town atmosphere, the riverside walks, the curious musty smell in the main theatre foyer, the late-night echoes in the streets of farewell conversations and of scurrying actors. There is a festive, holiday mood about the place that not even the passing of Mrs Richardson and the coming of McDonald's can destroy. The Old Town, with its low-slung red brick terraced cottage houses, hanging flower baskets, plethora of pubs and butchers' shops, is a permanent source of pleasure. For tourists, of course, the key haunt is Trinity Church, where hatchet-faced officials take good money off you for the privilege of gazing on Shakespeare's tombstone by the altar.

For committed Stratfordians like myself, the centre of all social life is the Dirty Duck. There are many reasons why this should be so. It serves good Flowers beer, it has pleasant views of the river and the food is honest and hearty. But the Dirty Duck is much more than just another inn. It is part of Stratford folklore, the actors' pub and a sort of informal dining club for company mem-bers, first-nighters, critics and other regulars. And for thirty years, save for a seven-year sabbatical in the 1970s, the main attraction, and best reason of all for darkening its doorstep, has been the formidable presence within of Pamela Harris, the greatest hostess in the British Isles, Mistress Quickly incarnate, the Brummagen Boadicea with a fine array of tent-like silk dresses in which she creates an impression of terrifying vastness and unanswerable elegance. Pam smokes untipped Piccadillys and drinks either champagne or brandy with water. She's a bona roba, she's a beagle, true bred. She works phenomenally hard, has a marvellous staff of young girls and boys, the loyal Roy and the considerate Wendy. She keeps late hours for the actors and runs the premises with a rod of iron. Woe betide any out-of-step townee, however large and macho, however drunk, who tries it on, or indeed any journalist or actor who fails to observe the unwritten rules of propriety and decorum. Pam has an uncanny instinct about people. She has an experienced and highly educated nose, you might say, for customers. Her brother, Bob Harris, is the sports editor of the Sunday Mirror, which explains Pam's natural affinity to journalists. She understands, and is interested in, our trade. Indeed, she usually accompanies me to the openings ever since some wretched publicity bureaucrat refused to furnish her with a ticket of her own; a typical corporate gesture of gratitude from the company whose individual members Pam does so much to keep cheerful throughout the increasingly long (April to January) season.

Even though the company nowadays would happily give her opening night tickets, I am pleased to say that Pam remains my preferred consort. I was deeply touched last year to be invited to her sixtieth birthday dinner party, along with Antony Sher, Terry Hands (who, alas, failed the feast), John Warnaby, Barbara Jefford, John Turner and a few local friends. For many years, when I worked for the Financial Times, I filed overnight notices from a bedroom in the Shakespeare Hotel (the rooms in the Shakespeare are all named in honour of the Bard; in my time, I have lodged in Ophelia, the Merry Wives of Windsor, Pericles and the Two Gentlemen of Verona, not to mention Oberon, Titania and Bottom; I have slept my way through the entire cast of characters in almost every major play). My work done, my freedom granted by my understanding Prospero, the sub-editor Henriques, I would repair at once for a late supper at the Duck. Pam has always insisted on entertaining the critics and was particularly fond in the old days of the company of the kosher butchers – Herbie Kretzmer, Milton Shulman, Bernard Levin and David Nathan – when she was assistant manageress to her friend and predecessor Ben Shepherd. Only Nathan of that vintage survives in harness, and he, along with Jack Tinker and myself, is the most assiduous and loyal of Pam's critical customers. If actors or directors are discomfited by our presence, Pam tells them they can like it or lump it or shove off somewhere else. All animosities are temporarily suspended, thanks in no small measure to Pam's genius for organising the tables in order to cause minimum embarrassment.

The great thing about having filed a notice was that I could discuss the play with Pam, or indeed anyone else, whereas now, with a weekly deadline hovering on Friday morning, I am necessarily more circumspect in my conversations. As a critic, you never really know what you think of a production until you sit down to write. The act of writing crystallizes the experience. So that night's play is always a tricky area, although I always feel safe in having a quiet exchange of views with Pam in the midst of the hubbub; also, you do not want to go too public with your impressions, or jokes, such as they are, in case they are filched or used in evidence against you when you write something completely contradictory.

I have enjoyed many of my most memorable and illuminating conversations with actors in the Dirty Duck: with Kenneth Branagh (making his mark in the 1984 *Henry V* season), Antony Sher (who, ten years ago, was embarking on his electrifying series of disgruntled, vengeful aliens: Lear's Fool, Richard III, Malvolio, Shylock, Vindice, Tamburlaine), Ian McDiarmid, Juliet Stevenson, Alun Armstrong, Malcolm Storry, Amanda Harris, Jane Maud, Roger Allam, Desmond Barrit, Robert Stephens, David Calder and Simon Russell Beale (who said at our last encounter, apropos of Michael Billington, whose reviews he admires, 'The thing is, there is always a paragraph that begins with a 'but'').

One incident I treasure above all others. After Michael Gambon's King Lear in June 1982, the roistering was especially vigorous. Gambon had gathered around him various actors in the cast including Sher (the Fool) and Sara Kestelman (Goneril). It had been an exceptional evening, I had safely filed my notice, it was very late, and I was feeling expansive. And, no doubt, expensive. I ordered champagne for the actors and Pam kindly offered to mark the occasion by pouring it in her finest and most treasured cut-glass goblets. The tray was prepared and I turned from the bar to bear it triumphantly to the carousing thespians. As I approached Gambon, I sensed the glasses slipping ineluctably across the surface of the

tray and, as I arrived, the whole invaluable set of them, and the
fizzing bottle, too, crashed into the mighty Gambon's lap and
thence to the floor, creating an uproarious confusion worthy of
some ancient scene in the Boar's Head Tavern itself. I am told that
at this point, though I have no remembrance of it, I merely turned
on my heel and, gesticulating extravagantly in the direction of the
temporarily dumbstruck Pamela, hollaed: 'And the same again,
mine hostess in the garters!'

Nothing so untoward happens on this trip. Caterham House is
jolly and sociable, though the traffic roars by very unsociably on
Rother Street from an early hour in the morning. The director,
Steven Pimlott, is also staying, so I have to explain to him rather
tortuously why I did not come up and review his revival of T S
Eliot's *Murder in the Cathedral*. Also in residence is a delightful
Irish lighting designer called Tina McHugh, with whom I sit at
breakfast. Tina works with Katie Mitchell, and is lighting tonight's
production of *Ghosts*. Everything is well in hand, so she is off to
find a horse and ride it mercilessly across the Warwickshire
countryside for a couple of hours. I go into the RSC offices and
bawl my complaints about the RSC bus shuttle down the telephone.
For the return trip, I have decided to forgo the bus altogether, and
to travel with Caroline Maude by taxi to Coventry and thence, on
the late train, to King's Cross (not Euston, for some reason or
other, though our final destination turns out, we are never told why,
to be Paddington), dining en route. On Coventry station at eleven
o'clock at night we tuck into an improvised feast of sandwiches,
chocolates and raspberries which I have bought earlier in Marks
and Spencers, and once on board we sip our beverages all the way
to London.

## *Just another not very boring week*

HALFWAY THROUGH THE YEAR, an account of a week, the last in June, lived on the job, in the sunshine, in the middle of the Test series with Australia and the Wimbledon tennis tournament. The most common thing people say to a critic is 'How can you face going to the theatre every night?' to which I always reply 'How can you face going to work every day?' All jobs have an element of monotony about them, otherwise they wouldn't be jobs, but there are two things a critic can never complain of: a set routine or a grinding sense of repetition. I know what those sorts of jobs are like. Most people do them. Most of the adults in my family did them, and for no great financial or spiritual rewards to speak of whatsoever.

SUNDAY: I feel ahead of myself for a change as I spent Friday and Saturday nights in the theatre, mainly to stack up against the domestic strain of the coming week. Sue's favourite uncle, a rather lonely old bachelor whose only enthusiasm was golf, died yesterday in hospital in Reading, and she has to make all the funeral arrangements. I simply do not know how people manage to get away to country cottages, or France, at the weekend. I like to enjoy being at home. Sue is a fanatical gardener and we have grass to mow and hedges to cut, raspberries to pick, plants to bed out. We take all our meals on our second-floor terrace, from which we can see the kites flying on Parliament Hill. Everyone is being very well-behaved this weekend: there is no loud music to pierce the membrane of the humming heat, the perfect summer sky, the glorious unaccustomed warmth. We both say that two weeks of this would do just fine as a holiday. We read all the papers, a melancholy task, and I work on a book review and a critical round-up for the Observer. Sunday is a good day to spend at the desk, for the telephone never rings. One immutable tradition of our weekends is the exchange of faxes with Toby Rowland, Binkie Beaumont's old sidekick, who lives in London off the Kings Road but who spends his weekends, with his wife Millie, and several dogs, in their beautiful house near Lewes in Sussex. The house once belonged to the impresario Prince Littler. It has a superb garden, pink shutters, exquisite furniture and a floating roster of house-guests who include Toby's old friends from New York and Hollywood, the actors Penelope Keith (and her family) and Christopher Biggins, the producers Thelma Holt and Michael Codron, director Patrick Garland and his wife Alexandra Bastedo, the florist Susan Pulbrook, the mother of all the Foxes, Angela Fox, restaurateur Richard Polo and his wife, and any number of people, mostly from the old days, who might be passing through Britain: Googie Withers and John McCallum, Michael Pearman, the singer Marti Stevens and the playwright Mart Crowley (who wrote *The Boys in the Band*). Toby is a flashpoint for the theatre in retreat, the theatre of yesterday. But he is the best news of that old-fashioned theatre, a real gent with an eye for talent and a need to know what is going on even if he doesn't like it very much. After a life well lived, with countless thousands of cigarettes smoked and bottles of gin and vodka downed, Toby has endured about fifteen operations on his throat for cancer. He can only speak by manipulating a voice box in the manner of the late Jack Hawkins. So the fax, for him, is a particular boon, and he always sends a resumé of his week and plans for the weekend some time on Saturday. Sunday, I reply. He and Millie are comparatively quiet this weekend, catching a matinée of Coward's *Relative Values* at Chichester and planning their trip tomorrow to BAFTA for the AIDS charity screening of *Suddenly Last Summer* produced by Robert Fox and the BBC, starring Fox's wife Natasha Richardson, Rob Lowe and Maggie Smith; Millie has been freezing their first homegrown peas and raspberries of the summer; Toby has had trouble with his ribs and is taking something called 'Knit Bone,' recommended by Katie Saunders (the former Katie Boyle, now married to 'The Mousetrap Man', Sir Peter Saunders). I reply, telling them that Sue is at 'National Music Day' on top of the BBC with the Heritage Secretary,

Peter Brooke ('a complete idiot,' she later declares, in that tactful, pussycat manner I admire so much), and the cast of *Starlight Express*, and what I thought of last week's openings and the major theatrical book of the week, Kenneth Williams's diaries, which are entirely compulsive and have been very well edited by Russell Davies. Another fax comes through from Paris thanking me for an article I have written about British dramaturgy for Le Monde: 'We acknowledge receipt of your text, which is presently being traduced.'

MONDAY: Early train to Reading to collect Uncle Bernard's death certificate and to find an undertaker. The hospital ward where he dies reeks of mortality, and I think of our visit last weekend when I suddenly understood the last act of *King Lear*. I don't have any experience of people dying. My family lives on for ever. Bernard had kept on looking at his legs under the sheet. They had turned blue with gangrene. 'I don't know what's going to happen,' he kept saying, and then something about a jockey. Sue wondered where I had put my car keys. Had I lost my car keys? 'Serve you jolly well right!' chuckled Bernard from his deathbed. A chaplain had come round, rubbing his hands in sympathetic unctuousness. 'He's Jewish!' declared Sue, triumphantly, and Bernard had chuckled again, a sort of 'Got you there!' pleasure flickering across his vague, uncertain face. We take the certificate and go to the registration office. They tell us of an undertaker nearby. In this anodyne, pink environment, bestrewn with pious memorial fatuities worthy of Patience Strong and such kitsch Christian paraphernalia as a plaster Virgin Mary, plastic crucifixes and sample funeral urns with suggested inscriptions ('Gladys and Wilf, together again at last' is a typically gruesome advert for posthumous commingling), we wrap up a man's life, choose the flowers and a casket, book a time on Friday for the cremation, track down a rabbi. There are no rabbis in Reading. There is one in Maidenhead, but he is departing on Thursday for a nationwide conference of rabbis in London. The one we finally trace will have to come from Muswell Hill and is obviously not on the conference list. He is, it transpires, merely a part-time rabbi, but he will have to do, as the British way of death dictates that a figure of religious authority officiates in the funereal departure lounge. We speed back on the train to Paddington, and share a taxi to our respective offices, Sue's in Chalk Farm Road opposite the Round House, mine downstairs at home on the lower slopes of Hampstead Heath.

TUESDAY: By train to Salisbury for the British premiere of Sam Shepard's *States of Shock*, his poetic one-hour blast about disintegrating America in the wake of the Gulf War. I missed last week's Press night, so I feel I am travelling incognito, under cover. The Salisbury Playhouse has been rejuvenated under the artistic directorship of Deborah Paige: a clever mix of daring new work (this Shepard is part of the National's 'Springboards' initiative) and smart, canny revivals of Coward, Somerset Maugham and P G Wodehouse to keep the military and cathedral factions sweet. The train hurtles through green, flat pastures and I feel as though I am on holiday. In Salisbury, the great market square is closing down for the afternoon as I ascend the stairs in Stoby's famous fish and chip shop for haddock, mushy peas and chips with vinegar on everything. Bliss. At the theatre, an extraordinary sight. A man with two false arms and two metal hooks for hands is buying drinks, folding his jacket, becoming an audience. With these hooks he quite naturally scratches his ear, fidgets with his nose, or knocks back his spectacles along the bridge of that nose. Who needs hands? He gesticulates generally and as successfully as if he had them. Everyone notices and is immediately becalmed by his relaxed and unselfconscious public manner. He is about 60, and obviously related in some way, by blood or friendship, to the actress Naomi Wirthner who is playing a waitress in the Shepard. She joins him and his lady companion, presumably his wife, for drinks beforehand and afterwards in the pleasant semi-circular theatre bar. The Shepard play is in part about mutilation. How did this man lose his hands? Was he a bomb disposal expert who was not quite as expert as he should have been, or an unlucky postman? The question that bugs me all evening is, how will he applaud the production? I am ashamed of my prurient concern. As the actors line up at the end, he simply taps his hooks together and creates the most marvellous and unexpected tintinnabulation.

The play is a sharp lament for an imperial nation in a surreal coffee shop, and this Salisbury production is much more effective than the New York premiere, which was blurred and impenetrable. That man Malkovich played the bullish Colonel off-Broadway in a fit of frenzied rage; David Burke, a more pedestrian, slightly older actor, goes towards the role's anger from the other extreme of placid ambiguity, and comes up with a memorably bullish version of 'Stormin' Norman Schwarzkopf, the general in the desert. Thanks to him, and Lucy Hall's design of a huge white canopy decorated with torn family photographs, I realise that this compact, poetic play discusses a nation's identity crisis in terms both personal and surreal. As the play is only about an hour long, I do not want to stay over; but the first train I can take to London (and the last) does not depart until 10.40 pm, so I amble around the cathedral close enjoying the free spectacular of the magnificent church as the dusk thickens and courting couples linger on the lawns. I gravitate towards the lounge of the White Hart hotel and address myself to my notes. Each play I see is scribbled about in a shorthand notebook and I transfer these doodles to a larger note-book (I am addicted to the thin-spaced red Silvine variety) in a more concise and legible form as a preparation for each weekly column. Eventually, I climb towards the station, leaving the city behind. I change trains at Basingstoke and arrive at Waterloo Station just before 1 a.m. A taxi drops me home fifteen minutes later.

WEDNESDAY: One of the biggest openings of the year is David Mamet's *Oleanna* at the Royal Court. Political correctness hits the stage, and a taunted professor, goaded beyond endurance, assaults his female student. She has come to have news of her grades and questions the way in which he talks to her. He asserts his authority as a teacher, someone who teaches, who is in charge in the class-room. She wants therapy and acquiescence, not his idea of what constitutes an education. And she wants a ceasefire in the sex war, but she only succeeds in extending it. The professor touches her arm in what he regards as a neutral gesture of sympathy and finds himself on a rape charge. In the last scene, ruined and bewildered, the professor is talking on the telephone to his wife, and calls her 'baby'. The student rips the 'phone from his hand and berates him for addressing a woman, any woman, in those terms.

At this point Harold Pinter's careful, atmospheric production explodes. Then something occurs which I never dreamed of seeing on, or hearing from, the hallowed stage where Jimmy Porter spawned the dissident movement in the post-war British theatre: sections of the audience loudly cheer the professor (David Suchet) while he turns brutally on his female student (Lia Williams) and kicks her to the ground. This is ugly, and repellent, and it's real drama. I know of at least one elderly colleague who joins in the unseemly uproar, the music critic Christopher Grier, who files a London drama column for the Scotsman. Nobody quite yells, as someone did in New York, 'hit the bitch', but the sentiment is all around, emanating especially from the back two rows of the stalls which are occupied by the production's commercial sponsors (American Airlines Inc) and their wives.

There are changes in the air at the Court, with Stephen Daldry taking over this year from Max Stafford-Clark. Sponsorship is on the agenda, and so are link-ups with BBC Radio, West End management and other producing venues. The Court under Stafford-Clark had become a rather enclosed, paranoid institution, in spite of some fruitful Anglo-American exchanges with Joe Papp's New York Public Theater in the 1980s. The traditional seven o'clock start on press nights was abolished by Stafford-Clark on the grounds that a 'real audience' was only obtainable one hour later; critics who had to file overnight notices were not part of his problem. He saw no merit in pandering to the requirements of newspapers, and his press relations were on the whole mediocre. Of course, the serious newspapers would always review his productions, however inconvenient the late start; and for many years I did so on the Financial Times while resenting his filching an hour of my reviewing time. In effect, his victims were his own writers and actors, not me. His response was always, well, take another day to think about the play and write later. Again, I objected to his high-handed manner in trying to dictate the pattern of my working life. An opening at the

Royal Court is always an event, if not of *Oleanna* proportions, and a daily newspaper's job is to report that event the next morning, at least in the London editions. Daldry will reinstate the early start later this year, and may indeed go to the other extreme, of emphatic friendliness, towards the press. He is welcoming, pleasant, stylish and considerate. Makes a change. And he is everywhere before the show: on the theatre steps, buzzing in the bars and foyer, checking out guests in the front stalls. Hooray for openness and this fresh, non-furtive approach to the tense experience of a first night.

THURSDAY: To Manchester for Vanessa Redgrave in a new play, *Maybe*, by the Soviet writer Mikhail Shatrov. This proves a fool's errand. Maybe? Not a chance. You have to take the rough with the smooth, the 'no chances' with the 'maybes'. Bump into Benedict Nightingale at Euston and we travel together. Second class, of course, with coffee and fruit juice from the trolley. A far cry from fifteen or twenty years ago when I regularly travelled first class, taking a full lunch on the train with such stalwart regional theatre-going colleagues as Ned Chaillet of The Times (now a BBC radio drama producer) and Eric Shorter (now an obituarist; *plus ça change*) of the Telegraph. Benedict has done a bit of homework and dug up a Nick Hern copy of Shatrov's collected plays, which has an authoritatively deadly introduction by Michael Glenny. I gratefully crib a few notes and resolve not to use them. Well, Ben, how about a bite to eat some time this evening? He visibly cowers, obviously having made his own arrangements. What are they? Merely to patronise the same old Indian restaurant he always patronises. Ben has an Indian food habit which could soon become a problem. Whenever I go to a theatre on the periphery of London – say the Hampstead, or Greenwich – I invariably find Ben sloping around the purlieu just before six, waiting for the favoured Indian restaurant to open. And he always orders the same stuff: chicken dhansak, boiled rice, cauliflower bhaji and a pint of draught bitter. (Benedict wrote a revealing book about his time on the New York Times as a Sunday commentator in which his social life seemed to consist of going back to his apartment to boil up a meal for one on a baby Belling.) I suggest a break with routine and an early supper at the Yang Sing, one of the best Chinese restaurants in Britain. Maybe I'll see you there, but I probably won't, says Ben, and dozes off. At Piccadilly Station, we slink away to our respective hotels. Mine is the grim Gardens on the Piccadilly Gardens square. I take a shower, change my shirt and head for the Yang Sing. I wouldn't say I enjoyed my own company (how would you like to live with a theatre critic twenty four hours a day?), but I am perfectly prepared to put up with it as long as I have a book and a few newspapers. Indeed, to sink into a restaurant, with or without Benedict Nightingale, for an hour before an opening is not, as I know it is for some colleagues, a dangerous soporific, but a relaxing preparation. Especially here. I was introduced to the Yang Sing many years ago by my wife's Manchester cousins, Jack and Janice Livingstone. I always think of them when I enter its splendid portals and descend to its open plan lower depths, the bustling kitchen visibly adjacent to the dining area. I order a few dim sum, then a special beef dish with Chinese greens and noodles. The portions are enormous, enough for two. I eat what I can and chat to some friendly folk at the next table who want to know about my Chinese greens, in between flicking through the Manchester Evening News. An interview with Vanessa is giving nothing away but is very well written by Alan Hulme, one of our best and most experienced local theatre reporters.

I settle the bill and head for the Exchange where I am meeting Jamie Buchan, an old friend from FT days and a novelist grandson of John Buchan, great writer, but dodgy anti-semite and arriviste snob. Jamie has been in touch lately over an article he is writing for Esquire magazine about the discredited Workers Revolutionary Party, in which Vanessa Redgrave was/is prominent. He has never seen Vanessa on stage before and is unlucky enough to have chosen a performance in which, uncharacteristically, she has muddled her political heart with her artistic soul. The result is a nothing portrayal of a left-wing teacher in Boston with a special interest in Russian literature. Shatrov's play, co-written over the fax wires with an American translator, posits a spurious parallelism between the Stalinist show trials of the 1930s and the Senator McCarthy witch hunts of the 1950s. But unlike Arthur Miller's *The*

*Crucible*, which I am increasingly disposed to consider the second greatest play of the twentieth century (after *The Cherry Orchard*), the reverberations are thin, the dramatic conflicts almost non-existent, the writing flavourless. Vanessa has refused point blank to meet Jamie, suspecting, rightly, that he is planning some sort of demolition job. So we decide to have a drink together and are joined in the theatre bar afterwards by my friends Vanessa Rawlings-Jackson, a theatre marketing consultant with more of an instinct for theatre than for marketing (the right balance), and Christopher Barron, a former associate director of the Edinburgh Festival, who is planning next year's Arts Council sponsored 'City of Drama' programme in Manchester. I ask Chris how his plans will be affected by the city's bid for the Olympic Games in AD 2000. 'If Manchester wins the nomination, City of Drama will gain enormously. And if we don't, our event will be a high-profile consolation. So we can't lose.'

The Manchester Olympic bid is led by the redoubtable Bob Scott, who was one of the chief agitators for this very Royal Exchange Theatre in the 1970s, alongside the late Michael Elliott and the director of tonight's play, Braham Murray. The work of these men, their commitment to making Manchester a great cultural centre removed from the cloying and patronising parochialism of London, has been consistently underestimated for twenty years. Admittedly Elliott sharpened his assault on Manchester once it was clear that the succession to Laurence Olivier as head of the National Theatre would fall on Peter Hall. But his vision of the Royal Exchange was undimmed from that moment. It opened in 1976, and the auditorium, with a space module cockpit which seems to have plummeted back to earth through the roof of the splendid old Corn Exchange, still sets the pulse racing every time I see it.

Vanessa and Chris depart for dinner and Jamie and I head back to drink up in the hotel bar. Later, I file the remains of my weekly column, punched into my laptop computer, over the telephone straight into the Observer system. Oh, miracles of modem! The wonders of technology truly are wonderful, provided everything works. I have always been lucky. Am lucky again. Sleep in the small hours. I hope Benedict enjoyed his solitary Indian meal as much as I have enjoyed my evening. Apart, that is, from the play itself.

FRIDAY: Very strange day, this. Uncle Bernard's cremation in Reading. Up betimes and onto the 7.18 am cross-country InterCity from Manchester Piccadilly to Brighton: via Macclesfield, Wolverhampton, Birmingham, Oxford and Reading. A lot of one's best work is done on such journeys. Thinking and reading. Sometimes, as the man used to say in the music hall, I sits and thinks; sometimes I just sits. The sun shines, a quiet breeze blows, the third Test Match with Australia is under way, the green fields glisten, untroubled cows stoop to their munching. England. Outside Reading station, in the taxi rank, in a dark suit and the boiling heat, I trap myself in a British Telecom phonebooth, unpack my laptop and unravel my notes for the crucial phone-call: to Ray Fox-Cumming, Observer super-sub, who will make my drivel fit for Sunday. We have to find thirty-odd lines to cut. I have prepared some cuts on the journey, we weigh my suggestions against his, discuss a headline and that's that. All done in fifteen minutes on a freephone call. These new booths have a useful, jutting desk-ish mini-counter which I have exploited to the full.

I return to the station to meet Uncle Bernard's great friend Jean Abelson. Bernard worked for many years as company secretary to her late husband's engineering firm in Birmingham. The Abelsons were very fond of Bernard. Jean, who lives in the pleasant Old Town of Stratford-upon-Avon, next door to the ballooning comic actor Richard Griffiths, has come from Leamington or Coventry by train and I have deduced from the schedules on which train she must, of necessity, arrive. We meet, we go to a grisly pub opposite the station for a quick fortifying drink. Taxi to the crematorium. A few family and friends. Jean Abelson's sons are both present and meeting them is like meeting old friends you have never met before. The elder son Edward is a writer of sports and assorted books, who lives with the novelist Grace Ingleby. The younger, James, is a photographer. Grace, kicking at a tuft of grass outside the 'chapel of rest,' says that this experience is like being in a Mike

Leigh play. Without the aggressive dialogue, I add. Had she ever seen, I wonder, the Mike Leigh television film about undertakers, *The Kiss of Death*? She had not, but knew what I was talking about. Sue, and Thomas, our fifteen-year-old son, arrive. Thomas is wearing his red suit. Sue sits in the bland 'chapel' next to her brother Nigel, a consultant neurologist. Halfway through the rabbi's platitudinous address ('I didn't know Bernard; you did; I cannot say what kind of a man he was but I know from speaking to one or two of you over the telephone that he was a kind man and I cannot say in words how you will miss him but you must know how much you do and think of him as if he lived among you still . . . ' etcetera) Sue's shoulders start to shake and I feel helpless. Nigel ignores his sister's emotional plight. So do I when I realise, with relief, that she is convulsed not in tears but in giggles. Some eerie taped music is flooded into the room and a hideous green curtain closes around the coffin. As we leave the crematorium, Bernard's life goes up in smoke. I can see the same spiralling black cloud every morning across Hampstead at the top of the Royal Free Hospital. But here, for some reason, I think of death camps. The clinical, impersonal efficiency of the modern crematorium. I'd rather my body was chopped up or ripped apart by careless students and parts of it made useful for medical science. Nigel has come up trumps with a booking at a nearby riverside pub for drinks and sandwiches. We have an exceedingly jolly party.

James Abelson, who has an office in Camden Town, drives Sue and Thomas and me back to London, very quickly. He drops me at Harrods, and I take a cab into the Observer. It is, after all, press day. About 4pm. The editorial upheavals have claimed another victim: Simon Kelner, the plump and affable editor of the Magazine, the man responsible for the controversial last-ditch £2m relaunch innovation by Donald Trelford. Kelner sits slumped in his office, tearful, swigging champagne and vodka. Sympathizers call by and swig with him for a few minutes. 'They don't know what they've got here' he blubs pathetically. I have grown to like Kelner and, as it happens, my first magazine article for some time – a profile of film director Mike Leigh – appears in his last magazine. This had come about at last April's Olivier Awards ceremony, where Kelner and I were sitting together at the dinner. He said he was from Salford. I said, so was Mike Leigh. He loved Mike Leigh's work, he said; was there a way of writing about him for the magazine? I said there was, especially in the light of Leigh's brilliant new film, *Naked*, which was about to be premiered at the Cannes Film Festival (Leigh won the best Director prize, and was afterwards honoured with the OBE in the Queen's birthday list); I had seen an early preview. I like Kelner and hope to cross his bows again one day. He was an ebullient and popular editor among the staff. He'll bounce back.

At home, the sun persists warmly into the late evening and we have supper on the terrace. Kites are flying on the heath, neighbours chattering beneath the trees. Fruits and salads on the table. In Bernard's aftermath, there is still life.

SATURDAY: To Dublin for the new Brian Friel play at the Abbey. Have decided to avoid Heathrow whenever possible, especially in the summery months, and am flying Ryan Air from Stansted. This entails going to the remarkably well renovated Liverpool Street Station, unrecognisable from my youth, when I had to cross the platforms from the incoming Essex lines to take (in the first place, in 1959) a steam train, and subsequently a diesel, out to Stamford Hill on the Enfield line to my Catholic grammar school. In those days, Liverpool Street was a foul mecca of fumes and walkways, strange pungent smells, begrimed stairways and peculiar announcements. Until recently, whenever I went there, I would absorb a Proustian tang of adolescent bygone days: sweets, short trousers, caps, homework, pens with calligraphic nibs, bottles of ink, the mud-clogged studs of leather rugby boots. The renovation has blasted all that away and I feel deprived of childhood memories. But there is the compensating clarity of the new station, train information simultaneously visible for all travellers to Billericay, Ilford, Cambridge, Ely or Hackney Downs. Going to Stansted Airport is a relaxing pleasure because so few other people are going there. You could get lost and speak to no-one for days between the embarkation platform and the flight check-in area. I eat breakfast, partly because I am hungry, partly to line my

stomach for the demands of the day ahead, and partly because
Ryan Air provides no in flight meals at all. The flight is half full.

In Dublin, I take a taxi to the Gresham Hotel in O'Connell
Street. Draw the bedroom curtains against the early afternoon sun
and jump into bed to watch the Wimbledon women's final: a
thrilling match. Novotna is 4-1 up in the final set against Steffi
Graf, having won the second set 6-1 to level the match. How can
she lose? Easy. She double-faults on her service game, 4-1 up, and
goes to pieces. She loses the next five games and the match. It is
almost too painful to contemplate. An amazing turn-around.
Accepting her runner's up prize from the Duchess of York, she
cries on the royal shoulder. This makes a great front page photograph in most of the next day's papers though not, I note, in my
own, which has the less interesting portrait of the victor.

Sally forth at six p.m. and take a pint in the Plough opposite the
Abbey before meeting Mary Holland, true friend and Observer
colleague. The theatre is buzzing, and has been since Wednesday
when the Irish president, Mary Robinson, and half the Irish cabinet
attended the premiere. Matt Wolf, the busiest of showbusiness
writing bees, representing the International Herald Tribune and
Variety, is interviewing Patrick Mason, the director of the play and
director designate of the Abbey itself, in a corner of the new bar
that juts out above the foyer into the street. John Gross of the Sunday Telegraph is calling at the box office to collect photographs.
Robert Hewison of the Sunday Times is proclaiming his arrival to
several Abbey regulars and asks me if I'd care to have dinner with
him afterwards. I would very much like to but have promised Mary
Holland that we shall discuss serious matters of state, the Abbey
and the Observer in strict privacy. We could not possibly share our
thoughts on these matters with the Sunday Times, however agreeable their representative. The foyer begins to hum. I meet Sean
McCarthy, a Cork playwright and one of the nicest men I know,
who tells me he has given up drinking and is writing for television.
I offer him my condolences and return with Mary to the bar.

There has been enormous interest in Friel's new play, *Wonderful
Tennessee*, chiefly because of the runaway success of his last,
*Dancing at Lughnasa*. In that play, Friel's most completely

enjoyable to date, the five sisters came alive in the kitchen and danced around the table. People are therefore expecting a musical. They will be disappointed. The choreography in *Wonderful Tennessee* is confined to the report of a natural apparition: a dolphin rose out of the sea and danced with 'a deliberate, controlled, exquisite abandon. Leaping, twisting, tumbling, gyrating in wild and intricate contortions.' This sighting was made off the Donegal pier where Terry Martin (Donal McCann), a bookie and concert promoter, has ordered a boat to the nearby island of Otherness and Mystery. It is Terry's birthday. He has taken an option on the property. Three couples arrive to the strains of 'Happy Days Are Here Again', a song unfortunately guaranteed to bring on a fit of the glums.

The boat never comes, but the idea of a pilgrimage is considered nonetheless. The play is about the need for ritual in our lives, and the dark consequences of that need. And, as in most of Friel's plays, the surface of the present is scratched at in the search for traces of the informing past. The flying dolphin may attest the mystery of a ritual slaughter and dismemberment on the island in 1932, perpetrated by a group of Dubliners returning from an Eucharistic Congress. This group are their successors; parallels are drawn with the Eleusian Mysteries, the harvest festivals held in honour of Demeter, the Greek goddess of agriculture. The play's power is cumulative rather than immediate. Complaints about the lack of dynamism are justified. The standing start is awkward. But Friel's poetic drama is about people drawn into contemplation of their cultural roots which, as in *Lughnasa*, are bifurcated in Christian and pagan soil. In his end of the pier show of the sacred and profane, Friel invokes the tragic music of society in search of its faith and identity. It is in this underpinning seriousness, so beautifully expressed in the set speeches of narrative and reminiscence, that the play takes hold.

Halfway through the first act I am aware of someone, probably an elderly usher, who has sneaked into the back of the stalls and is standing there jingling his small change in his pockets. Nobody around me turns to chastise the intruder for several reasons: there is an intense corporate concentration on the play; it might prove more of an embarrassment than an act of social responsibility to tell the jingler to put a sock in his jingling; it is impossible to move in the Abbey seats. These seats are the most uncomfortable theatre seats in Europe. They slope backwards at about forty five degrees, so that once seated in them, you are trapped for an hour or so right up to the interval unless you are willing to risk incurring a severe back injury. You might as well be wearing a seat belt. Patrons who have spent too long in the bar go straight off to sleep while the twentieth-century Irish drama unravels before their unheeding, firmly closed, eyes. Trying to make a note, as a critic, entails wiggling one's bottom until one's back is in a semi-upright position in direct contravention of the overriding requirements of gravity, and leaning violently forward, pen poised in the darkness, until one's chin meets one's knees and one's critical body is bent around the chair like a boomerang. By which time you have forgotten what it is you were going to make a note of, and you are already losing your hard-won position and sliding back into semi-recumbent helplessness. This explains why the reporting of Abbey productions is often so devoid of precise detail and telling quotation and why most Dublin drama critics suffer from curvature of the spine.

Anyway, just out of interest, I manage to corkscrew myself around to take a look at the phantom jingler. Good grief, it's the playwright himself, Brian Friel. I slam around immediately to face the stage and resume my critical task, despite a sudden cramp I have caught in my left leg and several painful new lesions in the lumbar region. At the interval, Mary and I are bidden to the theatre's reception room by the wonderful Lily (house manageress since the Abbey moved into these premises thirty years ago) along with the self-proclaiming Hewison, who is already giving vent to his displeasure with the evening when I tell him that he is seated next to the playwright's wife. The playwright's wife, Anne, arrives on cue and I am able to pronounce a formal introduction to her impatient neighbour in the sloping stalls. Hewison turns on the charm at once. The other guests include Pip Broughton, artistic director of the Nottingham Playhouse, and her handsome, bearded partner. Pip is brown and deliciously under-dressed. She tells me that her new baby boy is being baby-minded in the Gresham Hotel.

She is well on the way to having a fine old Dublin weekend, I can see. Also present is Gay Byrne, civilised and humorous host of 'The Late Show', easily the best chat programme on television. Gay and his wife are notably supportive figures in the cultural life of this city. I always meet them in intervals at either the Abbey or the Gate down the road. By now, Mary Holland has been telling Anne about Brian's coin campanology at the back of the stalls. Anne is furious and says that he is always doing this and it upsets the actors who can hear him on the stage. Brian, purple and bonhomous in the quietest possible way, now appears in the room himself, greeting the guests and looking reasonably fit for a man who has been on a bender since the play opened last Wednesday. To my horror, Anne goes straight up to him and tells him that his change-jingling is disrupting our enjoyment of the play in the rear stalls. The whole sorry saga reaches a humiliating (for me) conclusion when Brian lurches over and apologises. I say I hope he continues to jingle his small change for as long as he lives and he invents a funny reading of the phrase on the spot. We drink up and resume our semi-recumbent postures in the dastardly blue seats. Conversations are taken up again in the bar afterwards, and Brian mutters that he and the cast are going to a restaurant and that Mary and I would be very welcome to join them later on. We say that we might, but know that we won't. Finding our restaurant at last, a slightly swish joint called Tosca's, we are both dismayed and delighted to find the importunate Hewison completing his solo dinner at the table next to ours. The perfect social compromise is achieved. He joins us for a glass or two as he leaves, and then we begin.

Arrive home on Sunday to find Jovan Ćirilov, my friend and the artistic director of the Yugoslav Drama Theatre in Belgrade, and of BITEF, safely ensconced in our house. He has come to stay for a week and to see some London theatre. His journey, though difficult, was alright until he arrived in NW3. He got around the travel embargo in his chaotic country by making a six-hour bus journey to Budapest. He took a flight to Amsterdam and, a few hours later, another flight to London Heathrow. He then boarded the tube train to Belsize Park, our local station on the Northern line. Walking through the back streets he was assailed by a group of nine-year-old girls who hurled abuse, and stones, at him, redoubling their efforts when they discovered, as he remonstrated with them, that he was not from England and indeed spoke with a funny foreign accent. Welcome to London! Yugoslavia is tearing itself apart in the most obscene and upsetting way. We are indeed fortunate that here in England we can still lead by example when it comes to upholding the public virtues of decency, civility and hospitality.

# JULY

## *Running gags:*
## *to be fit or not to be fat*

IT HAS BEEN GOOD, dry running weather and my outdoor regimen on Hampstead Heath continues to keep me going. The quality of escape on this mercifully unchanging hillside is the same for me as it was for Keats: 'To one who has been long in city pent, / 'tis very sweet to look into the fair / And open face of heaven.' I run between fifteen and twenty miles a week, over four or five days, taking one of several routes from the lower side of Parliament Hill to Kenwood and back, or down by the ponds of South End Green, or snaking diagonally downwards on various paths. Once a fortnight I run twenty laps of the running track, five miles, at well under two minutes a lap (best time: 38 mins, 30 seconds). My athletic achievements may be paltry beside those of your average marathon runner, but they bring me immense satisfaction. My friend Chris Horsley, a wizard advertising consultant and genuine marathon man, dragged me round the Regents Park ten kilometre (just over six miles) course for the first time in May. My time was 46:32, and I hope to break 45 minutes before the year is out.

Critics are not renowned for their athletic prowess, though Milton Shulman claims to have once taken a set off the great Czech tennis champion Jaroslav Drobny. James Agate liked horses, and taking the air in Brighton, but his life was almost permanently sedentary: sitting in theatres and cinemas, in concert halls, at dinner in the Café Royal, at card tables in the Savage Club and, for half the night in a capacious armchair at home reading, writing, talking, and drinking whisky usually all at the same time. His successor on the Sunday Times, Harold Hobson, was severely handicapped with polio. At one time in the mid 1970s, the bitchier wing of the acting profession used to fly around asking which cripple did one read on a Sunday. The choice, at the time, lay between Hobson; the Observer's Robert Cushman, who suffered (suffers still) from rheumatoid arthritis; and the Sunday Telegraph's Frank Marcus, who juddered throughout his nights in the stalls severely afflicted with Parkinson's Disease.

Nor are critics particularly heavy drinkers, though neither Philip Hope-Wallace nor Alan Brien were remotely abstemious, and the Fleet Street veteran at the lower end of the market, Fergus Cashin, was as famous for sometimes being discovered in an undignified condition as he was for allegedly coining the phrase 'this one will run and run'. Billington and Wardle never drink before or during a play, though each can make up for it afterwards. Billington moreover is unapologetically unathletic, taking his sporting pleasures on the spectators' side of the cricket boundary (he is a member of the MCC), while Wardle is a committed swimmer and used to run round his local pond in Barnet until his knee joints registered a protest.

In my early school days I was a keen footballer – my one ambition in life, at the age of ten, was to play for Manchester United; I was a member of my primary school football team at Saints Peter and Paul in Ilford, defeated finalists in the H G King Cup of 1958/9 (losing 1-0 to the crack local schools side of the day, Barley Lane) – a keen, but less competent cricketer, and always an enthusiastic, untutored tennis player. In adult life, my exercise has been haphazard and, since giving up smoking over ten years ago, my weight steadily on the increase. At the start of 1992 I thought I should do something about this. I stopped drinking for the first three months of the year, began walking energetically every day on the heath and by Easter was, without really thinking about it, starting to jog the last mile or so home. I had other motivations. I had started to suffer from unpleasant twinges in my arms and back as a result of sitting at my word processor. The curse of Repetitive Strain Injury, the dreaded RSI, had struck, and was exacerbated by the panic of an approaching book deadline. The other deciding factor was the inevitable exclusion from my son's sporting life. Our days of kicking a ball around and of impromptu cricket were completely subsumed in his own physical development and involvement with his school teams. I was in serious danger of becoming an exercise-shy fattie, wheezing unhealthily between desks, bars and theatres. The time had come, the warning signs were all around. Critics ten years my junior – Paul Taylor and Charles Spencer – were even plumper than me. Michael Billington's skin was the wrong colour – a sort of smoke-fumed, bilious green. Benedict Nightingale had effectively lost weight for a few months then collapsed again into an unappetising muddle of incipient grossness. Sheridan Morley was busy setting new standards of giantism in the stalls.

Irving Wardle alone seems able to stay alert, lean and wiry on the job. It is as though he fidgets away his metabolic superfluity. In his pipe-smoking days, he developed a magnificent aisle-seat routine of pipe-smoker's business, conjured from the inner depths of his battered old leather briefcase. He filled in the empty minutes before the curtain rose by poking his pipe-cleaners along the stem, filling the bowl with tobacco for smoking later on, shuffling his books and papers, checking the screwtop cap on his hot coffee flask (this was an additional item in the repertoire, devised for the regional theatre and the bleak uncertainties of an inhospitable office backstage whence he would file his overnight review to The Times). I always admired Irving's fluency of performance, a lovely touch being the sure and silent way in which his biro would be slid comfortably along the spiral sheath of his reporter's notebook in those passages of the play where not a lot was going on. This latter habit I have shamelessly adopted. But the highlight of any Irving 'overnight' performance – some of the high tension has gone from his demeanour, and perhaps from his writing, since he went weekly on the Independent on Sunday – was the cracking of the knuckles. If the play was late starting, Irving's fidgetiness would be transferred from pipe business to knuckle-cracking, each bony protuberance of the left hand crushed like a nut in the right until the auditorium echoed with their impatient sound. On a really good bad night, Irving's exasperation would extend to the helpless gesture of brushing his hand through his thinning hair, raising it skywards, then bringing it down with a crashing thwack on the side of the seat. His eyes would roll and his very jaw would gape, and on one never-to-be forgotten West End occasion, as the seven-o-clock witching hour passed unregarded by houselights which refused to dim, and first-nighters who refused to hurry to their stalls, Irving, in his creased blue jacket and honest brown sneakers, banged his fist on the arm of his seat and yelled at an immutable stage curtain: 'Shop!'

Staying awake is a prime requisite of the job, and keeping fit helps. H L Mencken, the American hypochondriac and wit who said that he would rather be run over by a taxi-cab and have his hat smashed than sit through *Rosmersholm* again, used to itemise his illnesses and physical shortcomings in a correspondence with his friend and fellow critic George Jean Nathan. One morning, his ailments came to the following: a burn on the tongue (healing); a pimple inside the jaw; a sour stomach; pain in the prostate; burning in the gospel-pipe (always a preliminary of the hay-fever season); a cut finger; a small pimple inside the nose (going away); a razor cut, smarting; tired eyes. If Mencken had worked out and drunk less, he would have had none of these problems, apart perhaps from the occasional cut or pimple. On his fifty-first birthday, Nathan sent him a telegram announcing a parcel post gift box containing a set of false teeth, a toupé, one cork leg, six bottles of liniment and a copy of *What Every Boy Should Know*. Mencken wired back: 'Our Heavenly Father will reward you for that last-aid package but why did you omit bottle of asthma medicine? I am hacking and wheezing like Polonius.'

So I run. The hacking and wheezing are behind me now. In the first year, I would devise a route wherever the theatre took me. I have pounded the streets of Hull and Glasgow, of Leeds and Manchester, in the early morning hours. At last year's Edinburgh Festival, I attempted to combat the deleterious effects of late night sessions in the Assembly Rooms bar by lugging my guts around Arthur's Seat. This is a truly spectacular run, as anyone who saw *Chariots of Fire* will recall. I began on the Royal Mile, turned off at the Pleasance (Venue 33), smugly acknowledging all the one-man shows I was not going to see there, then climbed slowly uphill towards the international swimming pool and swung left into Holyrood at that point where the track rises steeply around the small mountain range just below Arthur's Seat known as the Lion's

Haunch. You level out at the top, with superb views across the Firth of Forth, and a couple of lochs on the left. The last mile or so back to the Palace and the city centre is a little too steeply downhill, and this was my undoing. I sustained a bad sprain which I thought I would run off the next day, but each day it felt worse. Without realising it, I had pulled my Achilles tendon and I was compelled to retire from the athletic fray for six weeks thereafter.

In London, on the heath, I pass other regular runners each day, and we nod and grunt our good mornings. The scenery is changing all the time, as the trees and bushes alter with the seasons, squirrels and hares dart in the undergrowth, crows and magpies circle overhead and the unspoilt fields and forests stretch across to Highgate on the right and Hampstead village on the left. I do feel a romantic communion on Hampstead Heath, with Keats and Shelley, but especially with Leigh Hunt, the first real theatre critic in our modern sense of the term, whose excoriation of the actor Pope is as cutting and uncompromised as anything written by Tynan or Levin in their pomp: 'His face is as hard, as immovable, and as void of content as an oak wainscot [Levin once said that a performance was as full of animation as the leg of a billiard table] . . . here is an actor, then, without face, expression, or delivery, and yet this complication of negative qualities finds means to be clapped in the theatre and panegyrised in the newspapers.' Upon plain subjects, Leigh Hunt said, he would rather be plain spoken. He was a fearless and radical editor and was imprisoned for two years in 1813 for an adjudged libel on the Prince Regent. On his release, he returned to Hampstead with a lover's ardour and wrote a couple of poems which perfectly express my own daily joy in the surroundings:

A steeple issuing from a leafy rise,
With farmy fields in front, and sloping green,
Dear Hampstead, is thy southern face serene,
Silently smiling on approaching eyes.
Within, thine ever-shifting looks surprise:
Streets, hills, and dells, trees overhead now seen,
Now down below, with smoking roofs between –
A village, revelling in varieties.

The northward, what a range – with heath and pond,
Nature's own ground; woods that let mansions through,
And cottaged vales with pillowy fields beyond,
And clump of darkening pines, and prospects blue,
And that clear path through all, where daily meet
Cool cheeks, and brilliant eyes, and morn-elastic feet.

Today's spring-heeled jacks with sparkling faces are the joggers and walkers who keep themselves, and the heath, alive by disporting themselves there each day. Whom do I see? The directors of Cheek by Jowl, Declan Donnellan and Nick Ormerod, have lately bought a house abutting the southern lowlands, and on most weekends can be spotted ambling idly round their newly acquired terrain. Adrian Mitchell walks his long-haired sheepdog. Max Stafford-Clark, now turned fifty but a former club-level rugby player, streaks past me in his black running strip. Melvyn Bragg has periods of activity in which he hauls himself around the perimeter. And, in between his exploratory world trips for BBC Television, Michael Palin has greeted me in tired but friendly fashion as he pushes on to Kenwood House.

There is no floral display in London to compare with the rhododendron bushes in the gardens of Kenwood. In the early months of the year I chart their transition from grey-green aridity to the full flush of orange, mauve and pink magnificence of this month. July is also the time of outdoor concerts on the slopes before Kenwood House, and I try to time my weekend runs to coincide with the jostle, hum and musical merry-making of the late afternoon rehearsals. Nothing like sprinting through the bracken to the noble and uplifting accompaniment of a Brahms symphony or a Rachmaninov concerto. I sometimes compose opening sentences as I run; everything in a review column depends on the first line. Sometimes I work off a head of steam about something or other, or else I try and think through a simile or metaphor, a particular phrase, a tactic of assessment. After a couple of miles, I hit the lovely wall of oblivion and my mind goes blank, the heart is pumping and my short fat hairy legs are obeying every twist and turn and rivet on the stony paths and woodland tracks. The sweat is up and my body glows from head to toe as I reach home base, walk slowly up the street and, after a few stretching exercises, plunge into the reviving, splashy splendours of a red hot shower. The whole business is complete within the hour and now I feel as though I am ready for anything: a deadline, a panic at the office, a new play at the Bush, a daunting classical revival at the National, or even an abusive post-card from John Osborne.

## Publicity angles and the hard sell

I AM HORRIFIED by a BBC radio broadcast about the theatre publicist Mark Borkowski. He says, without audibly blushing, that his job is 'all about getting people column-inches in the newspapers'. Most of these stories are either non-stories or non-existent stories, though not even Borkowski has peddled such delightful banalities as that which convinced one New York journalist to inform his less than amazed readers that 'Helen Craig, star of *Johnny Belinda* at the Longacre, yesterday was elected a member of the Book of the Month Club. She will start receiving books almost immediately.' I recall that the greatest theatre and film publicist of our age, Theo Cowan, who started at Rank and represented such stars as Dirk Bogarde, Peter Sellers, David Niven, Deborah Kerr, Sammy Davis Jr and Michael Caine, thought exactly the opposite: a publicist's job, said Theo, was to keep his clients out of the papers. By which, of course, he meant that only good and serious stuff should ever appear and that stunts and short-term tawdriness were to be eschewed. Above all, truth was, despite all appearances to the contrary, sacred. Because journalists and clients knew about Theo's moral probity, they all cooperated subliminally in keeping the stories sharp, clean, fresh and to the point. No-one ever became confused over the conflicting interests of feature journalists, who like to be jollied along and need certain privileges of information and intimacy with their subjects, and critical writers, who need facilities without frills or strings attached. And everyone on each side of the fence trusted Theo. The same cannot be said of Mark Borkowski. In the radio broadcast he says he seeks to work with people 'who will make the news'. Jeremy Beadle, the fatuous television presenter of silly games, offers the testimonial that 'he makes life more interesting than it really is;

Mark is the master of the silly story.' One such silly story, in his days at the Theatre Royal, Stratford East, involved a fictitious tap-dancing dog whose demise in a street collision with an articulated lorry led to a successful campaign to shut off that thoroughfare to traffic. The ends may be said to have justified the means. But at what price? The peddling of falsehood, for a laugh, courtesy of a lazy or dependent journalist, is the first step along the road to dangerous exploitation of the media for sinister and unreliable purposes.

It is a sign of the times that the arts editor of the Daily Telegraph, no less, should commend Borkowski's enterprise in this broadcast on the grounds that Borkowski is an essential part of his news-gathering activity, and 'one of the best PR men in the country'. So much for the Daily Telegraph. Borkowski affects a public manner of self-importance. He signs his name with a flourish and a peek-a-boo bow tie like the one he habitually wears. He comes across as a monumental prat, but to be fair to him, he probably thinks that that impression will do him least harm and probably quite a lot of good.

His operation seems to me to be a permanent campaign of deception and manipulation which will only fool some of the people some of the time. Most theatres are grateful for 'publicity' because it entails a lack of criticism, a boost to status and local credibility, and a justification of all that hard work, investment, talent and effort. The publicist treads a fine line between pleasing his or her employers, the producing management, and representing the interests of the media. Some PRs get the balance wrong, especially in the subsidised sector where it is easier to be the voice of management than the colleague of journalists. And in recent years, one or two PRs in the commercial sector have undermined their effectiveness, and the trust journalists place in them, by becoming investors in the shows they represent to the media. This conflict of interest results in a sort of unhelpful sullenness when a critic delivers an unfavourable notice or a showbiz writer goes digging for gossip. The critic is someone who comes along and spoils the party by telling the truth, or at least his or her version of the truth. Of course, if the critic is enthusiastic, that is to say, actually approves this production or that actor, then his or her verdict becomes the most powerful publicity of all: unsolicited recommendation from a supposedly disinterested and cynically hard-to-please source.

When they write unfavourable notices, critics are always berated for putting people out of work, or being unkind to some project that has taken years of preparation. No-one ever complains of the obverse effect, the commercial benefits that accrue when the notices are favourable. Ideally, as a critic, you want no thanks for a good review and no complaints for a bad one; unless you commit a howler which needs correcting, or have in some way overstepped the mark. If so, a good publicity agent will tactfully point out the error of your ways, and you will try to do better next time.

The big disaster at the moment is the muddling up of publicity and marketing departments. The two activities are totally incompatible; the first involves cooperation with the editorialising media, the second hard-nosed promotion and the placing of advertising. The Arts Council now thinks that marketing strategies are the way ahead. Last year I went to the opening of a new play in the Birmingham Rep Studio and fought my way through the thickest foyer throng I had ever seen at that venue. I assumed the main house must be showing a nude version of Alan Ayckbourn, or an evening with Jim Davidson. But then I began to recognise a few faces in the assembly; they were people in publicity and marketing from around the country and they were embarking on a marketing refresher course. The more of these meetings there are, the worse the overall standards of press releases, posters, and display advertising becomes. As a journalist, the personal touch is what you want in publicity, and nowadays what you get is a sort of disembodied marketing-speak, gushing and unconvincing, full of pre-emptive critical opinion and breathless bromide seemingly designed to put you off going anywhere near the production. The worst perpetrator of such stuff is Mark Borkowski, who sees himself as someone worthy of attention in the publicity process and whose disingenuous effusions are a godsend only to those sections of the media that are susceptible to the blandishments of the truly cynical.

Two of the last surviving publicists to learn their trade with Theo
Cowan are Sue Hyman and Peter Thompson. The first I married,
the second I talk to most days on the telephone. I sometimes
wonder if I have got them the right way round. They are the only
publicists who confirm interview appointments in a letter, with a
copy to the client; they never question your view of a particular
production; their manner with journalists hits the right sceptical
tone of neutral information and helpful hints; they know absolutely
everyone; they are not condescending in their dealings with local
journalists, radio stations or photographers; and they exude an
appropriate 'First Night' aura (Sue is easily the most beautiful and
best dressed publicist in town; Peter is not, but looks the part
anyway) in sharp contrast to the scruffy, furtive ministrations of
their rivals. Peter is generally known as 'Fucknose' Thompson
because he has an endearing habit of stonewalling the unanswerable question with a drawling, slow-motion 'fuck knows, dear'.
Whenever I telephone Sue at her office, she is usually dispensing
her considerable charm on the other line to Jack Tinker, or James
Christopher or Jeremy Kingston. In a world full of Michaels, I
am always 'Michael Who?' and our professional association, as
opposed to our private one, is conducted in chilly, matter-of-fact
language, rather as if she has used up all her cooperative instincts
on my more deserving colleagues.

Both Peter and Sue come to my aid this month on the most
nerve-wracking opening night of the year, the new Lloyd Webber
musical. It is difficult to experience *Sunset Boulevard* through the
miasma of hype and expectation which hangs like a suffocating fog
around the newly restored Adelphi Theatre in the Strand. I need,
even more than the stiffest drink, the mocking reassurance of Peter
in the foyer that this is just another one of those nights infested
with people who are not nearly as important or glamorous as they
think they are; and I need Sue sitting next to me to insulate me
against the crush in the auditorium and make me feel that I have
some justification for being there. On such nights, a critic, whose
job is the assessment of the patient's health, is likely to find himself
either swept away in an infectious panic of approval or, as is more
usually the case, struck with a stony-faced determination not to be

impressed by the brouhaha. Inspecting the corpse on the slab with a cold eye for detail becomes the hardest task in the world.

In the stalls, the critic of the New York Times, Frank Rich, who dislikes everything written by Lloyd Webber (and has been honoured by having a horse named after him in the Lloyd Webber stables; presumably so that he can be pummelled, kicked and sworn at while being ridden over the jumps), is being greeted as though he were minor royalty. Newspaper editors who steer well clear of worthier openings at the National or the RSC have stuffed themselves into dinner suits and hurried along the Strand in obeisance to the magnetic pull of a celebrity-rich media occasion (there is, of course, a large party after the show). There had been talk of Robert de Niro and Barbra Streisand showing up. The reality is slightly more mundane: Cliff Richard and Shirley Bassey. The atmosphere is not so much one of Hollywood as of the old Talk of the Town, with a strong whiff of Radio Two. Somebody points out a large, horsey woman called Eve Pollard, who seems to think the event has been arranged for her benefit. She edits the Sunday Express, which has lately run approximately one feature a week on *Sunset Boulevard*, and is married to another editor, Nicholas Lloyd, who was knighted for services to journalism by Margaret Thatcher. I think wistfully of strap-hanging on a bus from Lewes station for a Glyndebourne opening a few years ago with Alfred Brendel and Sir Isaiah Berlin. There was an outing, there was an audience, with a touch of class. Mercifully, the show proper begins and one almost topples with relief into the warm bath of one of Lloyd Webber's lushest, most melodious scores.

# AUGUST

## *Not getting away from it all on holiday*

AS PRINCE HAL RIGHTLY SAYS in *Henry IV, Part 1*, 'If all the
year were playing holidays,/To sport would be as tedious as to
work.' Even the absorbing and on the whole pleasurable activities
of a theatre critic need some relief, but I'm not very good at
holidays. It takes me about four or five days to relax and then I
start ticking off the nights before it is time to go home. This year
we are going to Corsica for the first two weeks of August. We have
taken a villa on the upper west coast of the island, half way between the noisy, Italianate city of Calvi and the more serene and
stylish, Frenchified town of Île Rousse. The climate is superb:
I wear sandals and shorts for the entire duration, evenings and all.
The sea is as welcoming as a warm bath, clean and green and
pellucid. Only in the last few days does it become contaminated
with offal, ambiguous bits of plastic, dirty tissues, cigarette ends.
Does this stuff come from ocean-going traffic or the nearby yach-
ting marina? I read somewhere that one in six persons who swims
in the Mediterranean these days comes out of it with an ear infec-
tion; both Thomas and I end up with a pain in the ear (it makes a
change, in my case, he says, from being a pain in the neck).

We play tennis. We hire a car and visit the mountain villages.
We have a puncture late at night. Sue tries to cut corners in the
kitchen by fuelling the dish washer with Fairy Liquid. Before you
can say Sheridan Morley, we are up to our knees in foaming bubble
bath and we spend an entire morning baling out the villa and trying
to prevent the offender from choking on her own giggling fits.
Some holidaymakers, I know, seek out museums and Renaissance
churches. We tend to amuse ourselves with domestic accidents and

paperback novels. The great treat is to snooze after lunch and go to bed before midnight. The last thing we crave is a 'night out' or an expensive restaurant, or a flamboyant discothèque. One has quite enough of that sort of thing at home. It always amuses me, though, how you never really escape your work on holiday. This year, the newspaper Le Monde is suddenly full of stories about upheavals at the Comédie Française and there is a front-page report one day of Heiner Müller's new version of *The Ring* at Bayreuth. Most of our time, though, is blessedly theatre-free and, although I have left unread novels of Mark Twain and George Eliot on the absurdly early morning flight from Gatwick, I am soon happily immersed in our pooled resources of Robert Harris, Dermot Bolger, Henri de Montherlant, David Lodge, Edith Wharton and Donna Tartt.

The worst holiday for not getting away from it all was a week we once took in Mykinos. It was the first time we had left Thomas, about one year old, at home. We travelled overnight and arrived at our villa where the sheets were damp and the bathroom full of unfamiliar faeces. The sun came up, we sorted ourselves out, settled down to a coffee on the communal terrace. An elderly English couple introduced themselves. As we exchanged names, I noted with horror that the old fellow was beginning to spoil for a discussion on a subject I was happy to have left behind. 'I shall be eternally grateful to you,' he said, 'for directing my attention to that Pam Gems lunchtime play at the ICA the other week.' We were lost. We spent the entire week scuttling behind rocks and secreting ourselves on beaches in order not to be sucked into a discussion on the state of the Royal Shakespeare Company or the uncomfortable seating at the Bush. Mykinos has, or had, a series of great beaches which become progressively nuder and gayer until you arrive at one called, I think, Super Paradise, where I half expected Bette Midler to be selling the icecreams. Instead, one day, on a quieter section of the beach, as Sue went off to find a toilet, and I sat on my towel reading an improving volume, a slim, middle-aged man with cropped hair approached me with his sun tan lotion and wondered if I would oblige him by rubbing some of it in for him. I readily agreed but I think my acquiescence was in some way misunderstood, for he promptly dived between my legs and buried his face in my crotch. Luckily, Sue's toilet expedition was on a minor scale, and she soon returned to save me from a f(ell)ate worse than death.

Chance encounters with professional colleagues can be more bracing. Ten years ago on St Lucia in the West Indies we booked on a boat trip around the island and discovered the Daily Express journalist Garth Pearce and his family on the same outing. It was rum punch all the way, and I can honestly say that I have never been more agreeably (in the short term), or catastrophically (in the longer term), drunk in my life. There had been a water shortage in the hotel and villa complex where we were staying and that evening, fortified, nay devastated, by liquor, I led a delegation of irate residents to lodge a formal, if muzzy, protest with the hotel manager. As he was married to one of Sue's best friends at the time – indeed, that was the only reason we had alighted on St Lucia in the first place – my outburst must have seemed doubly ill-mannered. I do not remember anything else of the evening except that I unwittingly exposed myself to my mother-in-law, who was neither shocked nor impressed by what she saw, and passed out on a bed before the sun had even gone down.

Still, we did see a one day Test Match, the first that had been played on the island since an earthquake some years previously. We blagged our way into the best stand on the slim excuse that I was a journalist. The West Indies were playing the already de-moralised Australians led by Kim Hughes. Clive Lloyd and Viv Richards were both absent on legal business, but the small ground, holding 8,000 people, was packed to the gills. The strangest sight was that of countless black umbrellas raised against the sun. We took our places and bought a couple of beers before realising that the rum was going at a few pence a shot. The Australians batted first. Within forty minutes, their innings was in ruins, three wickets down for about twenty runs as Malcolm Marshall and Joel Garner ran amok on a fast, viciously uneven pitch. But then the besieged Hughes, supported by Allan Border, played one of the most courageous innings I have ever seen, and the two Australians put on 150 fighting runs for the next wicket. Then another collapse. The score climbed to a respectable, though obviously insufficient, total of 220-odd. Meanwhile, we had a fine roast beef dinner on our laps and the rum kept flowing. It was a splendid afternoon. The West Indian openers, Gordon Greenidge and Desmond Haynes, knocked off the required total almost nonchalantly. The wicket held no terrors for them.

In the Caribbean, we spent one day with our friends before we all happily lost each other. Several years ago, the four of us (Sue, Thomas, Sue's mother and myself) reported to Gatwick for a flight to Sardinia, only to find ourselves checking in behind the film and stage director Mike Leigh, his wife, the brilliant actress Alison Steadman, and their two sons, Toby and Leo. They were on the same flight, and staying not only in the same resort, but even at the same hotel. Considering how miffed they must have been to find us there, Mike and Alison took the accident in good heart. Mike is not a 'holidays' person either and had, we later discovered, been dragged unwillingly towards sun and sea by his wife who, quite rightly, insisted on a break for the boys' benefit. We all played tennis together (except for Mike, who was perfecting his ball-boy skills) and shared beach barbecues. Mike is wrapped up in his work even by theatrical standards. When it comes to full-time obsessiveness, he makes Peter Hall look like a wilting flower. He knows and remembers every single frame of every film he has made. And quite a few million of other people's films, too. We had many happy hours of talking about his films: on the beach, in the sea (Mike does not swim; he wades in up to his waist and starts talking), in each others' rooms. When either of us got too heated or carried away, we invoked a codeword for either ceasing or beginning cultural altercations. That codeword was 'Simon Gray,' who, for some reason or other, had taken on the role of a bogeyman in our chats.

One day, the Coveney family decided unilaterally to take a trip around the coast to escape the relentless cultural debates. We boarded a boat and disembarked, just before noon, in a pleasant town square. No-one else was in sight. We ordered coffee and cognac. We sat back in our chairs and blinked vacantly at the sun. All was quiet. When suddenly, from another side of the square, wafted on the mid-day breeze, came the disembodied battle cry: 'Simon Gra-a-a-ay.' They, too, had decided to take a break in hostilities and had made exactly the same trip. Each side was, at first, severely disappointed with the other. But we had a fabulous day just the same. Mike is not at home on beaches. He stoops and scowls, has knobbly knees and uncoordinated limbs. His perennial demeanour is that of a hunched, rabbinical hamster, his busy mind ferreting out and storing information for future use. But he is wickedly funny, and merciless in both his pursuit of an argument and his powers of observation. The one dread legacy of a memorable holiday could still be a Mike Leigh film featuring one of his pimpliest actors playing a curmudgeonly theatre critic kitted out in less than state-of-the-art leisure wear.

In Corsica, I suggest we take the train across country to Bastia, stay the night there, and return. There are no takers for this scheme. The beach is too seductive. So I resolve to go on my own, on a day-return, my one solo adventure of the holiday. Corsica has a famous single-gauge railway. Bastia is only 100 kilometres away, but the journey takes three and a half hours. I catch a train at 6.30 am, two hundred metres from our front door. We follow the coast to Île Rousse then plunge across country, through the most sensational landscape of dense forests and death-defying precipitous ravines. It really does look as dangerous and romantic as those fine engravings Edward Lear made on his travels. In Bastia at ten o'clock I sip coffee and read about the latest defeat of the England cricket team in the international edition of the Guardian. I have not been to Bastia, or indeed Corsica, since I hitch-hiked my way through the country en route to the European mainland (I had taken a student's job for a fortnight in the summer of 1967 on an archaeological dig in Lucca, Tuscany; thence to Sicily and Sardinia, hitch-hiking all the way except for the ferry-crossings, through Corsica and back to England via the Rhine Valley and Holland; ten weeks in all, at a cost of my entire savings of £50). There is a marvellous statue of Napoleon attired in a Roman toga in the main square. I pass a pleasant day, climbing to gain the best vantage point above the magnificent harbour, visiting the excellent ethnographic museum, lunching on squid and spaghetti, and taking the last train home.

## Edinburgh strikes new blows for Europe

EVERY YEAR the Edinburgh Festival comes around and every year I think, 'Oh dear, here comes the Edinburgh Festival,' and every year I slog northwards, fearing the worst, and every year I have a really good time. For a start, the weather always seems to be fine. The last few festivals have been blessed with sunshine and mild breezes. It must be something to do with the ozone layer. In the rain, Edinburgh, though incorrigibly dramatic, can be deeply depressing. As he hurried forth to the Western Islands with Boswell, Johnson said that the city was 'too well known to admit description'. But it is never too well known to yield fresh delight and to set the pulse racing. There are certain things respectable critics should never do in Edinburgh: buy a ticket for the Tattoo, stay in the Caledonian, see a show about Sylvia Plath, watch television, or walk to Leith.

The aim is to discover some play or actor that nobody else has yet seen and bruit the news abroad. The sad fact, however, is that there are almost never any real discoveries made at the Edinburgh Festival. I can name only three in its entire history: playwrights Tom Stoppard and Doug Lucie, and revue performer Rowan Atkinson. What the festival *can* do, is provide a focus for emergent talent from the comedy circuit. But the whole 'showbiz' side of the fringe has become a sickening rush to cash in on flimsy radio and television reputations, and I'm afraid we critics too often, albeit unwittingly, cooperate in this vile commercialism. The days of finding rare Jacobean dramas in draughty church halls have long gone; rising costs of accommodation, and of rents in venues, have so increased, that the innocent gaiety of university and amateur theatre is virtually a thing of the distant past. Or at least that's how it seems. Maybe the critics are too easily beguiled by the publicity machine of the Assembly Rooms, the Gilded Balloon and the Pleasance, the three big fringe venues that are pooling their marketing and publicity resources this year but which all seem to be presenting the same things. Trouble is, quite a lot of these things one wants to see. The members' bar of the Assembly Rooms is one of the vilest places on earth, but it is essential to go there, not just for late-night drinking, but also for hearing who's in town and what's the goss.

Last year, the fringe was ignited by Thea Vidale, a huge, black, fright-wigged, filthy-talking American comedienne. She entered the gilded bar and saw my vertically challenged friend Jack Tinker perched on a chair at the far end. Jack, pony-tailed and dressed in black, was at his dinkiest, most animated and most fashionable that day. Vidale took a fancy to him at a distance, adjusted her sights, and stormed down the centre of the room, which divided like the Red Sea. She reached Jack and shouted at him from a great height: 'My dear, you are so sweet, I must fuck you.' To which the astonished Tinker bravely replied: 'Oh, my dear, if you do, I think I shall disappear.'

Emily Woof, one of this year's slightly less threatening one-woman shows, has broken her leg in rehearsal. Encased in plaster between left knee and ankle, she is therefore the only solo turn appearing with (and in) a full supporting cast. The talented Ms Woof, whom I have neither seen nor met until now, accuses me one night in the Traverse bar of having given her a bad review. I assure her that before I *do* give her a bad review, I will at least pay her the courtesy of going to see her performance. I go. She is good. The bad review is on hold. Ned Sherrin invites me onto his fizzing lunchtime chat show (well, it fizzes until I appear) at the George Square Theatre and introduces me as the drama critic of the Guardian-owned Observer, or 'The Obsurdian'. The other guests are Barry Cryer, Willie Rushton, Frank Delaney and Sir David Steel. Over drinks afterwards I remind Barry that the last (and indeed first) time we met was at a retirement lunch in the Savoy for Peter Hepple, the veteran editor of The Stage. I try out my Peter Hepple impersonation on him, he replies with an even better one, and we indulge for a few moments of celebratory Hepple-itis, scrunching our noses and shoulders, and intoning slowly our preference for a mediocre night of entertainment at the Rat and Vole Niterie, Thanet, over the prospect of a new play in the Cottesloe or the Bush. One or two people steal a pitying glance at two madmen apparently engaged in some terrible, argumentative ritual.

Anything can happen in Edinburgh, and frequently does. Someone with whom I studied Latin and Greek at school materialises at the book festival in Charlotte Square to see what I look like after thirty years. I arrange to meet the delightful Irish writer Hayden Murphy for a drink in the George, and he turns up with Jim Haynes. The festival is not really happening until you bump into Jim, who founded the Traverse in Edinburgh in 1963, lectures in Paris, and remains the most ageless person I know. He devotes his life to making friends, making love, bringing people together, giving them dinner. He is a charming, unreformed and sexually insatiable rapscallion, even though he must be pushing sixty. I go to my hotel room to collect my messages, and when I return to the bar he has chatted up the barmaid and discovered most of her relevant biographical details. Later that same evening, I am meeting two new friends, Amanda and Ruth, who work in the festival office, at the Traverse before Neil Bartlett's new piece. When I arrive, they say they have just had a drink with a wonderful man they've never met before called Jim Haynes who has invited them both to Paris. They're going.

Neil Bartlett's *Night After Night*, co-produced with Bartlett's own Gloria company, is a highly enjoyable camp meditation on post-war musicals and the etiquette of theatre-going. Bartlett was born in 1958 and presents himself in search of his own father (whom he plays) going 'up to town' for a show. In the first half, the gay underworld of ushers, barmen and chorus boys dedicated to heterosexual musical fictions is brilliantly conjured in monologues and swishing backstage scenes. Black ties and gilt chairs also evoke a sense of Pina Bausch's dance hall masterpiece, *Kontakthof*. It is a great night in the Traverse which, since opening in these new premises last year, has resumed its role as the focal meeting point of the festival. The bar is good and efficient, though I still sometimes guiltily yearn for the befuddled intimacy of the old Traverse, where you stood shoulder to shoulder with Roger McGough and Adrian Henri in puddles of beer. Roger, like Jim Haynes, is a festival perennial and is here again this year. The Traverse bar is packed, the atmosphere electric, in spite of the fact that most people are saying that the Traverse's own offerings – tonight's opera premieres with texts by John Clifford and Ian Heggie, two of Scotland's best young-ish playwrights – have been disappointing.

Brian McMaster's second term as the festival's director confirms all suspicions that the fringe has a real fight on its hands to compete with the main attractions. It is the best 'official' programme for years, certainly since John Drummond spent as much time and expertise planning the drama programme in the late 1970s, early 1980s, as his predecessors spent solely on the music side. This year we have work by two Peters, Sellars and Stein, Robert Wilson, the brilliant American choreographer Mark Morris, the Glasgow Citizens, the Gate, Notting Hill, and the Canadian Opera Company directed by Robert Lepage. On arriving in the city, Sellars takes one look at all the fringe comedy posters and wonders out loud why no-one is doing anything serious. He certainly is: re-jigging *The Persians* by Aeschylus, the only Greek tragedy to respond to contemporary events (the defeat of the Persian fleet by the Greeks at Salamis), to read as a bitterly enraged post-script to the Gulf War.

Festivals are all about conjunction and collision. If you mixed and matched writers and directors until blue, green or red in the face, the primal, posthumous alliance of Gertrude Stein and Robert Wilson would still sound like a dream ticket.

Trance and repetition, an iterating pulse of spare and beauteous incantation, a world of sighs and strange dark dreams: *Doctor Faustus Lights the Lights* is a real treat. Wilson's work, in twenty years, has been seen only twice before in Britain: his Hockney-esque *I was Sitting on My Patio This Guy Appeared I Thought I was Hallucinating* at the Royal Court in 1978, and his amazing quadraphonic version of Heiner Müller's *Hamletmachine* at the Almeida in 1987. In New York and Germany, he has lived through and lived down the reputation of being the most technically innovative and intellectually louche of all contemporary directors. He has done large-scale operas with Philip Glass and small, savage chamber pieces about autism and identity. Elements of both styles inform the new piece, which is a marionettish Faust feast of lighting, silhouette, shadow play and quiet misery. It is beautiful, colourful, surprising and funny. Stein's three acts play for ninety minutes and are performed in the original American English by a young cast from the Hebbel Theater in Berlin.

Jonathan Miller hates this *Faustus*. 'It's like a fashion window of Harvey Nichols,' he says, intending that as an insult (I happen to love the windows, and the interiors, of the new Harvey Nicks). 'Vacuous, meaningless tosh,' he continues in the lobby of the George Hotel a few days later, 'aimed merely at the morons who watch MTV and who work in modern schlock advertising.' His killer punch is one of cultural one-upmanship: 'It's all been done before, anyway, and with contextual and historical justification, at the Volkesbuhne in Berlin around 1916.' Anyone who liked Wilson's production was therefore both trivial and ignorant. I stagger back amazed, incapable of mustering any sort of response apart from my usual one of relishing the good doctor's fantastic fluency of wit, argument and unadulterated bile. He is here as president of the Fringe Society: the man who starred in the first real modern satirical revue, *Beyond the Fringe*, at the Edinburgh Festival in 1960, is putting something back in (apart from his boot).

On a different tack from Miller, I read in the Sunday Times that this Wilson sort of thing, and last week's *Persians*, is too much for the populist instincts of the Labour Party's former deputy leader, Roy Hattersley, who wonders what happened to 'fun' at the festival. People other than Mr Hattersley had fun last week at *The Persians*, which almost sold out, and at the productions of Mark Morris and Robert Wilson, which completely sold out. The 'elitist' charges simply won't stick this year in the face of box office evidence. The Edinburgh audience, at last, has outflanked the ignorant, knee-jerk reactionaries and cultural Jeremiahs. And the festival director, Brian McMaster, has cleverly demonstrated that you can enjoy 'art theatre' and music hall without selling your soul either to Mephisto or the trashy cultural ideology of people like

Hattersley, who once contributed to the so-called humorous magazine, Punch (ah, *that* was what 'fun' was about).

Even so, Hattersley conveniently overlooks McMaster's most delightful and 'populist' innovation of all: a night of Scottish Variety, the Fabulous Fifties, at the traditional home of Edinburgh pantomime and musical theatre, the splendid King's. This superb evocation of the vital humorous traditions in our islands is devised by Jimmy Logan and directed by Douglas Squires, with a fourteen-piece band in the pit, twelve high-kicking Tiller Girls, painted backdrops, illuminated number boards (to check the items against your programmes), brilliant jugglers and trampolinists, and wallows in musical nostalgia provided by Susan Maugham and the new 'Sounds of the Platters', the silken, harmonizing precursors of Motown. Enough 'fun' to be going along with there, Roy, I would have have thought. Jimmy Logan's Teddy Boy routine is a bit ropey, but his early incursion with Walter Carr and a ladder in the middle of Johnny Beattie's classic routine about landladies and seaside resorts is pure music hall joy.

Germany invades the last week of the festival's drama programme: Jakob Lenz, Goethe's unjustly forgotten contemporary, is celebrated by the Glasgow Citizens in Philip Prowse's exciting, classical revival of *The Soldiers*; the Deutsches Theatre of Berlin pieces together von Kleist's *The Broken Jug*; and Peter Stein's stark and monumental production of *Julius Caesar*, made for last year's Salzburg Festival, swirls and storms through the Royal Highland Exhibition Hall near the airport. Lenz in production is beefed up with Lenz in staged readings, as in last year's Granville Barker mini-festival. I would have preferred to see one or two more full-scale productions. But there was an outbreak of cold feet in the reps when Brian McMaster invited contributions. So he has turned to the Gate, who oblige with readings of two more Lenz plays: *The New Menoza*, in a felicitous, sprightly new translation by Meredith Oakes, which is not known in Britain at all and is obviously well worth reviving; and *The Tutor*, which is known here by reputation, Brecht's re-hash and a disastrous Old Vic production some years ago. Lenz sounds modern, urgent, jangling and even funny. I am sure that McMaster's programming will have consequences in the repertoire very soon.

In past years, the festival has followed up its productions with a series of rather anaemic Press conferences. McMaster has introduced a more robust support system of discussion and debate: improved background material in the theatre programmes, complementary publications and events, and an ambitious, well-planned series of festival conferences. At one of these conferences, Peter Stein regrets the shrinking tendency in modern theatre and comments how public speaking has become almost synonymous with not telling the truth. He is sharing a platform in the university's Old Senate House with Robert Wilson, Robert Lepage and the Citizens' Robert David MacDonald. Three Bobs and a Pete. They are, says chairperson Sheena MacDonald, 'at the innovative end of art forms' which means that they are all either very experimental, or completely washed up. It is hard to tell, looking at them, though three out of four wear top to toe black (two Bobs and a Pete) and the senior Bob (David MacDonald) wears a white jacket. They all utter interesting thoughts. MacDonald says that the trouble with British theatre is that it has a tradition of talk, not of words. Wilson is even more gnomically inspired. He suddenly declares: 'The stage is special. I hate naturalism. If your concept of the stage is artificial, the work becomes more natural.' I wonder what Jonathan Miller might make of that. I think he would probably agree. Then, even more suddenly, Wilson stands up to his full height of about seven feet and says that we should imagine Time as a vertical line and Space as horizontal: 'An awareness of this tension helps to make the difference between being onstage and being offstage.' Lepage does not have all that much to say, but anyone who has seen his unbelievable, water-logged staging of Schoenberg's *Ewartung* in the Playhouse knows that he doesn't have to add anything. They are asked about television. MacDonald says that a mouse looks very good on television, but that you can't do an elephant so well. Stein defends putting some of his work on television videos out of a mixture of vanity and greed; 'You think, also, that the work maybe in twenty years, like wine, will look better. Of course, it won't.' Wilson says, categorically, that theatre has been killed by television. He adds that he has seen Tony Kushner's AIDS-age

Pulitzer Prize-winner *Angels in America*: 'It's okay, but it's television.'

Wilson speaks so little in public that his pronouncements take on the immediate impact of a special event. But they are all so beautifully prepared and delivered that the suspicion dawns (and is later confirmed) that his statements are honed and held in readiness for any such rare occasion as this one. 'My theatre,' he says, 'is a formal theatre. It is non-interpretative. Interpretation is the business of the audience. Our responsibility in making theatre is to ask questions; to ask what it is, not say what it is. It's all too complex to know what we are doing. Perhaps the body is moving faster than we think. Words are like rocks. One letter within the word is all feeling, all emotion. I work on two premises: there is no such thing as movement; there is no such thing as silence. It is all of a continuum. So much of theatre I see is stop and start. It should be all one thing. Albert Einstein was once asked by a reporter to repeat what he just said. He said there was no need, as it's all the same thought.' Wilson is rapidly emerging as the star of the session, and his colleagues graciously yield him the final, enigmatic word. He reports how Jessye Norman was interviewed recently on television and asked what was her favourite recording: 'Martin Luther King.' Wilson waves his right arm in a huge gestural arc and stays quietly grinning through a silence of monumental proportions before a storm of applause and laughter bursts around the room.

The new Edinburgh Festival Theatre on Nicolson Street, on the site of the old Empire, will open next June and take its place at the centre of the 1994 festival. It looks certain to be Britain's most exciting new theatre building. Costing £20m, most of it raised by Edinburgh District and Lothian Regional Councils, and sponsors, it should compensate for all those years of disappointment over the 'Hole-in-the-Ground' and provide the city with a much-needed and long-overdue home for ballet, opera and great international companies. I am given a tour by general manger Paul Iles along with Neil Bartlett and his Gloria company. They all look slightly incongruous in hard hats, and as we pick our way through the rubble and filth there are many shrieks and exclamations about sizes of dressing-rooms, and a low coo of corporate approval greets Paul's news that the 1928 interior will be fully restored, with lots of silver foil and marble effects, lots of pinks and peaches, and a deep red stage curtain inlaid with gold bullion. It is like taking part in a camp episode of the BBC's building firm serial, 'The Brothers'. The huge stage, twice the size of that in the Theatre Royal in Glasgow, larger than Covent Garden, is completely flat, the stalls on a new rake. This atmospheric site, surrounded by university buildings, superb architecture and cheap shopping, has accommodated six theatres since 1830. The old Empire became a bingo hall in 1963 but stuttered back to life two years ago with occasional festival presentations. There are dressing rooms for 180 artistes, a superb orchestra pit, unprecedented flying and storing facilities, a proscenium which is 44 feet wide and an auditorium which hugs it most effectively. Even among the dust and debris, the concrete and drilling, I can envisage a night of style and glamour unequalled anywhere else in the British theatre. The restored venue will have a new glass frontage, with great bars on each level. Paupers have the best deal: the upper circle foyer has the most fantastic view back along Nicolson Street and out over the neo-Classical Surgeon's Hall to Salisbury Craggs and Arthur's Seat. An annual turnover of £6m is predicted. The only dangerous challenge to Paul Iles is that the operation must be 100 per cent self-sufficient within two years. Edinburgh will have to become as round-the-year culture-conscious as present-day Glasgow, and then some more.

My Edinburgh pleasures are doubled this year as my son joins me for a few days in the last week. He has never been here before. We take in a few comedians together. We agree that Jack Dee, who has the timing of Jack Benny and the frustrated intelligence of Dave Allen, is easily the best. He performs an immaculate self-deprecating routine for an hour and twenty minutes in the Queen's Hall. I only inflict one 'official' outing on him: the opening of the Deutsches Theater's *The Broken Jug* at the King's. Half-way through the uninterrupted two hours, leaning back in his seat at a quiet moment, Thomas involuntarily cries out, only half under his breath, 'This is so *boring*.' He is right, of course, and we soon rush off to the Traverse bar, thence to a late-night performance of the

Glaswegian comedian Bruce Morton, where we laugh ourselves almost sick. Three magical days. We meet up with Sue's nephew, a dentist who works in Edinburgh, and his hairdresser girlfriend, an astonishing half-Cherokee Indian blonde from Texas called Ladonna, we hang out in the Assembly Rooms, we have breakfast in the George and dinner in the Bar Italia on the Lothian Road, we walk around the New Town and up to Holyrood Castle, we meet friends and colleagues at every ten paces, we drink wine. Later in London, Thomas asks me if there is any other city in Britain like Edinburgh; and is there any other festival like the one we have just been to? My answer's a double negative. I'm already looking forward to next year.

# SEPTEMBER

## *Dashing to Dartington*

THEATRE CRITICS don't have much truck with literature. The exception is the writer and editor, John Gross, the critic on the Sunday Telegraph, who is as happy reading the text of a Shakespeare play on his knee as he is actually watching the production up on the stage in front of him. Gross is an intelligent man caught up in the reviewing dodge by mistake; he takes sly, superior digs at the 'world of theatre' and implies that theatre should somehow aspire to *his* intellectual plane. He is a good example of a fine writer who is perhaps too pure to be a drama critic. His predecessor in the post, the novelist Francis King, was another such, though Francis was much more likely to kick up his heels at the prospect of theatrical diversion. Gross himself is the most charming man in the world. My wife tells me that he is the most polite, amusing and considerate of all the critics. On the last Saturday of August, we meet off the beat at Philip French's sixtieth birthday party. Gross greets me, mysteriously, as 'maestro,' a term I can only accept in the cheerfully semi-sarcastic tone in which it is delivered. Philip has been given a stuffed eagle by his son, Sean, and this alarming beast, perched on a sofa, has already been christened 'Norman' after Anthony Perkins's Norman Bates in Hitchcock's *Psycho*. Philip wants to put a neon sign outside the front door: 'Bates Motel: Rooms Available'. His other non-paying guests include: novelist and critic Marina Warner and her husband, the painter Johnny Dewe Matthews; Alan Brien, the journalist and author, with his wife Jill Tweedie, the writer, tragically afflicted with motor neurone disease, and Philip Oakes, poet and journalist – Brien and Oakes were two reasonably debauched heroes of my

early theatre-reviewing career – and playwright Michael Frayn
with his partner Claire Tomalin, critic and biographer. For some
reason, I yearn for Sue to take a photograph of me flanked by
Frayn and Brien. But we have no camera. The moment passes, the
bonhomie rises. A rocket is launched in the back garden. We dine
informally around a table groaning with gravadlax and roast
moose. Star writers from my own generation, Hanif Kureishi and
Julian Barnes, pop in.

So, the world of books has intruded this month. The Observer is
sponsoring a literary festival, 'Ways with Words,' at Dartington.
On the last Monday of August, and the first Monday of September,
at either end of the proceedings, I am making an appearance. First,
with fellow critics on a panel where we must explain ourselves.
Second, on a solo platform to talk about my Maggie Smith
biography. The logistics of my trips to Devon are more than
usually complicated. For the panel discussion, I leave Edinburgh
on the first shuttle, aiming for the 9.45 am Paddington train to the
West Country. My plane is heaving with television executives.
Across the aisle, I am intrigued to see that Michael Grade, head of
Channel Four, reads his copy of Today before turning to The
Times and finally toying with the Guardian. I mention that I am
worried about getting across town in time for my train. He questions me about my journey and quickly comes up with a brilliant
proposal: I should take a bus or taxi from Heathrow to Reading and
join the train there, cutting out Paddington altogether. I congratulate
him on an outstanding example of executive-level lateral thinking.
'That's how I get the big bucks,' he responds, engagingly.

As a result of this smart manoeuvre, I am almost one hour early
for the train at Reading. The station, which has become one of the
busiest and most populous in Britain, is groaning with half-stoned,
half-alive, music fans who have spent the Bank Holiday weekend
turning on and sleeping rough at the nearby rock festival. When my
train arrives, I join my critical Observer colleagues Jann Parry
(dance), Kate Kellaway (books and theatre), William Feaver (visual
arts) and Philip French (cinema). We spend most of the journey
listening to Philip, who is on brilliant form. It emerges that Philip
is really called Neville French, but changed his Christian name by

deed poll in Liverpool at the age of sixteen a) because he disliked it and b) because he had just discovered Raymond Chandler and his hero was Philip Marlowe. Mind you, he has practised other deceits of nomenclature in his career. For a short while early on he was 'Philippe Sartor,' fashion correspondent on the Bristol Evening Post. He was, he says, the worst-dressed fashion correspondent ever known in that, or any other, part of the world.

Dartington Hall is in a wonderful setting of rolling green fields and superb, unimaginable gardens. Our panel is bouncily chaired by Kate Kellaway, who finally asks each of us if we have ever said anything in print which has made us tear out our hair. I dare not look at Philip French, bald as a billiard ball, half hoping he might chip in with something along the lines of having said something that made him go out and buy a wig. But the danger passes. There are no Rottweiler questions from the benign, mostly elderly, audience, and we are all given a ridiculously smooth ride. Afterwards I congratulate Kate on acquitting herself so well and jokingly refer to the 'tear out your hair' remark, but she remains blissfully unaware of any unwitting *faux pas*.

We meet up with Andrew Motion, who is delivering the festival's Observer lecture, on the subject of John Clare, the peasant poet whose bicentenary falls this year. Motion has been assigned the bedroom occupied last night by Michael Foot and his dog Dizzie; Foot has been rambling on about his favourite books to an enraptured audience. Motion, a fastidious and notably well groomed fellow (he wears a black Kenzo suit for his lecture), is already disturbed by the remains of dog-feeding apparatus in the room. I say it could have been worse. Remains of dog, period. Motion is unmoved. At lunch, he buys a bottle of wine and drinks most of it himself. At dinner, he drinks steadily and finally drains every one else's glasses, too. His lecture is brilliant and delivered without the hint of a slur, or the trace of a stutter. In the bar afterwards, we drink beer and whisky and adjourn to the lounge with more wine. The poet points out an eager, plain young girl, his very own celebrity-stalker, who is writing a thesis about him and who follows him everywhere. He is convinced she wants to kill him so that she can wrap up his work in a convenient package; we all agree that Dartington would be a perfect setting for such a crime. Motion just wishes that she was Italian, beautiful and sex-starved. In the lounge, he points out that Ben Okri is an anagram of Ken Biro before lapsing into maudlin regret over the only serious attacks on his Philip Larkin biography: 'Everyone loves it except two people and they're both called Amis.' Amis senior's response was in a way predictable, but Amis junior's, published in the New Yorker and reprinted in the Guardian, was a brilliant meditation on the ethics of biography, paternal relations and the prose life of poets: in my view, for all its contentious judgements, it did nothing but flatter Motion's labours, at the very least by taking them so seriously. But Andrew, understandably perhaps, does not quite see it that way. 'Taste your legs, sir, put 'em to motion,' cries Sir Toby in *Twelfth Night*, encouraging Sir Andrew Aguecheek to hop about a bit. Motion has tasted his legs in his time, and done a bit of hopping about. We all retire to bed, with fulsome partings and frank kissings on the landing of the residential wing where we are billeted. Jann Parry, who is in utter thrall to Motion's slinky bed-room voice and watery bedroom eyes, slopes away, and as I go through my own bedroom motions, I wonder if Andrew next door has at last conquered his queasiness over canine detritus. Hairs of the dog, after all, are what we shall all need in the morning.

I am up betimes and back to Edinburgh on the 6.52am train from Totnes to York, where I coincide with my son Thomas. We travel together to Edinburgh. My umpteenth visit, his first, and I enjoy this last leg of the festival ever more keenly through his eyes. Returning to Dartington at the end of the week, I catch a second bar-and-lounge session, this time with Anthony Thwaite, poet and editor of Larkin's letters; his wife Anne, biographer of A A Milne; the poet Peter Porter; the novelist Penelope Lively; and Elizabeth Gaskell's biographer, Jennie Uglow. Another memorable evening! I am able to confirm my suspicion that this Jennie is the same Jennie I knew at Oxford twenty-five years ago as Jennie Crowther, a fine actress and an unforgettable Masha in *Three Sisters*. What has she been doing since? Raising a family and running a pub-lishing house, that's what. Touchingly, I discover she speaks almost every day on the telephone to her old Oxford friends

Hermione Lee (the academic and author) and Fran Hazelton (good egg and political activist). I keep in touch with no-one, and suddenly feel strangely isolated, all at sea, a social failure. Maybe this book is my flare, my public announcement to old friends in Ilford, in Oxford, in south London, abroad, next door. Next morning, I am dismayed to learn that Philip French played to an audience of just three persons for his talk on his 'Movie Verse' anthology. I talk about Maggie Smith to an infinitely larger audience, at least seventy, most of whom buy books and trade badinage outside on the lawn afterwards. One of the enthusiasts is Lady Cottesloe, a fascinating orphan whose husband was chairman of the National Theatre and who is related in some remote way to Lord Florey, the Nobel Prize-winning scientist with whom Maggie's father worked, during and after the last War, at the Dunn School of Pathology in Oxford. Small world, as ever.

## New home and new look for the Observer

WELL, HUGH McILVANNEY *has* left the Observer, bought out and bought up like so many others by the shopping mall emporium otherwise known as the Sunday Times. The paper is re-designed and re-launched on 26 September, with mixed success but at least with a sense of things happening. The arts and books are ensconced in, or rather crammed into, the sixth floor of the Guardian building on Farringdon Road. The rest of our colleagues will arrive from Battersea in a few weeks. We have a new arts editor, Lucy Tuck, from the Independent magazine, who is agreeable, hard-working and very bright. All the critics have been kept on and we are all refreshed, and relieved, by her arrival. It has been a dreadful few months in Battersea. The new editor, Jonathan Fenby, has been slow to let people know whether their services are still required or not, with the result that people have been working under conditions of appalling strain and anxiety. To be fair, Fenby and his Guardian masters have had to play the waiting game in order to work out what they are looking for. The identity of the new Observer is up for grabs, which is why McIlvanney's departure, and that of the political columnist Alan Watkins, is not, finally, all that dispiriting; these brilliant wordsmiths are part of an old Observer that may need overhauling and indeed may no longer exist.

The dangers surrounding our new arts section, for instance, are obvious: the tabloid format has immediately dispensed with one of the paper's most distinctive features, top-class black and white arts photography. Lucy wants her photographs with the features, and the review columns are now headed by mug shots of the critics. Revealing what a critic looks like is not, in my view, a tactic guaranteed to boost the circulation figures. These, as it happens, have leapt anyway, but this is the start of a vicious autumn circulation war which promises jaunty new arts-oriented sections in the middlebrow Sunday Express and Mail on Sunday, as well as a revamped Independent on Sunday. On the back page, our television critic John Naughton appears in postage stamp colour, looking slightly blobby and blotchy. Under his second postage stamp appearance, Naughton thanks readers who have written in asking if all Observer critics are in the habit of wearing full make-up and lipstick. Education and science have been lumped into our new section. On successive Sundays, 'education' writers talk about their inability to see the point of Shakespeare or great American literature ('I had been bored out of my tree struggling through Melville, Henry James and Sylvia Plath'). I am delighted to see that we subsequently publish a letter from Donald Trelford's wife Kate, an English teacher, asking if this stuff can possibly be appearing in the newspaper of Ivor Brown and Kenneth Tynan. So perhaps the debate about the Observer's identity is still a live issue. I sincerely hope so. Dispiritingly, we have already published crass, second-hand nonsense in the news section about 'luvvies' (a word I hope to see banned forthwith in the Observer; the Private Eye coinage has become a lazy, sneering generic term for creative artists whom too many journalists simply despise out of envy) and speculation over which celebrities attended, or did not attend, the first night of Harold Pinter's new play. Not only is the story base and sloppy, it is written by someone who wasn't actually there but is reproducing inaccurate stories from other newspapers, including the Guardian!

From a practical point of view, the most important task of the month is to make my computer system at home fully compatible with the Guardian Atex system. This proves much easier than I anticipated. Our deadlines have come forward on Friday morning, so it is imperative I send in my column overnight on Thursday, or first thing on Friday morning, followed by a quick scamper into the Farringdon Road offices to make it all fit in the allotted space. My fears are those of a man who can change a plug or a lightbulb but is mystified by the contents of a car's bonnet. I am tragically impractical in almost every area of everyday life, but I have learned just enough about new technology to make it work to my advantage. My Elonex (IBM-clone) word processor uses the WordPerfect programme. Next to that on my desk, I have a Tricom modem which takes me into the British Telecom system, and next to that my Panasonic fax/phone machine which means I can both screen incoming calls and meet foreign deadlines at the last minute. I have a Panasonic printer which can do a million things (I exploit about three of them), and I also work continuously, when travelling, on a Tandy laptop computer which, thanks to a tiny null modem, can either upload into, or download from, my main computer. I can therefore write anywhere, but preferably from home. The thing is: how can I arrange for all the shows that I have to review to come to my study? If I can pull that off, I need never step outside the front door again.

At the Observer, as previously at the FT, I have become accustomed to the SII system. There is a different, more left-handed, keyboard at the Guardian, and it takes getting used to. My tutor on a morning's training session is John Shirley, a former news editor of the Observer and a friend from way back. At Oxford, he had a girlfriend called Barbara Gravenor, who was a superb Maria in Jonathan Miller's production of *Twelfth Night* for the Oxford and Cambridge Shakespeare Company (I was billed as Jonathan's 'assistant director,' which mostly meant rolling around on the floor, clutching my sides with laughter during his rehearsals). Years later, I learned that Barbara had taken the veil and become a nun. Speeding round some mountain roads in France with a few other nuns, she fell out of a car and hurtled, also with a few other nuns, several hundred feet to her instant death. I have never really recovered from the shock of hearing either this peculiar story, or indeed the news that she had become a nun in the first place. Nor, perhaps, has John (who has since been through many other relationships and fathered the delightful child of my colleague Kate Kellaway). But we do not discuss private matters while trying to unravel the mysteries of the Atex keyboard and its stunning array of complicated commands. It is pleasant to be in the Farringdon area of London after Battersea, where going out for lunch was a major expedition usually sacrificed for the compensating low-priced splendours of the Observer canteen, catered by Justin de Blank. I now live only two or three miles from the office as the crow flies, and my journey on the tube via King's Cross is much preferable to slogging over to south London via Victoria or Waterloo Station. As for everyone else who commutes on the underground in London, going to work has become a lottery. Each single journey holds the same promise of uncertainty: will there be a bomb hoax, a real scare, a defective escalator, a go-slow, a fire alarm, a body on the line? Going anywhere renders you exhausted before you arrive. At least we are now within a stone's throw of the Quality Chop House and the Eagle on Farringdon Road, two street markets, coffee bars and shoe-repair stalls and a wonderful array of pubs and wine bars.

The first issue of the new Review section is celebrated with champagne in the office, and an expedition to the King's on Clerkenwell Green, next to the spartan Georgian church which has free lunchtime organ recitals every Thursday. The toast is not so much a gesture of self-congratulation as a statement of hope for the future. Spirits are comparatively high for the first time all year.

# OCTOBER

## A day at the National with David Hare

THE FIRST SATURDAY of the month is spent at the Royal National Theatre watching David Hare's trilogy of plays about the church, the law and the Labour Party. The general critical feeling is that the first play, *Racing Demon*, is something like a masterpiece; the second, *Murmuring Judges*, flawed and superficial; and the new play, *The Absence of War*, somewhere in between, a political tragedy too closely modelled on recent political events. John Thaw has joined the company to play George Jones, the Labour Party leader who loses the election campaign through giving the appearance of compromising his ideals. His case reflects the defeat of Neil Kinnock. But just as J M Barrie's *What Every Woman Knows* (1908) is no longer discussed in terms of its central character's resemblance to Ramsay MacDonald, so *The Absence of War*, I am convinced, will outlive its immediate, topical application.

I make no bones about stating in my review of the trilogy that my colleagues have been grudging and condescending. For me, these plays are the highlight of the year. They also strike me as constituting the real reason why Richard Eyre went to the National in the first place. The Hare Trilogy comes out of his twenty-year commitment to Hare's work, dating from their time together at the Nottingham Playhouse, a period which yielded Hare and Brenton's *Brassneck*, Brenton's *The Churchill Play*, Trevor Griffiths' *Comedians* and two classic Ken Campbell extravaganzas, *Walking Like Geoffrey* (in which an entire village affected to walk in a silly manner in order to avoid paying their taxes) and *Bendigo* (about a lunatic boxer with mysterious, evangelical powers).

Apart from anything else, it is a great occasion at the National, starting at 10.30 am with a play in each segment of the day. The night before, we have had IRA bombs going off in the Finchley Road, a couple of miles away in north London, and the most tremendous storms. Fearing the National Theatre might have been washed into the Thames before I get there, I book a taxi for nine o'clock and duly arrive on the South Bank at 09.25 hrs with over an hour to kill. Other early birds are stoking up on toast and bagels in the coffee bar in preparation for the long haul. I submit to a muffin. There is a palpable sense of communal excitement.

My theatre-going life is dotted with such extended events and experiences: the RSC's *Wars of the Roses* cycle in Stratford; the RSC's *The Greeks* (ten plays) and *Nicholas Nickleby* (two plays, eight hours) in the same year, 1980, at the Aldwych; Peter Brook's ten-hour *Mahabharata* in Glasgow; Ken Campbell's 22-hour *The Warp* at the ICA (we entered the building for coffee one morning and came out after breakfast the next day; only Ned Chaillet, formerly of The Times, and myself can claim not to have missed a single word); the indomitable Campbell's paranoid eight-hour *Illuminatus* in Liverpool (later at the Cottesloe); Michael Bogdanov's Shakespeare Histories in York; Ariane Mnouchkine's *Les Atrides* in both Paris and Bradford; Andrei Serban's 'Ancient Trilogy' across twenty years in Belgrade and Edinburgh; Peter Stein's Oresteian trilogy in Paris, Peter Hall's in London. Bill Bryden's 1985 *Mysteries* was the last all-day event at the National: I recall arriving in the foyer at about the same early hour to be greeted at the bar by Robert Stephens, who had managed to convince someone to open up way before the licensing hours and had lined up an imposing battery of triple vodkas and lime which he was airily dispensing among friends and critics while remembering to down several of same himself. Shortly afterwards he embarked on his tremendous double act of King Herod and Pontius Pilate, not noticeably the worse for wear, but certainly not holding anything back.

Unlike Stephens, the great Wilfrid Lawson, a similarly robust toper, sometimes forgot to go on the stage. Lawson was playing the Button Moulder in Ibsen's extended epic, *Peer Gynt*, which meant he only appeared in the last act. His guests at one performance were Richard Burton and Elizabeth Taylor, and he sat with them for the first few acts in the front of the dress circle. Many drinks had been taken over a long lunch, and many more were taken in each interval. Half way through the fifth act, Lawson, who had been reluctant to leave his guests and their bibulous hospitality, leaned across Taylor and said to Burton, 'Now, this is a very good bit, watch carefully; this is where I come on,' and sat back in his seat fully expecting to see himself appear on the stage below. The worst that happens today is that I am shown to a seat in the middle of a row. Not much really gets my goat about going to the theatre, but being seated in the middle of a row is one of the things that does. As a critic, I am there to work, and that means an aisle seat for easy access and quick exit, and a little more space to spread with the essential accoutrements of book bag, notebook, pens, programmes, papers, mackintosh, spirit level, compass and climbing boots. Nothing worse than being stuck between paying customers on either side who are becoming irritated with one's persistent scribbling. So it's as much for their convenience as for mine that I dash to find press officer Stephen Wood and make good the seating error. For the rest of the Trilogy I am seated on the aisle with Jack Tinker. For lunch, I repair to the Festival Hall with Michael Billington, his wife Jeanine and two colleagues on the radio arts programme, 'Kaleidoscope'. There is some Czech folk music going on. In the second Hare play, the one about the law, a rotund magistrate and part-time journalist called David Fingleton actually has the temerity to fall asleep directly behind me and snore roundly down my neck for most of the duration. Nothing in the world, let alone in the theatre, is more annoying than this. Verily, the aisle is full of noises. The fat Fingleton recovers consciousness in time to punctuate the onstage dialogue with wise comments to his companion. One of these is a clever remark about a menu. Another, as the terrorist character has a five-year sentence reduced to four-and-a-half on appeal, is a dismissive rebuttal of this legal likelihood: 'That would never happen,' he announces fatly, and loudly. Well, it happens in the play, and I guess he'll just have to put up with it.

Trilogies have been all the rage this year. Soon after the Hare trilogy, we had Ken Campbell whipping off his pork-pie hat to reveal a gleaming pate and 'the bald trilogy,' also at the National. And earlier this year there were Billy Roche's *Wexford Trilogy* at the Bush and Bill Morrison's stern, Protestant counterpart, his 'Irish trilogy', *Love Song for Ulster*, at the Tricycle. Campbell, Roche and Morrison have significantly moved the idea of 'theatre as event' into the realms of new writing and bang-up-to-date personal expression. But the Hare plays have an additional resonance: they seek to take the moral temperature of the nation in a big public arena and to investigate, through formalised, anti-thetical structures of drama, how it is that our good intentions, good faith and basic instincts are continuously disappointed and battered by the institutions of religion, law and politics, instead of harnessed to making those institutions a glorious expression of a nation's aspirations.

The topics of the plays are the church, and the hunger for faith, in *Racing Demon* (1990); the law and the prisons, and the reactive instinct for radicalism, in *Murmuring Judges* (1991); and politics and the packaging of socialism in the new piece, *The Absence of War*. The new play uses the events of last year's general election to define the tragedy of a Labour leader. And sure enough, the Labour Party politicians, Roy Hattersley and Gerald Kaufman, have leaped into print like guard dogs whose patch had been trespassed on, conveniently overlooking this tragedy of a fictional character while moaning about alleged trivial misrepresentations of real people and events. Hare did indeed go on the campaign trail with Neil Kinnock, but Kinnock's colleagues in the Shadow Cabinet seem to think that Hare's job was to soothe their vanities and reproduce faithful characterisations and truthful reportage, rather than a work of imaginative fictional drama. The reportage does in fact exist in the very fine companion book Hare has published alongside the plays, *Asking Around*.

John Thaw's magnificent, rasping George Jones is an impetuous Cockney bachelor who likes the theatre ('which I suppose is meant to be an endearing touch,' sneers John Gross in the Sunday Tele-graph; heaven forfend that a drama critic should actually *endorse* an enthusiasm for theatre as a virtue) and whose political fire is extinguished in a campaign devised to make him seem sober and responsible. Incidentally, a nice, twofold irony hovers about the name of George Jones: the Daily Telegraph's political correspondent, George Jones, finds himself filing a commentary about a hero who shared his own name; and when, two weeks later, Stephen Daldry's electrifying production of a forgotten American Expressionist drama, *Machinal*, opens next door in the Lyttelton, George Jones sheds another self: as the boss and the husband of the suppressed, murderous stenographer played by Fiona Shaw.

There is a great moment in Thaw's performance when he seizes up at the big Manchester rally and fumbles for his script. Afterwards, he bemoans the fact that he is not allowed to talk about Northern Ireland (John Smith, the real-life Labour leader in succession to Neil Kinnock, did not mention the subject in his keynote address at the Labour Party's annual conference); that he cannot denounce nuclear weapons; nor mention the royal bloody family. This country, he says, 'spavined with ancestor-worship, can never prosper until it escapes from its past.' It is entirely beside the point that Gerald Kaufman dismisses the dramatic validity of this scene because such sentiments lost Labour the 1983 election. On radio, the ubiquitously aggrieved Hattersley says that the play fails because 'It doesn't carry any universal truths.' One universal truth that *is* established concerns Hattersley's journalistic opportunism: invited to review the play for the Daily Telegraph, he preempts that commission by breaking all critical embargoes on the production and shopping a piece of fatuous self-justification to the London Evening Standard for a fee reported to be £2000. The Telegraph's editor, Max Hastings, is said to be so furious that he disinvites Hattersley to deliver his commission and declares he will never again invite him to write an article for his newspaper. This all sounds like a scene tactfully omitted from Hare's play.

*The Absence of War* is a political tragedy precisely because it *does* lament the failure of inarticulate decency to prevail against the PR machine, the trimmers and spin doctors, and all those who think that a radical party can fool the electorate by adopting the mannerisms and even the arguments of its enemies. The way in which this dilemma relates to last year's events is secondary to the power with which Hare states the central thesis. Which is, that the quality of your conviction is all that really matters. The charge against him, therefore, might be one of romanticism. The excitement and backstage campaign skulduggery are well communicated. To what extent it reflects the reality is neither here nor there. Who cares? Hare is writing about passion, conviction, belief, and how these virtues may or may not be made effective in public life.

Exactly the same question of faith underpins both *Racing Demon* and *Murmuring Judges*. In the first, Oliver Ford Davies's distraught South London vicar is at odds with 'the Arch' because he regards his job as listening to people's anger; 'people' includes the black girl who needs an abortion, but does not include his wife, heart-rendingly played by Barbara Leigh-Hunt, an unloved husk lumbering among her potted plants. In the second, Irina, the young black barrister (Alphonsia Emmanuel) and the inquisitive policewoman (Katrina Levon) bring their scruples to bear on a male-oriented system of connivance. Their concluding, respective decisions to take professional action are balanced against the 'making of a terrorist', the case of an Irishman (Paul Higgins) trapped in an unsafe conviction perpetrated by Mark Strong's brilliantly fly and sympathetic detective constable. I love the contrapuntal flow of *Murmuring Judges*, the ironic, and climactic, use of the overture to *The Magic Flute* as Irina goes to the opera with the oleaginous head of chambers (Richard Pasco) while the prison world slops out. This play is less engaging than the others, but no less cleverly controlled. It is all argument. Every line works forward to make a point, each situation illustrates a problem. *Racing Demon*, like *The Absence of War*, has more emotional depth. Michael Bryant's gay vicar is hounded from his parish by a campaign in the gutter press, leaving Ford Davies's gauche and gawky vicar sobbing with rage and sorrow. He sums up the unequal battle with the establishment: 'They give knighthoods to people who publish this stuff.'

The Financial Times critic crassly avers that Hare is 'a whacking great conservative', presumably because he represents the Savoy Hotel, the Opera House, the Cenotaph and the Lobby of the House of Commons, on stage. On BBC's The Late Show, the journalist

Polly Toynbee accuses Hare of dragging down mighty matters of state to his own flip theatrical level ('and a standing ovation each night,' rejoins a justly peeved author), while Michael Ignatieff sneers pompously from the chair. Such patronising responses cannot stand up against the effervescence of Hare's writing and the sheer sensual buoyancy of Richard Eyre's direction which, together with the all-round energy and commitment of the acting, and designer Bob Crowley's magisterial array of photographic blow-ups, has not only produced the most important and enjoyable theatrical occasion of the year, but has justified, at long, long last, the National Theatre's claim to be exactly that. A theatre for the nation, talking to the nation about the nation. This Trilogy is a truly exciting achievement, and the culmination of a writing career that is the most consistently interesting and adventurous of all contemporary British dramatists, including Pinter and Stoppard.

## Regional variations, Cardiff celebrations

HAROLD HOBSON'S predecessor on the Sunday Times, James Agate, was once tentatively approached by his editor wondering if he, Agate, might consider forsaking his usual West End beat in order to review a production in Kew. 'Sir,' blustered the old phoney, swishing his cape and adjusting his monocle, 'I should remind you that I am your esteemed newspaper's dramatic critic, not its foreign correspondent.' Things have changed a good deal, although not completely. Sheridan Morley once published a collection of reviews in which the furthest afield he ventured in the course of one year was Chichester and Swindon. Mind you, going to Greenwich is often more complicated and unpleasant than going to Leeds these days. On the other hand, I have found that trips on the South East network out of Waterloo Station this autumn – to Salisbury, Winchester, Southampton and Eastbourne – have been quick and almost entirely painless. But with the threatened Arts Council cuts of £5 million looming [the cuts, in the end, were £3.2m], there is a special irony in the fact that the Theatrical Management Association, the TMA, which represents theatres all over the country, this coming year celebrates (or, at least, marks) its centenary.

The occasion comes into focus over the third weekend of October, when the TMA holds its annual conference in Cardiff and also hosts, with its sponsors Martini & Rossi Ltd, the third annual regional theatre awards, a conspicuous attempt to redress the balance against the metropolitan flavour of all the other awards. Admirable spokesmen such as Ian McKellen and Richard Eyre keep saying that the regional theatre matters, that if you amputate the extremities of the theatrical body, you stop the heart and cause death of the patient. The theatre on Broadway is customarily described as a fabulous invalid. In my peregrinations these days I often feel like Algernon in *The Importance of Being Earnest*, who tells Jack early on that he has invented 'an invaluable permanent invalid called Bunbury' in order that he may disappear into the country whenever he chooses. The out-of-town reps are my Bunbury. And while there is not much that is fabulous about them, it is essential to recognise their worth. Politicians sometimes boast of our great national companies. But their existence would be both pointless and impossible without the network of regional theatre which supplies them with new talent, new ideas, new writers, new actors and new audiences. It is easy to sound pious about the regional theatre. The very term implies a degree of condescension. The truth is, for a comparative ha'porth of tar, the politicians and the Arts Council between them are vandalising the very backbone of our national cultural life, and it is important to spell out the historical complexities and inter-relationships that have established this tradition.

One hundred years of British theatre is, to a large extent, the story of buildings, ownership and the rise of the acting profession. Most of these important shifts have been registered in the regional theatre, where the music hall gradually elided with the legitimate stage and the great repertory movement gathered around several extraordinary characters with a mission. The Theatrical Management Association was formed in 1894 to protect the interests of the managers. Its first president was Henry Irving, who was knighted in the following year. There were various unions for performers (the Actors Association was formed in 1891, the Actresses' Franchise League in 1908). But the more powerful Equity was not founded until 1929, by which time the control of the theatres had passed from the actor managers (Irving, Beerbohm Tree, George Alexander and Charles Wyndham) to businessmen and syndicates such as Howard and Wyndham and H M Tennent. The touring productions at the beginning of the century played the old variety houses and the big city Victorian theatres. But the wind of change which led to our own repertory system blew first in Dublin, where the Abbey was opened in 1904. In this same year, *The Cherry Orchard*, possibly the key dramatic masterpiece of the century, was first produced in Moscow, and Harley Granville Barker and J E Vedrenne presented their first season at the Court, now the Royal Court, in Sloane Square. In three years, the Court famously established the reputation of Bernard Shaw, and gave London its first international repertory programme, with plays by Ibsen, Schnitzler, Hauptmann, Maeterlinck and W B Yeats.

Almost everything stems from this early period. The Abbey had been an upshot of Yeats's Irish literary theatre at the turn of the century, but the patronage was provided by an English woman, Annie Horniman, whose family fortunes derived from Horniman's Tea. Ironically, Miss Horniman loathed Irish nationalism. But, by the time she finally fell out with Yeats and his co-director Lady Gregory, she had financed England's first repertory theatre, the Gaiety in Manchester, which she bought and refurbished in 1908. Key innovations thereafter include the formation of the Birmingham Rep in 1913 by Barry Jackson (later responsible for establishing Stratford-upon-Avon as a serious producing home of Shakespeare); the Education Act of 1944, which liberated an entire new generation through the teaching of the humanities and the arts at school; the formation of the Arts Council by the Cambridge economist Maynard Keynes in 1946; the first Edinburgh Festival in 1947; and the building of the first post-War civic theatre, the Belrade, in Coventry in 1958. The Belgrade was so named because of a large donation of Yugoslav timber; it was thus a symbol of the peace effort, and the building financed entirely by the municipal authority. It is sad to contemplate both the disintegration of Yugoslavia and the shaky current status of the Belgrade in particular and of our regional theatre in general. The big push in the modern theatre building programme came in 1962 with the opening of the privately financed Chichester Festival Theatre and of the powerhouse Hampstead Theatre. In both cases, the projects were inspired by men with a dream of public service and a hyphenated surname, Leslie Evershed-Martin in Chichester, and James Roose-Evans in North London. The Nottingham Playhouse and the Edinburgh Traverse opened in 1963, followed by the Yvonne Arnaud in Guildford (1965), the Bolton Octagon and the Northcott, Exeter, in 1967, the Young Vic in 1970, the Sheffield Crucible in

1971, the Leicester Haymarket in 1973 and the Royal Exchange in Manchester in 1976. All of these venues survive, some are struggling. Hampstead and the Traverse, alongside the Royal Court, are at the heart of British new writing.

The Court's early pioneering spirit was renewed in 1956 when George Devine, a self-sacrificing agitator in the tradition of Horniman, Jackson and Lilian Baylis at the Old Vic, formed the English Stage Company and presented John Osborne's *Look Back In Anger.* Over the next ten years, the National Theatre grew out of the early seasons at Chichester under Laurence Olivier before settling down at the Old Vic, and Peter Hall founded the Royal Shakespeare Company in Stratford and London. We are a small island, and Peter Hall once described the British theatre, or the people who work most regularly within it, as one company. This sense of comradeship and interdependence has increased, or at least become more manifest, in the current economic climate.

At the TMA ceremony in Cardiff, an award is given to the directors of the Glasgow Citizens 'for their innovative achievements in theatrical style, their absolute commitment to their community over more than twenty years and for making Glasgow's theatre internationally famous.' In accepting the award, the director, Giles Havergal, is in no mood to rest on his laurels: 'Survival is the achievement, no more than that. The secret is to go four hundred miles away and stay there. Then they dig you up for a lifetime's achievement award. Many times this year I have thought, am I going to keep my job? Do I *want* to?' Arnold Wesker, who confirms the astounding news I first heard at Dartington from Andrew Motion, that he is no longer living with his wife of thirty years, Dusty, but beavering away in solitude in Hay-on-Wye, welcomes the opportunity to present the Best New Play award as 'the playwright is an endangered species; power and respect have moved from the playwright to the director.' Unfortunately, the recipient is Neil Simon's *Lost in Yonkers.* It is indeed a very fine play which toured the country before opening in the West End with Maureen Lipman and Rosemary Harris, but it does not reflect the valiant efforts to present new work this year in Leeds, Salisbury, Manchester, Bristol, Stoke, Mold and Southampton.

Wesker does not look exactly dismayed when he announces the winner, but you sense that he is disappointed. He knows, of course, that this is always what happens with awards: the glitzy wins over the truly deserving, the powerful magnet of showbusiness glamour draws juries into their predictably venal decisions. The judges seem to have missed other golden opportunities by honouring the touring version of *Me and My Girl* as Best Musical and the well-travelled *Juno and the Paycock* from the Gate, Dublin, as Best Overall Production. The Best Actor, however, is justly celebrated: Niall Buggy as Captain Boyle in that same *Juno*. Several stalwarts had sat up late the previous evening with Niall in the hotel bar as he regaled us with an impromptu concert of impassioned Irish singing. He receives the award from Sylvia Syms, who declares herself unshakeably devoted to touring, even if she is older and larger than she once was and suddenly considered for the same parts as Joan Sims. Buggy is visibly moved by his award and says how much he enjoyed himself travelling, and presumably singing, around the country: 'Be proud of the regional theatre,' he exhorts the audience, 'you have the greatest theatre in the world in this country; look after it.'

I am summoned to present the award to the Best Regional Theatre Critic (David Isaacs of the Evening Chronicle in New-castle). I say how pleased I am to be invited, but I think I know why: I'm cheaper than Ned Sherrin, I eat less than Sheridan Morley and, unlike Jack Tinker, I am at least tall enough to speak into the microphone. I also say that it is crucial for critics to relish the low esteem in which they are held. The minute a critic thinks he is important, or perhaps I mean *becomes* self-important, he is lost. He-e-e-e-e-e-lp! I also pay fleeting tribute to my colleagues and friends on newspapers around the country: Joyce MacMillan and Robin Thornber on the Guardian, Michael Schmidt on the Daily Telegraph, Alan Hulme on the Manchester Evening News, Phil Key on the Liverpool Echo, Richard Edmonds on the Birmingham Post. Theirs is a difficult task: maintaining space in their newspapers for the live theatre, and reporting it thoroughly and fairly, sometimes unfavourably, while at the same time retaining the cooperation and confidence of the managements. This occupation, it often strikes me, is far more complicated than that of being a national critic with no-one really to answer to except your editor.

One of my favourite regional critics was Desmond Pratt of the Yorkshire Post, a purple-faced gentleman with a walking stick who left every first night, regardless of its running time, at 9.20 pm. He would retire to the nearest pub, sink a couple of pints and proceed to compose and file his copy one hour later in a reasonably unhurried fashion. If the play had been an old one, he would know it, and would almost certainly have re-read it. If it was new, he would have obtained the script from the theatre well in advance. His notices, year in, year out, were models of clarity and appreciation. Like Milton Shulman, he always got the plot right. Unlike Milton Shulman, he was agreeably susceptible to change and new ideas. He used to telephone his copy into the Yorkshire Post and was occasionally undone by the process of dictation. He was alarmed to see, one morning, that the title above his account of a new Robert Bolt play had been considerably enlarged by a copytaker who had taken down his speech, like Bottom, cues and all: 'Vivat, Vivat – that's Vivat again – Regina!' At least the copytaker got his V's and R's the right way round.

Thanks to the laptop computer, the modem and the wonders of telecommunication, the days of the telephoned notice are almost gone. And all the errors that appear are the critic's alone, not the copytaker's. I used to hate phoning copy; 800 words down the line from a hotel in Manchester or a backstage office in Watford could take anything up to forty minutes to convey. But I always loved the sense of achievement once it was done and the satisfaction of seeing the notice in next morning's paper. Pratt, rather like the late Philip Hope-Wallace, had the gift of instant phrase-making. Hope-Wallace was famous for leaving a theatre, picking up a telephone and fluting his copy down the line before repairing to supper and a good bottle or two of wine. And, most mornings, his reviews in the Guardian read as though they had been slaved over for a couple of hours, so jewelled and erudite was his prose.

Except, of course, when the copytaker had been deaf or drunk. There was the famous review of *The Merchant of Venice* in which the leading character was referred to throughout as one 'Skylark'. When Janet Baker made her Glyndebourne debut in 1953 as Purcell's Dido and moved the house to rapture with her rendition of the final tragic aria, 'When I am laid in earth', Guardian readers learned the next morning of Miss Baker's matchless, doom-laden and impassioned delivery of 'When I am laid enough.'

Lunch in Cardiff is an extremely convivial affair, although I have evidently blotted my copy-book by referring in my speech to yet another dull season at the Chichester Festival Theatre. As I uttered these words, I simultaneously remembered that Martini & Rossi Ltd sponsor not only these awards, but also the Chichester Festival Theatre. Glancing down from the stage, I noticed that Rupert Rhymes, the TMA's chief executive, sitting on the top table with various dignitaries from Martini & Rossi, had slid a little deeper into his chair and covered part of his face with his right hand. Undaunted, I ploughed on, telling myself under my breath that no party is a really good party until someone volunteers to insult the host.

I am fortunate in my table-mates: no-one from Martini & Rossi, but Arnold Wesker; Giles Havergal; the Old Vic administrator, Andrew Leigh; the actors Georgina Hale and Don Warrington – and Bernard Hill, who compères the proceedings with a droll, lugubrious charm. Hill's presence, in fact, illustrates better than could any argument the value and the tragedy of our nation's theatres. Hill is today well known and much loved as a top flight stage and film performer, and immortalised as Yosser in Alan Bleasdale's television series, *The Boys from the Black Stuff*. Twenty years ago, when I started reviewing, he was a mainstay of the Liverpool Everyman, a theatre today facing closure right in the face. Acorns grow into oak trees. The Everyman was founded in 1964 by Terry Hands (of the RSC), Peter James (of the Lyric, Hammersmith) and Martin Jenkins (the BBC Radio producer). Hill's colleagues in the early 1970s included the playwrights John McGrath and Willy Russell, the singer Barbara Dickson, and the actors Jonathan Pryce, Antony Sher, Julie Walters, Pete Postlethwaite, and George Costigan. Their considerable reputations and brilliant careers are all grounded, they would be the first to acknowledge, in the soil of the Everyman.

Where do the politicians think the next generation of actors is going to come from, or don't they care? And if the Liverpool Everyman *does* close, what are the chances of the Treasury and the country reaping the benefits of the career of another Willy Russell, for one, whose plays and films today contribute so much to the gaiety, and the exchequers, of several nations, including our own. In Britain, the arts pay more back to the government in Value Added Tax than they receive in grants. The income from tourism, even in a recession, is incalculable. Subsidising the arts is indeed a modest form of investment with huge returns. Any sensible government should therefore be glad not only to preserve the glories of our regional theatre, but also to ensure the health of tomorrow's entertainment industry and the vivacity and variety of our national culture.

## *Prince Charles cheers up at the Buck House buffet*

IT IS NOT VERY OFTEN that I spend two consecutive days in the company of Prince Charles, whose lately assumed presidency of the Royal Shakespeare Company has become a raging enthusiasm. On the last Wednesday of the month he comes to Stratford-upon-Avon to chair the annual governors' meeting. And on the following evening, he hosts a party in Buckingham Palace 'to celebrate the works of William Shakespeare'. The prince's Stratford appointment falls between two press nights, so the assorted hacks are invited to attend the meeting in the Buzz Goodbody studio of The Other Place, and to have a buffet lunch thereafter in the theatre restaurant. HRH's first appointment of the day is in Oxford, where he has delivered a forthright speech in the Sheldonian about the Middle East that is both a well-timed jolly-up for the Moslem community in Britain and a Foreign Office-approved attack on the atrocities committed in Kurdistan and Iraq by the troops of Saddam Hussein. His helicopter lands half an hour late, but we keep ourselves going on coffee and conversation with Adrian Noble, the RSC's artistic director, who has become a royal chum.

The prince's interest in the RSC stems in the first place from his friendship with Kenneth Branagh, who recruited him as patron of the Renaissance Theatre Company, which he founded, ironically enough, partly as a result of not having had a wholly satisfactory time with the RSC. Noble directed Branagh as a memorable Henry V in that 1984 season and remained in touch. Branagh has returned to the company this season to lead Noble's production of *Hamlet* in London and Stratford. With Prince Charles accepting the RSC presidency two years ago, this triumvirate of near-contemporaries has a Shakespearean neatness, with Noble and Branagh playing a cross-party amalgamation of Hotspur, Peto and Poins to Charles's Prince Hal. The parallels can be extended to include Robert Stephens lumbering benignly in the background as Falstaff, Pam Harris of the Dirty Duck as Mistress Quickly, and Joanne Pearce, who is married to Noble, a mixture of Doll Tearsheet (which role she played opposite Stephens's Falstaff, directed by Noble) and Lady Hotspur. When the prince went to see Stephens as King Lear this summer, he told him afterwards that the performance was the best argument against abdication he had yet encountered.

The governors' meeting is populated with serious-looking middle-aged ladies, one or two local officials in Mayoral chains, various RSC officials and a motley crew of critics, as well as two most congenial arts reporters I have not met before, Susannah Herbert of the Daily Telegraph and Alison Roberts of The Times. The only governors I recognise are Stanley Wells, the brilliant academic husband of the novelist Susan Hill; Sir Eddie Kuluk-undis, the impresario (who was not knighted for services to the arts, as is incorrectly minuted at the meeting, but for services to athletics, about which he is possibly even more passionate than the RSC); and my friend Peter Holland, fellow in English Literature at Trinity Hall, Cambridge, and an excellent reviewer in the more intellectual Press and on BBC Radio. Anticipating the cuts in arts funding in the Government's November budget, the pin-striped prince says, 'I never understand why we're so bad at appreciating what we do really well . . . the RSC and our other flagship companies represent the great in Great Britain.'

He then launches into an enthusiastic and highly personal sum-mary of his recent visits to Stratford: '*The Winter's Tale* I thought was remarkable. Tears were pouring down my face at the end, and I was delighted to learn that the actors had the same problem themselves every evening . . . I experienced a slight shock when the curtain went up on *The Merchant of Venice* [the setting was a contemporary financial centre with high-tech scaffolding and computer terminals] but the whole thing was finally masterly . . . *King Lear* with Robert Stephens was one of the great experiences of my life; I felt privileged to see such a great performance by such a great actor . . . *The Venetian Twins* rather alarmed my policemen [there is a fake rumpus in the auditorium each night], and some of the actors were very nearly arrested, but that, too, was a wonderful experience . . . Every time I come here it raises my spirits, and I invariably feel better coming out than when I went in.' This last comment may have been part of the 'script' Prince Charles seems to be acting out as a melancholic, friendless monarch-in-waiting whose marriage has collapsed in public, but there is no disguising the sincerity of his remarks. HRH retires with the governors for an informal buffet while the rest of us cross the road for finger food in the main theatre with the RSC publicity department. Afterwards, I am heading up Waterside to my lodgings – on this visit I am experimenting yet again, and staying as a bed-and-breakfast guest with Jean Abelson (the widow of Sue's deceased Uncle Bernard's employer) in the Old Town – when Pam Harris hails me from the upstairs window of the Duck. Am I coming in? 'What on earth for?' 'The prince and Adrian are going to walk by in a minute on their way to visit the theatre workshops.'

I scoot in and order a bottle of champagne from Pam's fridge. We are just in time. 'More rushes, more rushes! The trumpets have sounded twice. 'Twill be two o'clock ere they come from the coronation. Dispatch, dispatch.' (*Henry IV, Pt 2*, Act V, scene 4.) Glasses raised, we stand on the terrace of the Duck as Adrian and Prince Charles, Geoffrey Cass (the RSC's chairman), David Brierley (the RSC's general manager) and assorted officials and private policemen saunter briskly past. 'God bless you, Sir' is the toast, our own version of Falstaff's 'God save thee, my sweet boy!' and Pam receives a friendly royal wave in return. No grim rejection scene here, no icy injunctions to fall to our prayers and to keep our distance by ten mile on pain of death. I wonder in an absurd little fit of vanity whether or not Adrian feels impelled, as they sweep past, to excuse our impromptu conduct and explain to HRH who the hell comprises this cheerful, disorderly knot of loyal patriots on the stone-flagged, pot-planted entrance to the actors' hostelry. The scene, this late October afternoon by the sleepy Warwickshire river, is instantly pasted in my scrapbook of memory.

The event at Buckingham Palace the following night is a private party hosted by Prince Charles for 350 guests. The minute my invitation arrived, I had telephoned the prince's secretary, Belinda Harley, to accept, unequivocally and with the greatest pleasure. After all, I never thought they'd let *me* into Buck House. Also invited – and in attendance – are RSC actors and personnel, media celebrities (David Frost, Jonathan Dimbleby – like Neil Kinnock, much shorter than you thought he'd be, Brian Redhead, Melvyn Bragg, etc), arts world panjandrums, and assorted businessmen: the prince is mindful that the RSC still has a deficit of £2.3m, and the company has still not replaced the three-year sponsorship of Royal Insurance.

In the weeks building up to the beano, I have been sidling up to colleagues to sniff out if they, too, have been invited. Michael Billington tells me at the opening of *Hair* at the Old Vic that he has been invited, but that he doesn't think Benedict Nightingale has. A small amount of inner gloating takes place. It turns out, of course, that Benedict *has* been invited. So have Irving Wardle, Charles Spencer, Paul Taylor, John Peter, Nicholas de Jongh, Uncle Tom Cobleigh and all. Still, the apparent absence of any particular cachet on the jaunt has been forgotten in the excitement of having been asked at all. My invitation sits proudly on my office mantelpiece, ostentatiously displayed between the usual (and usually ignored) cardboard come-ons to private views, screenings, press conferences and minor awards ceremonies. My son Thomas remains unimpressed. 'They let anyone in there these days,' is his only response; 'and now you can even pay to get in.'

On the day itself, I taxi from Stratford to Coventry station. Train to Euston. Tube home. Work all day on my column, which I send from my office, in the usual way, through my trusty modem straight into the Observer system. By 4 pm, Ray Fox-Cumming, our sub-editor, is ready to discuss cuts, meanings, clarifications and spellings. At 5 pm I down tools, switch off the screen, take a shower and climb into black tie, dress shirt and dinner suit. We are summoned for champagne at 7 pm. I go by tube to St James's Park and walk around the palace walls. It's only 6.30 pm. So to prove to myself that I am not entirely seduced by the high life, I pop into the saloon bar of the Bag o'Nails for a fortifying Scotch whisky. Saunter round the walls once again, passing Ted Hughes, the poet laureate, walking in the other direction, possibly into the Bag o'Nails. It is still only ten to seven. I wander over towards the main entrance where two small figures are crouched by the gates. They must be autograph hunters or tourists. They are not. They are Cicely Berry, the RSC voice director, and Brenda Bruce, the distinguished RSC actress, keen to be first through the portals and straight at the champers without a minute to lose. Good girls. We form a tripartite phalanx of expectancy. Guests with cars are being waved through, much to our annoyance, but eventually the signal comes to admit the foot soldiers, and we cross the courtyard and invade the great hall.

There's a cloakroom, just like a theatrical cubby hole. Up the grand stairway and into the blue drawing room for bubbly and nibbles. Lashings of the former, disappointingly dull bowls of the latter. Even at home we run to something more exotic than peanuts and salt and vinegar crisps. There is a magnificent flower display against one wall. Mirrors, chandeliers and red flock wallpaper everywhere. It is rather like being in a very expensive Indian restaurant. The actors congregate. Penny Downie, this season's Portia, has improvised a splendid black taffeta knee-length cocktail dress. Norman Rodway has affected a silken and velvet look, a Dublin look, you might say. Katie Mitchell, the director of *Ghosts* at The Other Place, sports a striking grey Chairman Mao tunic. David Thacker, the RSC resident director, asks me why I always give him only B double minuses for his productions. I answer as tactfully as I can without wanting to hurt his feelings any more than I obviously have already. Peter Hall is as immensely friendly as ever, although I think I've only liked approximately two of his last five productions. And as we talk, I flash up in my mind's eye the rather tart paragraphs I've written this afternoon for next Sunday's paper about his latest. Grin and bear it. I eavesdrop on Peter Shaffer and Iris Murdoch discussing the irreducible radiance of the greatest theatrical performances.

Suddenly, two large mirrored doors swing outwards from the room, and there, captive within and preparing to take the plunge into the thespian maelstrom, is the royal party, with Adrian Noble and Joanne Pearce. They move forward into the body of the reception. There are no announcements, no formalities, they just walk through: Prince Charles, Princess Margaret, Queen Anne-Marie of the Hellenes, the Duke and Duchess of Gloucester, Prince and Princess Michael of Kent, Princess Alexandra and Sir Angus Ogilvy, the Earl and Countess of St Andrews. What will happen? There is an intake of breath as the prince suddenly surges forward, his arm outstretched to greet . . . David Frost. A great cry of 'David!' echoes around the room and the hubbub rises generally once more, as if summoned by this royal pleasure in the presence of the arch transatlantic interviewer and television mogul. Frost is an ingratiating symbol of the Nosy-Parker-ism which has both trivialised and undermined the monarchy itself, and convinced the royals, or at least the younger generation, that mingling with the media is the way to democratise the image and justify your place in the world. If you live by such principles of participation, you will surely perish by them, or end up feeling betrayed and disillusioned, as the sad tales of Princess Di and Fergie have resoundingly proved.

We are summoned to the ballroom for the recital. The prince says, disarmingly: 'The whole evening's my fault,' confessing he has become something of a 'groupie'. He wants to save the company from death by a thousand cuts. He hopes some financial aid might be found in city boardrooms as a result of this evening. After all, even Buckingham Palace is sponsored these days. The prince offers personal thanks in the programme 'to Allied-Lyons for the helpful effects of Lanson champagne; Corney and Barrow for the Falstaffian quantities of excellent wine; Edward Goodyear for the magnificent flowers.' Sitting on gilded chairs, we hear Derek Jacobi, Judi Dench, Robert Stephens, John Wood, Dorothy Tutin. Antony Sher, Michael Pennington, Barbara Leigh-Hunt and Simon Russell Beale join battle against unkind acoustics. The compere, Jeremy Irons, finally brings on John Gielgud with Samantha Bond. Prospero and Miranda? Instead, a complete surprise: Lorenzo and Jessica in the antiphonal opening to Act V of *The Merchant of Venice*: 'The moon shines bright. In such a night as this, when the sweet wind did gently kiss the trees, and they did make no noise . . . ' through to Lorenzo's great speech, 'How sweet the moonlight sleeps upon this bank!' Gielgud fluffs his lines catastrophically, but nobody minds. He beams and twinkles pinkly, refusing to consult his script and muddling through with dignity and poise, edged safely into harbour by the tug-like ministrations of Samantha Bond. The applause is generous, the actors bow, and thoughts turn to dinner.

We are seated in the state apartments at small round tables. There are indeed liveried footmen scattered around the place, but here's the rub: we are not to be waited on. It's help yourself, if you please, at the Buck House Buffet! The poached salmon is glazed in aspic, as at all the best parish parties and fêtes. The celeriac tastes as though it has come out of jars. The salads are unexciting. There are no potatoes. I ask at the serving table for potatoes. I am told there are none to be had. The dessert, however, is delicious. The red wine is indeed excellent. My company is splendid: I find myself seated between Timothy West and Zoë Wanamaker, opposite Emily Richard, Simon Russell Beale and a deaf old Greek princess in a wheelchair. Everyone wants to know what democratic left-winger Max Stafford-Clark is doing here. 'Research!' he replies, triumphantly, adding that he is hoping to pull his first princess by the end of the evening.

After the meal, the company congregates in the outer rooms and the party continues. At midnight, all the wine disappears, and so does the royal party. At one o'clock, Michael Pennington drives Robert Stephens, Patricia Quinn and myself to Primrose Hill, and I walk the last half mile home in the cool early morning air thinking that, on the whole, it has been a good night out, certainly an interesting one, and that I'd better pull myself together and get ready for tonight's opening on the fringe at the Gate, Notting Hill, where the actors are unpaid and where the same company which supplied our Palace champagne, Allied-Lyons, has generously, and more crucially, paid for the refurbishment of a powerhouse theatre which is the source of tomorrow's RSC actors and directors – tomorrow's guests, we hope, at Buckingham Palace.

# NOVEMBER

## *Standards high and low*

I HAVE JUST BEEN TOLD by two colleagues, both employed by the Evening Standard, that Andrew Lloyd Webber and David Hare have no talent. I am so appalled by these outbursts that I am seriously considering my position as a member of the Evening Standard Drama Awards panel. I am prepared to listen to all manner of arguments against both writers, and I would especially welcome any evidence in their submissions that a) Nicholas de Jongh knew anything about music, or b) Milton Shulman knew anything about contemporary drama. (What I really mean by all this, of course, is that I don't agree with either of them.) Such evidence is not forthcoming. De Jongh splutters indignantly that he simply abhors Lloyd Webber in all his works and deeds, and Shulman dismisses Hare, as he has dismissed him consistently for the past twenty years, as a left-wing charlatan buoyed up by a phoney reputation. This allegation is delivered by the man who failed to recognise any worth in Brecht, Osborne, Pinter or Beckett when they first crossed his bows and who laboriously denounces current critical standards on the grounds that our ranks no longer include such giants of discernment and personality as Herbert Kretzmer and himself, who could be relied upon to keep the West End tills ringing through the 1950s and 1960s with all manner of tosh and nonsense.

At first sight of *Waiting for Godot*, Milton was already bored before the dust settled, as if here was just one more pretentious play deliberately conceived, written and produced for the sole purpose of causing him maximum irritation: 'another of those plays that tries to lift superficiality to significance through obscurity.'

And although he boasts of supporting Osborne's claim to be 'promising' in the first days of the Standard awards, he actually said after the first night of *Look Back In Anger* that the play 'aims at being a despairing cry but achieves only the stature of a self-pitying snivel.' In spite of his howlers and his blazoned, unapologetic ignorance, I am secretly fond of old Milt. I always say that if I had to be marooned on a desert island for a day, or stuck in a lift for an hour, with one colleague of my choice, I'd probably choose him because of his endearing fulminations and bottomless fund of good stories. He is right to be proud, on the whole, of his part in the history of the Evening Standard Awards, but entirely wrong to be so adamant about their respectability. Nothing pleases me more than being instrumental in winning a battle over a nomination which, in his view, subverts the dignity of the Awards and undermines the whole fabric of Western civilisation as he thinks he knows it. Thus it was last year, with my campaign to instal Steven Berkoff's *Kvetch* as the Best Comedy of the Year. And in the same category this year, surprisingly but crucially supported by Benedict Nightingale, I achieve an equally unexpected and significant victory for Ken Campbell with his delirious monodrama, *Jamais Vu*.

Our deliberations are conducted on the first night of the month in the upstairs dining room of the Ivy restaurant, restored these days to something like its former theatrical glory of famous clientele, brown panelling and spangled stained-glass windows. In the past, these dinners have been held in the Café Royal, or the upstairs room of the Gay Hussar. On the last two or three occasions, we have been billeted in the Standard's new headquarters behind Barker's in Kensington High Street, pleasant enough but uninspiring. The Ivy puts some pezazz into the proceedings, although Milton is followed across the front door by a tramp asking him for twenty pence. Milt is affronted: twenty pence is far too little, five pounds would have been far too much. If he'd asked for one pound, he might have had more success. As it is, the tramp is ushered penniless from the premises.

As we foregather over a glass of champagne – the judging panel this year is Pamela, Lady Harlech, de Jongh, Shulman, Nightingale and myself – with our host, the Standard's ebullient and good-humoured editor, Stewart Steven, I am encouraged to recount my own theatrical tramp story. The scene is Times Square in New York, busy with well-dressed theatregoers rushing to catch their curtains. A decrepit hobo intercepts a shark-like, callous impresario nervous about the prospects of his latest musical. 'Can you spare a dime for a cup of coffee?' pleads the tramp; 'Coffee, coffee . . . ?' snarls the mogul without breaking his stride, ' . . . look what it's *doing* to you!'

Dinner is excellent – smoked salmon, venison, wicked dessert – and the discussion, to put it mildly, heated. There is no quorum for Hare, so Stoppard wins Best Play. I was hoping to secure Best Actor for either Mark Rylance's West End Benedick or Antony Sher's athletic RSC double of Tamburlaine and Henry Carr in *Travesties*, but Ian Holm wins for returning to the theatre after many years of stage fright and sitting in bed for seventy minutes, a sentimental vote for an indubitably great actor. Best Production clearly should have been *Machinal*, but there's an inexplicable swing towards Terry Hands for *Tamburlaine* (the televised excerpt at the awards ceremony in the Savoy Hotel later in the month, with its simple, jigging choreography, makes the mighty Marlowe play look like some primitive ethnic cabaret such as *Ipi Tombi*, or *Kwa Zulu*). Michael Owen, the Standard's arts editor, who has long given up drinking, sits patiently, soberly taking notes of our babblings, and the whole affair is affably chaired by Stewart Steven, with one or two decisive interventions on his part in favour of Ken Campbell and Terry Hands.

At the Savoy luncheon, Steven delivers the best speech on the arts by a newspaper editor that I have ever heard. Art belongs to the people, he says, and people do respond to art: 666,000 Londoners watch Arsenal play football in a calendar year; over the same period, 727,000 people visit the Royal National Theatre. He cites more statistics: 16.3m people, that is 36 per cent of the British population, attended a live performance last year; 4.3m went to the National Gallery, 1.8m to the Tate, 500,000 to the Royal Opera House. 'The artist,' he says, 'illuminates our society. If you eliminate the lamplighter, you soon descend to darkness and barbarism.' He pledges the Evening Standard's support in the campaign to save the Lyric, Hammersmith, and in the campaign to save all of London's orchestras, and he announces a £25,000 sponsorship for the visit to London next year of Peter Brook's *L'homme qui*, Brook's Paris adaptation of Oliver Sacks's *The Man Who Mistook His Wife For A Hat*.

The ceremony is compered as usual by Ned Sherrin who says that Pinter's *Moonlight* really is a full-length play; it only lasts for 75 minutes, but Harold has put in all his pauses at the end. At a table close to mine, where I sit with Sue, Timothy Spall, John Sessions, Sian Thomas, Peter Eyre, Susan Fleetwood and Richard Olivier, Pinter's unyielding features turn to grey granite and thunderous, unamused anger. As if by divine intervention, there is a power cut in the generator feeding the television lights that are no longer flooding the rococo splendours of the Savoy's Lancaster Room. In the semi-gloom, Miriam Margolyes, who is on the verge of presenting an award, seizes the microphone and regales us with a selection of Jewish jokes, notably the one about the Jewish grandmother at Bournemouth who loses her grandson in a storm at sea and goes down to the beach where his half-dead body has been washed up on the tide. Keening gratefully at full stretch and raising her eyes to the heavens, she yells at the cruel but merciful Almighty: 'He had a hat!' Ned trots out a few of his own after-dinner anecdotes, but there's a feeling here that Miriam is auditioning for his job next year and doing rather well.

The lights eventually come back on, although some people have by now had to return to work. They miss Alan Rickman, presenting the Best Actress award to his friend Fiona Shaw, congratulate the Evening Standard for taking the survival of the theatre so seriously when actors are continuously trivialised as 'luvvies' in some sections of the press: 'Actors are not a luxury. Nor is the Lyric, Hammersmith, nor is any Theatre-in-Education company. Any society defines itself by the stories it hands down, and we are part of that chain. We are in danger of being remembered as the first generation to teach our children *less* than we know.'

## Meetings with famous directors, part 1:
## Peter Brook

AT LAST I CAN NOW SAY that I have been directed by Peter Brook. On Guy Fawkes Night, the greatest stage director of our day gives an informal Platform Performance at the RNT to publicise his new book, *There Are No Secrets*. The Olivier auditorium is jam-packed. Brook is introduced, sweetly but gauchely, by Genista McIntosh, the RNT's executive director. Brook changed her life twice, she says: once when she sat in the audience for the Beckettian *King Lear* with Paul Scofield; second, when she worked with him at the RSC on his all-white gymnasium *A Midsummer Night's Dream*. Brook beams about him at the vast stage and says that this is the biggest Empty Space he has ever been in. The ice broken, he asks us to prove the communal power of theatre and the value of concentration. He asks us to stand up when he claps his hands and, when we feel like it, to sit down again. We do so, all eleven hundred of us, with a certain amount of shifting about. He then asks us to think a little harder next time, to exercise peripheral vision, awareness of our fellows, to weigh the moment in our thoughts and, as if personally responsible for a corporate entity, to sit down again. He claps. We stand, we feel each others' eyes and breath upon ourselves, we wait and, miraculously, we all sit down almost simultaneously. Brook assures us that we were twenty times better the second time than we were the first, and we know he is right. The old magic is still working.

Tynan once said that the young Peter Brook gave the appearance of never having travelled anywhere, but of having been borne by others, wrapped in soft silks. His 40-year career has continuously redefined the sensuality of theatre, what he calls tonight 'the breathless moment' that is unique to the live performance, the irreplaceable quality of pure theatre in which all argument melts. He used to cook, said Tynan, with cream and blood and spices; bread-and-water addicts were advised to look elsewhere. And the young Brook himself said that he was growing tired of people who claimed their lives had been changed by a chance visit to the Chinese theatre. He produced opera with designs by Salvador Dali, the musical *Irma La Douce*, Robert Morley in a West End comedy, Gielgud in Restoration Tragedy and Shakespeare, the backwoods melodrama *Dark of the Moon*, a film of *The Beggar's Opera*, Christopher Fry. He learned his trade eclectically, long before he became renowned for the Scofield *Lear*, the great RSC production of *The Marat/Sade*, the film of *The Lord of the Flies*. But his generosity of spirit was deepening with a channelling of his creative seriousness into pushing back the frontiers, and at the moment of his greatest fame – the RSC *Dream* in 1970 – he left London to form his Centre for International Theatre Research in Paris in the derelict Bouffes du Nord.

This uncomplicated devotion to the moment of truth in theatre, or at least a version of the truth, has informed all his great epics ever since. As Irving Wardle says, the critical scepticism which often greeted his excursions to Iran, Africa and India was finally blasted away by the 1988 tours of *The Mahabharata*, 'which confirmed all the travellers' tales in the most majestic fusion of Eastern and Western theatre ever to electrify a performance space.' As in his new book, and his other writings, Peter Brook has nothing to hide, nothing to fear, nothing much to regret. He seems to feel lucky in his calling, and to rejoice in the variety and imperfections of humankind. He has become a hero, perhaps a guru, simply because his talent, his curiosity and his confidence in himself have freed him from the small-minded pettiness and silly vanities that infect the majority of us, inside or outside the theatre. Near the start of his Platform Performance, a baby cries. He uses the sound, feeds off the contact, keeps smiling at the interruptions when most of us in the audience think it is high time the mother took the child outside.

I recall the last time I attended an audience with Brook in London. Someone asked what was the most important single factor in the future health of the British theatre. Some held their breath, some craned forward, there was a slight pause. Brook replied: 'Cheap seats.' In a single phrase he reminded us that the point of subsidy, in the first place, is to make art available to people at prices they can afford, not at prices they sometimes feel grand and superior in meeting (as at the RNT, the Royal Opera House, and in the West End).

Tonight, he is asked how directors should treat actors. 'Praise sparingly, bully never.' This receives a volley of applause which Brook interprets (rightly) as signifying the presence of lots of actors in the audience. He says he has only once reduced an actor to tears and was immediately ashamed of himself. 'It is a disgusting, unnecessary and, more importantly, unproductive thing to do.' It is also, he might have added, an abuse of power and a sign of weakness of character. And yet some of the most brilliant directors of our day, many of them associated with the Royal Court, are renowned for having made the life of some poor actor a total misery from the first day of rehearsal. Brook reminds actors that they should always consider the role bigger, and more interesting, than themselves: 'It is a mistake to patronise the role you play, whether it is Rosencrantz or Othello. If the character you play is mean, then he should be *intensely* mean.'

Finally, the *Oleanna* question. In disguise. A woman teacher objects, on behalf of her pupils, to Brook's use of the words 'man' and 'actor' throughout his first book, *The Empty Space*, and denounces him for still using today these 'gender-specific terms'. Brook looks momentarily dumbstruck. A flash of anger at last crosses his face but is soon gone. He says he does not like what lies behind this question and simply reports that he has run a company of mixed race, mixed gender ('at least two') actors in Paris for twenty years and not once – *not once* – has this question arisen. He leaves the stage to prolonged and sustained applause.

Brook's publishers, Methuen, are hosting a dinner for him afterwards in Gabriel's Wharf, near the National. First of all he signs books for an hour and a half. I am fortunate in being seated opposite the maestro at table and take full advantage of my luck. I have never interviewed him professionally, partly because he has not really been here for twenty years, partly because I assumed, wrongly, that he was too intimidating. We once sat next to each other in Belgrade at one of Yuri Lyubimov's Taganka Theatre productions; I remember him saying how disappointed he was in the circus-style, old-fashioned animation of John Reed's exciting account of the Russian Revolution, *Ten Days That Shook the World* (so was I). We have chatted at the Round House. And during the all-day marathon of John Barton's *The Greeks* for the RSC at the Aldwych in 1980 (an event eclipsed, quite unfairly, later in the same year, by *Nicholas Nickleby*), we exchanged pleasantries in the supper interval at Joe Allen's. Other guests tonight include Nicholas Wright, the playwright and associate director of the National; Nina Parry, Brook's sister-in-law and administrator in Paris, who is immensely jolly; the intelligent young journalist James Woodall; Geoffrey Strachan, the chairman of Methuen; and Neil Mullarkey, the gifted young comedian and writer who is married to Brook's actress daughter, Irina. The conversation is lively and general. Every question put to Brook is met with a straight answer, sometimes a joke, a story and a counter-question. I note that he instinctively found the strongest place to stand on the Olivier stage. Olivier called it, he says, 'the point of command'.

He surprises me by being more informed than I thought he would be about what goes on in London. He is constantly in touch with Peter Hall, Adrian Noble, and Richard Eyre and is affectionately admiring of them all. He loved Theatre de Complicité's outrageous version of *The Visit*, the Dürrenmatt play he famously directed for the RSC in 1960: 'It was much better than mine.' I ask him what he felt about Tynan's dismay at the turn his work took after he went to Paris and in particular at the admission at the end of *The Ik*, based on Colin Turnbull's book about a threatened African tribe, that nobody knew if they still survived or not. Tynan wanted to know why nobody on the production could be bothered to go and find out. Brook says that Tynan knew full well that it was impossible to do so because of the civil war raging at the time. He remained great friends with his early chronicler, though he saw less of him later on, and never bothered to reply to his strictures.

As the party breaks up, I ask him to sign my copy of his book. On the fly-leaf he writes: 'On Guy Fawkes night we made our own

rockets; to Michael with warm wishes, Peter Brook, 1993.' I dance
elatedly up to Waterloo Bridge in search of a taxi home.

## Meetings with famous directors, part 2:
## Max Stafford-Clark

EARLIER THIS YEAR, on Hampstead Heath, Max Stafford-Clark, director of the Royal Court these past fourteen years, ran by me in his black strip and said 'Hello.' Now, to many, this may not seem a particularly promising exchange, but, given the state of our recent relations, it was an expression of cordiality on a par with a bear-hug. I have always admired Max's directing skills, but I have often expressed the not very heretical view that he has remained at Sloane Square for far too long. He is now starting a new company, Out of Joint, an obvious successor to Joint Stock, the touring troupe dedicated to new writing that he inaugurated in the mid 1970s with William Gaskill, David Aukin and David Hare. Max has invited a few critics and colleagues for lunch at the new headquarters, which he shares with Theatre de Complicité, off the Holloway Road in north London.

Lunching the critics is quite a tradition at the Royal Court; it used to be held on the stage in the days of Lindsay Anderson and Oscar Lewenstein (ironically enough, the regime that shut Max and his fringe generation out of the theatre). 'It's a strange time to be starting a company,' says Max. 'The times couldn't be worse. But this last year was the first year I've never done a new play [he had directed *King Lear* for the Court and *The Country Wife* for the RSC in Stratford] . . . my problem was not getting into the Court [not strictly true] but leaving it [never a truer word] . . . if I'd known what fun it was to leave, I'd have left years ago.' He says that these are sterling times for new work and that the commitment towards it of both the theatre profession and the audiences is very strong, citing the public's appetite for the plays of Stephen Jeffreys, David Hare, Tom Stoppard, Neil Bartlett; the promise shown by his own Court stable of Martin Crimp, Winsome Pinnock and Adam Pernak; and a new writer, Philip Kingston, whose recent play about drugs at the Hen and Chickens pub theatre he has found particularly promising.

His own plans, he explains, as we gather at the appropriately frugal but supremely adequate lunch table – chicken and vegetables, dessert, red and white wine, coffee – are governed by the fact that Out of Joint is to be funded by the Arts Council merely on a project basis (£65,000 has been earmarked for the first year so far), renewable for three further years before they might qualify for a franchise grant. The biggest problem in the British theatre, he says, is not a scarcity of new writing, but an erosion of the ideal of the ensemble company as a desirable goal. Out of Joint would try and rectify this, and the model for the structure of work would be the back-to-back juxtaposition of new and classical work with a permanent company, along the lines of his own 1988 Royal Court double-header of Farquhar's *The Recruiting Officer* and Timberlake Wertenbaker's *Our Country's Good*.

In the first season, next year, Out of Joint will co-present with the Royal Court and the Leicester Haymarket a large-scale tour of *The Queen and I*, adapted by Sue Townsend from her own bestselling novel, with Pam Ferris in the lead, and a revival of Jim Cartwright's *Road*; the second tour, middle-scale, will comprise a new play by Stephen Jeffreys about Rochester, *The Libertine*, and a revival of George Etherege's Restoration comedy *She Would If She Could*. David Hare has promised a play for 1995. The administrator is Sonia Friedman, sister of the brilliant actor-singer Maria Friedman, and daughter of Clair Friedman, a musician and teacher, composer for the children's Christmas show at the RNT, *Jo-Jo the Melon Donkey*, who has floated the company's first month of operation with a small loan.

After lunch, Benedict Nightingale mutters his apologies and leaves for urgent business at the Critics' Circle. This sounds like a man excusing himself from the Long Room at Lord's in order to go and watch a scratch game on the village green. Max announces that the remaining critics are to be divided into three teams charged with planning, costing and casting the 1995 Out of Joint season of two tours, one large, one-middle scale, incorporating the new Hare piece. Nicholas de Jongh is paired with Jane Edwardes (we'll call them Team A). Michael Billington and Paul Taylor form a triple threat with Matt Wolf (Team B). And my partner is James Christopher, Jane's sidekick on Time Out (Team C).

We disperse into corners, taking turns to visit first the Arts Council in an upstairs office (represented by Sonia Friedman sitting behind Max's desk while we, her supplicants, huddle on Max's casting couch); then we go to Graham Cowley, the Court's general manager, to learn expectations of sponsorship; and finally to Stephen Jeffreys in the passage, who is shuffling cards and opening pages of Spotlight at random in order to illustrate the precarious procedures of casting. Max drifts between us all, goading and supervising in a friendly, but somewhat enigmatic, manner, refusing to be drawn into direct discussions. Halfway through, Michael Billington leaves to chair BBC Radio's 'Kaleidoscope', but his team seems unnervingly confident of victory, while de Jongh and Jane Edwardes are making an absurd kerfuffle, banging doors on eavesdroppers with the ruthless determination of a new Bill ('Binkie') Kenwright and his shrieking West End associate, Helen Montagu. James and I play it cool, keep calm, wait for the ideas to fall into place, take professional advice but keep our own counsel. It's looking good.

Max calls us to order and we are invited to resume our places at the table and to present our plans. Team A has been carried away on a tide of wishful thinking and misplaced enthusiasm: the large-scale tour, for which a guarantee of £40,000 has been secured from the Arts Council, comprises the Hare play (untitled), about a theatre critic who exposes corruption at the RSC and the RNT, with some finagling by the Minister for the Arts himself, and, somewhat limply, a double-bill of Sheridan's *The Critic* and Molière's *Le Malade Imaginaire* in which Nigel Hawthorne is more than interested; the medium-scale fare is the first British tour of *Angels in America*, in tandem with *Ghosts* (Helen Mirren as Mrs Alving), translated by Stephen Jeffreys, with Steven Berkoff as both the satanic Roy Cohn in *Angels* and Pastor Manders.

Team B has obviously suffered some sort of collective nervous breakdown. Their big tour is Botho Strauss's latest incomprehensible epic, *Equilibrium* (raved over by Billington at his most lip-smacking in Salzburg this year), translated by Neil Bartlett, and a new version by Winsome Pinnock of Billy Wilder's *Double Indemnity* in which Emma Thompson has committed to the Barbara Stanwyck femme fatale role; the medium-scale tour will be the David Hare play (no details) and Granville Barker's *Waste*, with David Jason leading the company.

James and I remain quietly confident. Our major tour is an inter-linked project of Chekhov's *Three Sisters* and a David Hare play about three sisters in a university town in various states of profes-sional and matrimonial disarray, with the tentative participation of either Joan Plowright or Sian Phillips and possibly Emma Piper (the Spotlight pages had fallen open at 'P'), and an Arts Council guarantee of £30,000. Secondarily, as our trump card, we propose the re-launch of Debbie Isitt's promising career as both actress and playwright (she founded, and writes and acts for, the Snarling Beasties) in her new contemporary Birmingham comedy, *Street* (we have to get her off that beanbag and out of her bedroom), paired with the same ten actors in an overdue revival of Middle-ton's great city comedy *A Chaste Maid in Cheapside*, in which Debbie will play Moll Yellowhammer, with promises of support from Alan Strachan's Theatre of Comedy set-up.

Max asks his colleagues – Sonia Friedman, Stephen Jeffreys, marketing man Guy Chapman and Graham Cowley to consider these proposals and to award a total of three marks each where appropriate. James and I blame our unexpected failure with the judges solely on the order in which Max chooses to collect these votes. First, the sorry Chapman awards two votes to Team A, one to Team B. Jeffreys: two B, one A. Friedman: two C, one A. Stafford-Clark: two C, one B. Cowley (I'll never speak to him again): two A, one C. The result is computed: six A, five C, four B. A bottle of champagne goes to de Jongh and Jane Edwardes, last year's win-ners, too. I console James with the plain fact that the artistic direc-tor and the administrator, the people who really matter, have given us top marks. We decide on a career in movies or Channel Four.

On the last Sunday of the month, there is a benefit for Max's new company onstage at the Court. It is hosted by Pam Ferris and

Richard Wilson, who allude satirically to their own television fame in, respectively, *The Darling Buds of May* and *One Foot in the Grave*; while the actor Allan Corduner plays Chopin's revolutionary polonaise with a fine self-deprecating frenzy on a half-tuned piano. Thereafter, a vanishing era is brought alive in highlights from Max's finest shows as artistic director: *Three Birds Alighting on a Field* and *Our Country's Good* by Timberlake Wertenbaker, *My Heart's a Suitcase* by Clare McIntyre, and *Falkland Sound*, a moving collection of letters between a doomed officer and his loving father during the Falklands campaign, edited by Louise Page.

Ian Dury and Micky Gallagher's 'futures song' from *Serious Money* is rapped out by many of the original cast, including Gary Oldman, Lesley Manville, Linda Bassett and Danny Webb. Adrian Dunbar as George Farquhar in a mangy wig replies to Max (an injoke referring to Max's *Letters to George*, allegedly penned while rehearsing Farquhar's *The Recruiting Officer*), William Armstrong and Lesley Sharp perform, brilliantly, two monologues from *Road*, Maria Friedman sings Sondheim, expressively accompanied by Jeremy Sams, and five of Max's female authors – Wertenbaker, McIntyre, Sharman MacDonald, Sarah Daniels and April de Angelis – perform the great historical restaurant scene from Churchill's *Top Girls*. In this last excerpt, Max's successor, Stephen Daldry, hovers awkwardly in the background as the waiter. The general consensus is that Stephen should hang on to the day job. Receipts from tickets and a bucket collection realise about £10,000 and the Joint Stock of the 1990s, the new focus of new writing on the road, is well and truly launched.

# DECEMBER

## *Curtain calls and seasonal salvoes*

CHRISTMAS CREEPS UP ON CRITICS with a terrible predic-
tability. Early in the month, the dread word goes out from editors
in search of 'pantomime previews' and 'round-ups of the year.'
This year at the Observer we must also supply quiz questions, top
tens and picture choices. A lot of this leg-work I complete by the
end of November in providing my annual update on the British and
European stages for the Encyclopaedia Britannica. So by the time I
am asked for awards nominations and lists, I am reeling them off
like nobody's business. Top tens, usually the province of film
critics, I find particularly invidious, but I grit my teeth and propose
the following in order of preference:

1. *The Hare Trilogy* at the National
2. *Angels in America* at the National
3. *Much Ado About Nothing* in the West End (with Mark
   Rylance and Janet McTeer)
4. *The Picture of Dorian Gray* at the Glasgow Citizens (with
   Rupert Everett)
5. *Father's Day* (an extraordinary new play about Alzheimer's
   disease by 56 year-old local author, Maureen Lawrence, at the
   West Yorkshire Playhouse)
6. *At the Black Pig's Dyke* by Vincent Woods (a powerful Irish
   play at the Tricycle, Kilburn)
7. *King Lear* with Robert Stephens at Stratford-upon-Avon
8. Mike Leigh's *It's A Great Big Shame!* at the Theatre Royal,
   Stratford East

9. Neil Bartlett's *Night After Night* (a musical journey around
   the author's father in the West End of 1958) at the Traverse in
   Edinburgh, on tour, and at the Royal Court
10. *Jamais Vu*, Ken Campbell's final episode of his one-man
    'bald trilogy' at the National and elsewhere

I don't feel particularly perverse in omitting Pinter, Stoppard and
Mamet from this list, though a few eyebrows are certainly raised.
Both Pinter and Stoppard, after all, have written their most sub-
stantial new work for the theatre in several years; and Mamet's
*Oleanna* induced genuine cultural debate and arguments which
spilled over from the arts pages. But my innards were not churned
by any of them, really, and you have to obey, in these and in all
theatrical matters, the instinct of the gut. Excuses and rational-
isations come later.

Performances one wants to salute are, as ever, multitudinous.
Immediately springing to mind are Penelope Wilton giving the
performance of her life in *The Deep Blue Sea*; Clare Higgins,
skittish and exotic as the RSC's Cleopatra; Patti LuPone glittering
like an armour-plated armadillo in *Sunset Boulevard*; Maggie
Smith as a whirlwind Lady Bracknell; Fiona Shaw as the murderous stenographer in *Machinal* at the National; Elaine Paige as a
foul-mouthed, scuttling, vocally tremendous Edith Piaf; Ian Holm,
bed-bound but raging at the dying of the light in Pinter's *Moonlight*; Kenneth Branagh as a really fine RSC Hamlet; Antony Sher
athletically virtuosic as both Henry Carr and Tamburlaine for the
RSC; Michael Siberry turning in a truly notable support double of
Parolles and Macduff, also at the RSC; Iain Glen as Macbeth at the
Tron, Glasgow (easily the top Scottish tragic hero of the year,
beating Alan Howard and the newly knighted Derek Jacobi by
several lengths) and in the underrated new Michael Frayn comedy,
*Here*; John Thaw as the besieged and defeated Labour Party leader
in Hare's *The Absence of War*.

I often ruminate on the manner in which actors take their bows,
receive our plaudits, feed off the noise we make in their honour.
When I say 'we,' I mean audiences, not critics. Critics tend to sit
on their hands at the curtain calls, or make a sensible dash for their

deadlines through the green exit lights. But as so few critics write overnight these days, we tend to perch politely on the aisles for a few minutes proffering a few desultory claps. Michael Billington is the most sphinx-like of us all, often the most chucklesome of critics in print but the most sombrely undemonstrative in the theatre. You feel that he is hoarding his responses for print and not letting on; good thing, too. Charles Spencer, on the other hand, almost goes out of his way to indicate what a good time he is having, laughing out loud in a rather forced manner and looking for comradely signs of approval or solidarity across the aisle. None of this bothers me very much, though I am occasionally distracted by more barbarian forms of Irving Wardle's knuckle-cracking exercises. John Peter, for instance, has a 'don't forget I'm still here' sort of little cough. And Nicholas de Jongh is given to slumping in his stall with his legs stretched out in a rather boorish manner; he has even been known at times of acute stress in overheated fringe venues to strip off to the waist. Ladies, in the past, have sometimes been asked to remove their hats, but no-one, as far as I am aware, has ever requested a gentleman to remove his shirt.

The commonest critical tick, though, is the unnecessarily noisy turning of notepad pages at moments of high drama, or even of low drama; chief page flickers are Nightingale (who does battle each night with something the size of an artist's sketchpad on his knee), Spencer, de Jongh and Paul Taylor. The latter has otherwise developed a most sophisticated notepad technique: his left thumb moves slyly down the page in the dark while his right wrist scribbles away almost without remission and his eyes remain fixed on the stage. You never sense that Taylor is doodling pointlessly or drawing attention to himself. Nor do you feel that Robert Benchley's job description could be, in his case, appropriate: 'Jotting down nasty remarks in the margin of our program alongside the Rogers Peet advertisement, which we are unable to decipher the next morning owing to having written one thing on top of another in the dark.' Benchley – of whom it was once said that he rarely slept through an entire play; he woke up for intermissions – was responsible for my second favourite short review of all time (my first is Walter Kerr's curt dismissal of John van Druten's *I Am A Camera*: 'Me no

Leica'). This review was not written, but uttered in situ during a trite play called *The Squall*. A gypsy girl was whining on to her loved one 'Me Nubi, Nubi good girl. Nubi stay here,' at which point Benchley stood up and shouted 'Me Bobby, Bobby bad boy. Bobby leave here,' and promptly headed for the exit.

Paying members of the public usually reserve their displeasure and approbation for the curtain calls. The majority of standing ovations on a first night are totally unconvincing, as they are perpetrated by investors, producers and friends of the cast. This year, though, the standing ovation afforded Elaine Paige at the end of *Piaf* was the most untaintedly spontaneous since that given to Michael Crawford at the end of *Barnum*, many years ago, a tribute vociferously led, I seem to recall, by the late Robert Morley. Fiona Shaw, most uninhibited of actresses, stripping naked to don her death robes for the electric chair, was also greeted with wild enthusiasm at the end of the RNT's *Machinal*, but she became almost shyly diffident at the calls, anxious not to offend her own democratic impulses by hogging the applause, retreating bashfully into her company line-up at the first opportunity. Maggie Smith is the exact opposite: taut and ferocious as Lady Bracknell, she reverts to a girlish, unimpeded state of grace and glee at the curtain calls, almost making love to her audience. 'They're ovating again' she says of them as she leaves the stage.

On the whole, though, curtain calls are not what they were. Donald Wolfit used to milk the applause and indicate his exhaustion by hanging on to the drapes and hauling himself back into the spotlight. John Gielgud received his acclamation with a beaming, almost tearful acknowledgement of his unalterable place in our affections as the applause crashed about his pink and gleaming dome. Olivier used to amble slowly on at the Old Vic like a matador, eyeing every nook and cranny of the house, scanning it to the rafters and frequently holding his open right palm on his left breast, in a mock humble salute, the undisputed first warrior and war lord which, of course, he was. More recently, Ian McKellen was visibly overwhelmed by the reception of his National Theatre *Coriolanus* when the company took Peter Hall's production to the Herod Atticus in Athens, in the shadow of the Parthenon. I shall never forget McKellen walking out into a wall of sound for which he was totally unprepared and translating his astonishment, and faint embarrassment, into a reaction of joy, gratitude and sharing. These few minutes were as moving and impressive as any that had preceded them in a generally moving and impressive performance.

When the Rustaveli Theatre of Tbilisi came to the Round House with *Richard III*, McKellen and Simon Callow were the first on their feet at the end. That memorable visit had been sponsored and supported by the late Robert Maxwell, the posthumously disgraced newspaper tycoon. The Russians had just invaded Afghanistan, and a noisy demonstration against Soviet imperialism was in full swing outside on the Chalk Farm Road. Maxwell, huge and sinister in a black floor-length coat and dyed black hair, sought to quieten the disturbance, and the customers' anxiety, by saying a few words before the performance began. As he strode into the middle of the arena, an American tourist sitting behind me, conversant with the fact that the play began with a soliloquy, whispered loudly but in all innocence to her companion, 'Gee, what an incredibly evil and ugly portrait of Richard this guy is!'

Nowadays, actors shuffle on and shuffle off in lines without waiting around too much. Thus they deprive the audience of its right to complete the circle of experience, to answer back to the performance and prove the communal success or failure of the night's endeavour. This year, two plays did not invite any audience response at all: DV8's performance drama about cottaging in men's toilets, *MSM*; and the Young Vic's *Thérèse Raquin*, in which the doomed couple were left expiring behind a glass encasement like the laboratory human specimens Zola envisaged. In both instances, the tactic was perhaps justifiable. The characters at the end of *MSM*, it is implied, are AIDS-age victims of the impersonal search for sex, and ascend on trapezes to the great lavatory in the sky. The Zola adaptation made a point of inviting our inspection of this tragic story with a series of cinematic, alienatory devices of both scenography and sound. But even as a critic I felt cheated as a member of the audience.

The Glasgow Citizens, in many respects our most admirable theatre company, rarely returns to face the music of applause after two perfunctory cast line-ups (there was a time, in the early years of the current artistic regime, when curtain-calls were never taken at all). My own view is that if the audience is still clapping, the actors are called, and should return. If the play is an ensemble piece, each actor should take a solo turn before, or during, the company call. And if the piece is a hierarchic tragedy, or even a comedy with leading roles, each actor should take his own applause at some stage in the finale. The habit of perfunctory curtain calls is an upshot merely of perfunctory performances and the fear of there being no applause to endure when the time comes. Standing ovations are no place for a critic. But I like to know they are happening, and I reserve the right to cheer, or to boo, even if I rarely exercise that right.

Almost the most exciting moment of the entire year was during the frightful musical *Eurovision* at the Vaudeville. A few minutes into the second act, Alan Drury, a BBC radio producer and playwright who was accompanying Louise Doughty, the new critic on the Mail on Sunday, let rip a 'boo' of such snorting ferocity that it quite unsettled the hitherto undisturbed, incipiently comatose audience. Most people pretended they had not heard the eruption and went back to sleep. Drury was driven to his outburst by exasperation, and he probably should have held his peace until the curtain calls. But the incident reminded us, with an almost shivering intensity, of the important part we play as an audience at the theatre, and the nature of our collective intervention which derives in the first place from an individual membership of that audience, a membership that entitles us to the ultimate privilege of standing up and shouting approval, or its opposite, of walking out or, in special circumstances, governed by an agreement with the management, of simply writing a review in a national newspaper and getting paid for it.

Perhaps I enjoy pantomime because of the curtain calls. The cast invariably has a complete change of costume and appears, in sedate style and in pairs of rising hierarchical ascendancy, at the top of a staircase. I also love in pantomime the idea of audience participation which is not based on coercion. It is also important to remember that the economic cornerstone of most repertory theatres is its annual seasonal entertainment. I am as suspicious of people who say 'I don't like pantomime' as I am of people who say 'I don't like musicals': the limp generalisation betrays cultural snobbishness on the one hand and, invariably in my experience, a tin ear on the other. And it is always a dead giveaway when some pompous theatre management or other – this year it was Hampstead Theatre – advertises a December production as 'a perfect antidote to traditional pantomime', thereby implying an ignorant contempt for the popular art form. Pantomime is one of the great British inventions. Charles Dickens, who loved pantomime, said the form was a mirror of life. Leigh Hunt, our first theatre critic, said that 'not to like a pantomime is not to like love, not to take a holiday, not to remember we have been children ourselves.'

Pantomimes are never what they used to be. The Times said as much in 1846, well before the Victorian heyday of Augustus Harris's Drury Lane spectaculars. But the traditions of Joseph Grimaldi, 'the Garrick of clowns', and of Dan Leno, the first great dame, are honoured and reanimated each Christmas by performers like Roy Hudd, the perfect Idle Jack, and Jack Tripp, an elegant 72-year-old dancing dame blessed with a great pair of legs, both on the bill in *Babes in the Wood* at the Pavilion, Bournemouth, this year. Hudd and Tripp exemplify all my Christmas memories of pantomime, which are invariably associated with great vaudevillan artists: Stanley Baxter, Ken Dodd, Les Dawson, Danny La Rue ('I know what you're thinking, ladies; I wonder where he puts it'). I love the balance in pantomime between incipient licentiousness and moral rigour, the direct contact with the audience, the aspirations to magical escapism, the will to please, the holiday high spirits. And I even love pantomime when it goes wrong or looks cheap. I have quite enough expensive, serious-minded perfection during the rest of the year, thank you very much.

So, Christmas holds no terrors for me. This year we have snow, and the whitest Christmas in Britain for over 20 years. In West Yorkshire, where Sue, Thomas and I spend a few restful days with Sue's mother in a dramatic valley just outside Halifax, the hilltops are whitened with frost and snow on Christmas morning, the sun shines palely in a slate blue sky, and we enjoy an immensely jolly sit-down lunch in the local pub. On Boxing Day we go for a long walk and then drive to Harrogate for lunch in the Old Swan Hotel. This is a real treat, in spite of the fact that the bars and foyers are clogged up with crowds of cheerful wrinklies bumping into each other on their zimmer frames. 'What is all this,' I sarcastically enquire of our waitress, 'a block booking from Saga Holidays?' 'Yes, that's right!' she replies.

On the Bank Holiday Monday, the weather is still crisp and dry, the hilltops frosted, the roads relatively clear, so Sue and I drive over to Saltaire, the village built on the river Aire, near Bradford, by the philanthropic 19th-century manufacturer, Titus Salt, for his factory workers. Today, the converted Salts Mill is a wonderful, buzzing emporium run by Jonathan Silver which houses the most extensive collection of David Hockneys in Britain and plays regular host to such other Yorkshire cultural heroes as the poet Tony Harrison and the actor/director Barrie Rutter and his Northern Broadsides company. Jonathan is at work, as usual, on the premises, so we take coffee and fruit sodas with him in the restaurant before he shows us the latest Hockneys, a series of violently colourful abstract and geometric paintings that look very well against the deep red, newly painted brick walls of the upstairs gallery.

It snows heavily overnight and on the Tuesday morning we have a natural white carpet around the house laying four or five inches thick. After much digging and scraping, the drive and the pathways are cleared. A thaw quickly sets in under the mid-day sun and the afternoon rain ensures that we are not trapped or isolated, a frequent occurrence in this part of the world. Our holiday break is completed, surprise surprise, by a visit to the theatre. Halifax, whose old industrial town centre has been imaginatively restored around the architectural glories of the Gilbert Scott church, the Venetian-style Piece Hall, Wainwright's Tower and Sir Ernest Hall's magnificently reanimated Dean Clough warehouse complex, is now the home of Northern Ballet. The company is occupying the Victoria Theatre with a new production of *Cinderella*. The witty and vigorous new score by Paul Feeney, the choreography by artistic director Christopher Gable, the magical designs by Tim

Hatley and the sheer bubbling effervescence of the young company, all contribute to an evening, as the critics might say, of sheer delight. The audience is wildly appreciative, and the curtain calls, needless to say, are sensational.

## Ring out the old, ring in the new

THE YEAR HAS ENDED with a nice little babble of controversy initiated by a lecture to be delivered in the New Year by the outstanding playwright of the old one, David Hare. Hare suggests that the theatre is unfashionable because journalism treats theatre with disdain. These thoughts were prompted by an encounter with Peter York, a 'style journalist' who first identified the 'Sloane Rangers' in the 1980s, at a farewell party for the defeated Labour Party leader Neil Kinnock. On being introduced to Hare, York asked, 'Are you the one who wrote the play where that baby is stoned in its pram?' The inference Hare draws is that a reasonably intelligent person in the media or its allied trades thinks 'controversial' or 'left-wing' playwright, presses a button and comes up with that 1965 image of the layabouts pelting a baby with stones in Edward Bond's *Saved*. Hare says that York would never have confused Manfred Mann with the man who sang 'Jailhouse Rock', nor designer Jeff Banks with 'the one who runs Gap,' nor Gillian Armstrong with her fellow feminist film maker Jane Campion (the one who made *The Piano*). The proper attitude of any successful 'style journalist' to the theatre, concludes Hare, 'had immediately to be one of boastful ignorance.' The arts correspondent of the Independent, David Lister, responds by saying that Hare is right; theatre is not 'trendy' and should jolly well try and become more so. And Jenny Topper, artistic director of the Hampstead Theatre, rallies behind Lister and says that 'unless we grab the interest of a younger audience, theatre will be dead within 25 years.'

Becoming trendy and 'grabbing' younger audiences are the last things the theatre should be self-consciously doing. If it is any good it will do that automatically. The theatre must cherish its specialness: a devotion to ideas of truth in performance and production, a respect for its audience's intelligence, and a sense of its own history. I think Hare has a point in noting the media's increasing trivialisation of actors and theatre writing. Every day, some journalist or other says that the theatre is boring, or boasts that he or she never goes within spitting distance of a proscenium arch. But most people in the country, including those who do not go to the theatre themselves, do not share this journalistic contempt for the medium. It is indeed a depressing fact that many people who work on arts pages these days do not take the theatre all that seriously. And Hare is correct in identifying a sort of spiritual poison in the water. To admit to liking the theatre is seen to be a sign of weakness or silliness. And yet if I stay at home and watch television I rarely see anything fictional – no, not a play by Dennis Potter, nor a series by Alan Bleasdale or Andrew Davies – that begins to approximate in talent, authenticity, daring and imagination to most of what I see night in, night out, in the theatre. And I suppose the theatre critic, in spite of clearly having a vested professional interest, stands in some ways as a final bulwark against an engulfing tidal wave of hype, second-hand smugness and cultural indolence.

Theatre haters used to be intellectual snobs or moralists. Plato admired Aeschylus and Sophocles but thought everyone else a waste of time and the theatre, on the whole, a swamp of grossness and impropriety. Several centuries later, Jeremy Collier, in his *Short View of the Immorality and Profaneness of the English Stage* (1698), excoriated the Restoration dramatists we nowadays revere and effectively drove Congreve from the theatres, an act of vandalism for which his name shall be reviled in perpetuity. Puritanical objections to the theatre have been replaced nowadays by something else; a sort of blasé, know-nothing contempt which finds the whole business old-fashioned and either naff or distasteful, or possibly both. Theatre does something to people, gets up their noses and under their skins. And the majority of commentators in the media, secretly aware, and envious, of the fact, seek to trivialise that power lest the magical, life-changing properties of theatre diminish and swamp the evanescent cultural values that are more readily and habitually endorsed.

*This* is I think the point Hare is making, and a very serious point it is, too. On the last day of the year Bernard Levin rolls into action in The Times to put Hare in his place. He challenges him to admit that fully 97 per cent of plays that are staged are rubbish without a redeeming feature. His proof for this exaggerated statistic? The fact that he, Levin, has spent hundreds of evenings in the theatre. I think Levin, though amusing, is wrong. There are bad evenings to be had in the theatre; but these days, there are indeed so many evenings to be had in the theatre, that you can, with a little care and attention, avoid the worst of them quite easily. Milton Shulman weighs in on the same theme, turning his fire on the critics and sneering at any sign of undue appetite for the job or sense of duty in its execution: 'The present crop of regular critics are devotees of theatre. They will travel to distant, unsalubrious [sic] places, sit in playhouses the size of telephone kiosks on back-breaking benches, try to find something kindly to say about the most formidable rubbish, and give the benefit of the doubt to any performer with a smidgeon of talent.' Shulman's stance, like Levin's, is adversarial before he begins. The difference between them, of course, is that, in his heyday, Levin was a brilliant and destructive drama critic on the Daily Express and the Daily Mail; the minute he graduated from the popular journals to the Sunday Times, he discovered he really didn't have all that much to say about a theatre which had broadened its constituency and radicalised its obsessions. Sniping was no longer enough, and Levin honestly admitted that he simply did not have the stomach for a more protracted war of attrition. Life, he felt, was too short to bother with playwrights called David, Howard or Trevor. I can fabricate the put-downs as well as the next man when required, but I tend not to go out in the evening with that possibility uppermost in my mind. If that confession makes me a devotee, so be it, and if it makes be an unabashed enthusiast, I shall readily own up to the charge. For devotion and enthusiasm are indeed unfashionable, unprized qualities in arts commentary in these dog days of reactionary bromide on the one hand and cheer-fully paraded Philistinism on the other. The vocational dignity and intellectual respectability of the critic are not virtues particularly worth defending; his independence of spirit and freedom of

expression most certainly are. And a critic, even a retired critic like
Shulman or Levin, makes an ass of himself when he exposes the
limitations of his knowledge and cultural experience by declaring,
as Levin declared in his end-of-year Times article, and without a
jot of remorse or self-deprecation, that indeed, à propos of Hare's
comments on Peter York's inability to distinguish between Edward
Bond and Hare himself, he, Levin, had never consciously so much
as heard of any of the other names Hare had cited. Never heard of
Manfred Mann, or Jeff Banks, or 'Jailhouse Rock,' or Gap, or
Gillian Armstrong, or Jane Campion. Where do these commentators live? To whom do they speak? With whom do they travel?
What do they do in the day time? What, in short, is their
connection to the imperfect world they describe, beyond their own
confidence of their place in it and their right to vent their
considered opinions?

Critics are obliged to be critical of the culture produced by their
times. But they also have some sort of obligation to live in those
times. I am frequently embarrassed by my lack of knowledge of
certain kinds of music and whole areas of literature and the visual
arts. But I don't think I'm ever proud of that ignorance, and I try
assiduously to repair the gaps whenever I can. The trouble today is
that the minute a critic, or even an artist, puts his head above the
parapet on the subject of the intrinsic meritoriousness or importance of art, the canons of derision are fired from every quarter.
Our national talent for theatre is rapidly being corroded by our
national talent for denigration.

In this climate, the critic's task is clear: to fight for the serious
assessment of the theatre in every word he writes, whether the performance is a farce, a tragedy, a musical, an installation, a serious
new play, a dance drama, a political cabaret or a one-man show.
And even though the subsidised theatre is under threat from
economic cuts, and the West End struggling to survive, the critic
should beware those wiseacres who counsel only 'supportive'
writing designed to keep the show on the road and the theatres
open at all costs. Hard times may call for desperate measures, but
they also call for tougher criticism. If you knock the hell out of
everything, goes the argument, you will have no shows left to

review. Poppycock and balderdash. Bland, kind and 'supportive' critical writing merely alienates readers and theatre-goers, as well as contributing to a sense of conspiratorial clubbiness.

The trick is to be tough, but to support your opinions with arguments and description. All criticism is subjective. But all subjective criticism is a pain. The value set by an individual critical judgement will only rise if the reader considers that the critic has earned the right to his opinion, and that he writes blisteringly well. The minor consolation of the professional critic can only be that theatre artists themselves respect your efforts while understandably hating the fact that you're making them. As Sir John Gielgud used to say of reading Kenneth Tynan in full flight: 'It's wonderful when it isn't you.'

This year may have been one of only average significance, but the same could be said of almost every other theatre year, with its inevitable roster of highs and lows, triumphs and disasters, flash points of debate and troughs of inanity. The creative theatre moves on, its lights on the blink and its spirit under threat. For, wherever people gather in a community, from Glasgow to Plymouth, from Montreal to Sarajevo, there will be a performance; and, with any luck, a critic on the aisle with a notebook, ready and eager to make an account of the proceedings and to remind his fellow creatures of their shared, flawed and glorious humanity. Tynan discovered early on in his career that the theatre was not apart from life. It was a part of life. There is, in truth, no such thing as an average year. Roll on such another. I'll bounce around as best I may and hope to catch some pleasure on the wing.

# *Index*

# INDEX

Abelson, Edward 102
Abelson, James 102, 103
Abelson, Jean 102, 166
*Absence of War, The* 149, 152-4, 186
Adler, Larry 86-7
Agate, James ix, 9, 10, 84, 111, 156
*All God's Chillun' Got Wings*, ix
Allam, Roger 91
*American Clock, The* 34
Amis, Kingsley, 142
Amis, Martin, 142
Anderson, Kevin 51
Anderson, Lindsay 180
*Angels in America* 134-5, 182, 185
*Anna Christie* 4
Ansorge, Peter 12, 71
*Arcadia* 58-60
*Archers, The* 2
Armstrong, Alun 91
Armstrong, Gillian 194, 197
Armstrong, William 184
Ascherson, Neil 63
Ashcroft, Peggy 18
Ashford, John 76
*Aspects of Love* 51, 56-7

*At the Black Pig's Dyke* 185
Atkin, Pete 33
Atkins, Eileen 20, 48
Atkinson, Brooks 15
Atkinson, Rowan, 52, 128
Aukin, David 180
Ayckbourn, Alan 5, 120

*Babes in the Wood* 191
*Backroom Boys, The* 12
Bailey, Derek 41, 42, 44-5
Bailey, Gill 41, 42, 44-5
Baker, Janet 162
Banks, Jeff 194, 197
Barba, Eugenio 75
Barker, Howard 6, 44
Barnes, Clive 16
Barnes, Julian 140
*Barnum* 188
Barrit, Desmond 91
Barron, Christopher 101
Bartlett, Neil 130, 135, 180, 183, 186
Bartlett, Peter 45, 76
Barton, John 86, 178
Bassett, Linda 184
Bassey, Shirley 122
Bates, Alan 5

Baxter, Stanley 191
Beadle, Jeremy 118-9
Beattie, Johnny 133
Beaumont, Hugh ('Binkie') 2, 5, 94
Beckett, Samuel 6, 16, 171, 175
Benchley, Robert 187-8
Benjamin, Louis 4
Bennett, Alan 5, 16
Berkoff, Steven 3, 172, 182
Berry, Cicely 168
*Best of Friends, The* 36
Biggins, Christopher 2-3, 94
Billington, Michael 3, 15, 16, 18, 19, 66, 85, 91, 112, 113, 151, 167, 182-3, 187
*Birthday Party, The* 16
Black, Don 51, 56
Blakemore, Michael 5
Bleasdale, Alan 162, 195
*Bluebeard's Castle* 81
Bogdanov, Michael 3, 150
Bolton, Erica 41, 42, 45
Bond, Edward 6, 194, 197

Bond, Samantha 169-70

Borkowski, Mark 118-20

Boyd, Michael 77

Boyle, Katie 94

*Boys from the Black Stuff, The* 162

Bradwell, Mike 12

Brady, Ian 73

Bragg, Melvyn 46, 50, 116, 167

Branagh, Kenneth 52, 80, 85, 91, 164-5, 186

Brassard, Marie 82

*Brassneck* 149

Brecht, Bertolt 6, 133, 171

Brenton, Howard 6, 47, 74, 149

Brien, Alan 112, 139-40

Brierley, David 166

Brightman, Sarah 50, 54

*Broken Jug, The* 133, 136

Brome, Richard 22

Brook, Peter 11, 29, 75, 79, 84, 150, 175-9

Brooke, Peter 94-5

Broughton, Pip 107-8

Brown, Ivor 145

Brown, Tina 70

Bruce, Brenda 168

Bryant, Michael 154

Bryden, Bill 150

Buchan, James 100-2

Buckman, Rob 32-3

Buggy, Niall 160

Burchill, Julie 71

Burgess, Anthony 71-3

Burke, David 97

Burton, Richard 151

Buzo, Alexander 12

Byrne, Gay 108

Cadieux, Anne-Marie 82

Calder, David 91

Callow, Simon 189

Campbell, Ken 149, 150, 152, 172, 173, 186

Campion, Jane 194, 197

*Carousel* 26-7, 28

Carr, Walter 133

Carteret, Anna 48

Cashin, Fergus 112

Cass, Geoffrey 166

*Cats* 31, 36, 56, 57

Chaillet, Ned 99, 150

Chapman, Guy 183

Chéreau, Patrice 22

*Cherry Orchard, The* 101, 157

Chisholm, Jimmy 77

Christie, Julie 48

Christopher, James 121, 182-3

*Churchill Play, The* 149

*Cinderella*, 192

Čirilov, Jovan 108-9

*Class Enemy* 46-7

*Clockwork Orange, A* 72

*Cocktail Party, The* 20

Codron, Michael 3-5, 11, 94

*Comedians* 149

*Conference of the Birds* 29

Cook, Christopher 60-1

Cooper, James 8-10

Corduner, Allan 184

*Coriolanus* 79-82, 83, 188-9

Costigan, George 162

Cottrell, Richard 32-3

Courtenay, Tom 5

Coveney, Martin 8, 10, 88-9

Coveney, Thomas x, 58, 103, 112-3, 123, 124, 126, 136-7, 142, 167, 191

Covington, Julie 32-3

Cowan, Theo 118, 121

Coward, Noël 5, 8, 49, 94, 96

Cowley, Graham, 182-3

*Crazy for You* 1, 3-4

Crawford, Michael 188

Crewe-Read, David 53

Crimp, Martin 181

Crowley, Bob 27, 155

Crowley, Mart 94

*Crucible, The* 100-1

Cryer, Barry 129-30

Curtis, Richard 52

Cushman, Robert 112

*Daisy Pulls It Off*, 49, 50

Daldry, Stephen 98-9, 153, 184

*Dancing at Lughnasa* 105, 106

Daniels, Sarah 184

Darras, Jacques 23

Davies, Andrew 195

Davies, Russell 32-3, 95

Dawson, Les 191

de Angelis, April 184

de Jongh, Nicholas 3, 17, 18, 167, 171, 172, 182-3, 187

de la Tour, Frances 67

de Wend Fenton, Rose 76

*Death of a Salesman* 34

Dee, Jack 136

*Deep Blue Sea, The* 18, 186

*Déjàvu*, 17

del Rio, Dolores, 76
Delaney, Frank 129
Delfont, Bernard 1
Dench, Judi 169
Dent, Alan ('Jock')
    10
*Desire Under the*
    *Elms* 21-5
*Destiny of Me, The* 37
Devine, George 159
Dewe Matthews,
    Johnny 139
Dickens, Charles 191
Dickson, Barbara 162
Dimbleby, Jonathan
    167
*Doctor Faustus Lights*
    *the Lights*, 131-2
Dodd, Ken 191
Donnellan, Declan
    116
Dossé, Philip 69
Doughty, Louise 190
Downie, Penny 168
*Dragon's Trilogy, The*
    79, 82
Drummond, John 60,
    76, 131
Drury, Alan 190
Dunbar, Adrian 184

Eddington, Paul 16,
    19-20
Edgar, David 24-5
Edmonds, Richard
    160
Edwardes, Jane 18,
    182-3
Elliott, Michael 101
Elton, Ben 5-6
Emerson, Sally 69-70
Emmanuel, Alphonsia
    154
*Europeans, The* 44-5
*Eurovision* 190
Evans, Harold 70
Everett, Rupert 185
*Evita* 51, 52, 55, 56

*Ewartung* 81, 134
Eyre, Peter 174
Eyre, Richard 41, 45,
    47-8, 155, 156, 178

*Falkland Sound* 184
*Father's Day* 185
Feaver, William 62,
    140
Feeney, Paul 192
Fenby, Jonathan x, 65,
    144
Ferris, Pam 181, 183-
    4
Fielding, Harold 4
Filer, Roger 4
Fingleton, David 151
Fleetwood, Susan 174
Foot, Michael 141
Ford Davies, Oliver
    154
*42nd Street* 40
Fox, Angela 94
Fox, Edward 5
Fox, Robert 4, 94
Fox-Cumming, Ray
    102, 167
Frayn, Michael 5, 64,
    140, 186
French, Sean 139
French, Philip 59-60,
    62, 139-41, 143
Friedman, Clair 181
Friedman, Maria 16,
    181, 184
Friedman, Sonia 181,
    182, 183
Friel, Anne 107-8
Friel, Brian 104-8
Frost, David 167, 169
Fry, Christopher 2,
    176
Fry, Stephen 6, 52

Gable, Christopher
    192
Gagnon, Gerald 82
Gale, John 2-4

Gale, Listel 2-3
Gambon, Michael 91-
    2
Garland, Patrick 94
Gaskill, William 180
*Ghosts* 85, 87, 92,
    168, 182
Gielgud, John 28, 36,
    80, 169-70, 188,
    198
Gill, Peter 75
Gilliatt, Penelope 16
Glen, Iain 77, 186
Glover, Brian 48
*Goodbye Girl, The* 35
Grade, Michael 140
Gravenor, Barbara
    146
Gray, Simon 5, 126
*Greeks, The* 150, 178
Greenspan, David 34
Grier, Christopher 98
Griffiths, Richard 102
Griffiths, Trevor 47,
    149
Grimaldi, Joseph 191
Gross, John 105, 139,
    152-3
Grotowski, Jerzy 75
Guinness, Alec 5, 77
Gummer, John
    Selwyn 52
Gurdon, Madeleine 53

Hack, Keith 11
Hadary, Jonathan 37
*Hair* 2, 167
Hale, Georgina 162
Hall, Lucy 97
Hall, Peter 3, 11, 16,
    47, 48, 101, 126,
    150, 159, 168, 178,
    188
*Hamlet* 24, 27-8
Hampton, Christopher
    16, 51, 56
Hands, Terry 86, 90,
    162, 173

Hansford Johnson, Pamela 73
*Hapgood* 59
Hare, David 5, 47, 74, 149-55, 171, 173, 180, 181-3, 185, 186, 194-7
Harlech, Pamela 172
Harris, Amanda 91
Harris, Bob 90
Harris, Pamela 89-92, 165, 166
Harrison, Tony 192
Hart, Charles 56
Hastings, Max 153
Hatley, Tim 192-3
Hattersley, Roy 132-3, 152-3
Havergal, Giles 11, 159, 162
Haynes, Jim 130, 131
Hazelton, Fran 142-3
Hedley, Philip 8
Helpmann, Robert 10
Hemming, Sarah 58-9
Henri, Adrian 131
Henriques, Kevin 7, 12, 47, 63, 90
Hepple, Peter 18, 129-30
Herbert, Susannah 165
*Here* 186
Hewison, Robert 105, 107-8
Higgins, Clare 186
Higgins, Paul 154
Hill, Bernard 162
Hobson, Harold 5, 15-16, 111-2, 156
*Hobson's Choice* 29-30
Hockney, David 192
Hoffman, Dustin 32, 34
Holden, Anthony 11, 70
Holland, Mary 105, 107-8

Holland, Peter 165
Holm, Ian 47, 173, 186
Holmes à Court, Robert 4, 53
Holt, Thelma 94
Hope-Wallace, Philip 112, 161-2
Hopkins, Anthony 73-4
Horniman, Annie 158-9
Horsley, Chris 111
Howard, Alan 77, 186
Hudd, Roy 191
Hughes, Dusty 11-12
Hughes, Robert 73
Hughes, Ted 167-8
Hulme, Alan 100, 160
Hunt, Leigh 115-6, 191
Hyman, Bernard 93, 95, 102-4, 166
Hyman, Nigel 103
Hyman, Sue 41, 76, 93-6, 103, 123-6, 166, 174, 191-2
Hytner, Nicholas 2, 21, 27, 30

Ignatieff, Michael 155
*Ik, The* 29, 178
Iles, Paul 135-6
*Illuminatus* 150
*Importance of Being Earnest, The* 4, 29, 157
*In the Native State* 60
Ingleby, Grace 102-3
Ingrams, Richard 26-8
*Irma la Douce* 16, 176
Irons, Jeremy 12, 169
Isaacs, David 160
Isitt, Debbie 183
*It's a Great Big Shame!* 185

Jackson, Barry 158-9
Jackson, Glenda 88
Jackson, Richard 15
Jacobi, Derek 169, 186
*Jamais Vu* 172, 186
James, Clive 33, 62
James, Peter 162
James-Moore, Jonathan 32-3
Jameson, Derek 52
Jefford, Barbara 90
*Jeffrey Bernard is Unwell* 62-3
Jeffreys, Stephen 22, 180-3
Jenkins, Martin 162
*Jesus Christ Superstar* 50, 55, 56
Jones, George 153
*Jovial Crew, A* 22
*Julius Caesar* 133
*Jumpers* 59
*Juno and the Paycock* 160

Kahn, Madeline 36
Kaufman, Gerald 152-3
Kaye, Danny 8
Keeler, Ruby 40
Keith, Penelope 5, 94
Kellaway, Kate 140-1, 146
Kelner, Simon 103-4
Kenyon, Nicholas 58
Kerr, Walter 15, 187
Kestelman, Sara 91
Key, Phil 160
Kilroy, Thomas 22
King, Francis 139
*King Lear* 22, 67-8, 73, 74, 85, 91, 95, 165, 175, 176, 185
Kingston, Jeremy 121
Kingston, Philip 181
Kinnock, Glenys 46
Kinnock, Neil 45-6, 47, 149, 152-3, 167, 194

Klaić, Dragan 45
*Knuckle* 5
Kramer, Larry 37
Kretzmer, Herbert 18,
    19, 90, 171
Kulukundis, Eddie
    165
Kureishi, Hanif 140
Kustow, Michael 41,
    42, 44-5
*Kvetch* 172

La Rue, Danny 191
*Lady Chatterley's
    Lover* 70-1
Land, David 4
Langhoff, Matthias
    22-3, 25
Larkin, Philip 5, 142
Lau, Patrick 12
Lawrence, Maureen
    185
Lawson, Wilfrid 150-
    1
Lee, Hermione 32,
    142-3
Leigh, Andrew 162
Leigh, Mike 102-4,
    126-7, 185
Leigh-Hunt, Barbara
    154, 169
Leno, Dan 191
Lenz, Jacob 133
Lepage, Robert 76,
    79-84, 131, 134
Lerner, Alan Jay 10
*Les Atrides* 43, 150
*Les Misérables* 18, 31
Levin, Bernard 19, 90,
    115, 196-7
Levon, Katrina 154
Lewenstein, Oscar
    180
*L'homme qui* 174
*Libertine, The* 181
*Lila, the Divine Game*
    7
Lindsay, Robert 6

*Lipstick on Your
    Collar* 71
Lister, David 194
Lively, Penelope 142
Livingstone, Jack 100
Livingstone, Janice
    100
Lloyd Webber,
    Andrew 1-2, 13,
    49-57, 121-2, 171
Lloyd Webber, Julian
    50, 55
Logan, Jimmy 133
*Long and the Short
    and the Tall, The*
    10
*Look Back in Anger*
    17, 25, 159, 172
*Lord of the Flies, The*
    176
*Lost in Yonkers* 159
*Love Song for Ulster*
    152
Lowe, Rob 94
Lucie, Doug 128
LuPone, Patti 51, 52,
    186
Lynne, Gillian 36
Lyubimov, Yuri 75,
    178

McAnally, Ray 11
MacBain, Kenny 12
McCallum, John 94
McCarthy, Sean 105
McDiarmid, Ian 91
MacDonald, Robert
    David 134
MacDonald, Sharman
    184
McGlone, Jackie 78
McGough, Roger 131
McGrath, John 162
McHugh, Tina 92
McIlvanney, Hugh 64,
    144
McIntosh, Genista 175
McIntyre, Clare 184

McKellen, Ian 156,
    188-9
MacLean, Jack 78
McMaster, Brian 131,
    132-4
MacMillan, Joyce 160
MacMillan, Kenneth
    27
McTeer, Janet 185
*MSM* 189
*Macbeth* 77, 79, 82-3
*Machinal* 153, 173,
    186, 188
Mackenzie, Ruth 83-4
Mackintosh, Cameron
    1-4, 52
*Mahabharata, The* 29,
    150, 176
Malkovich, John 34, 97
Mamet, David 34, 80,
    97, 186
Manfred Mann 194,
    197
Mansfield, Blagdon 9
Manville, Lesley 184
*Marat/Sade, The* 176
Marcus, Frank 112
Margolyes, Miriam
    174
Mason, Brewster 88-9
Mason, David 53
Mason, Jackie 37-40
Mason, Patrick 105
Maud, Jane 91
Maude, Caroline 87, 92
Maugham, Susan 133
Maury, Dominic 87
Maury, Olive 87
Maxwell, Robert 52,
    53, 189
Mayall, Rik 5-6
*Maybe* 99-101
*Me and My Girl* 6, 160
Medved, Michael 68
Mencken, H L 114
*Merchant of Venice,
    The* 85, 161-2, 165,
    169-70

*Midsummer Night 's Dream, A* 11, 82, 83, 175, 176
Miller, Arthur 11, 30, 34, 100-1
Miller, Jonathan 19, 67, 132, 134, 146
Mitchell, Adrian 116
Mitchell, Katie 87, 92, 168
Mnouchkine, Ariane 43, 150
Montagu, Helen 5, 182
*Moonlight* 173-4, 186
Morahan, Christopher 48
Morley, Robert 176, 188
Morley, Sheridan 2, 15, 17-18, 113, 123, 156, 160
Morris, Mark 131, 132
Morris, Michael 76, 84
Morrison, Bill 152
Morrison, Blake 63
Morton, Bruce 137
Motion, Andrew 141-2, 159
*Much Ado About Nothing* 185
Mullarkey, Neil 178
Murdoch, Iris 168
Murdoch, Rupert 68-70, 73, 74
*Murmuring Judges* 149, 151, 152, 154
Murphy, Hayden 130
Murray, Braham 101
*My Heart 's a Suitcase* 184
*Mysteries, The* 150

Nachoma, Rivka 33, 35-6
Nathan, David 17, 18, 90

Nathan, George Jean x, 114
Naughton, John 62, 145
Neal, Lucy 61, 76
Neeson, Liam 4
Neil, Andrew 52, 68
*New Menoza, The* 133
*Nicholas Nickleby* 150, 178
*Night After Night* 130, 186
*Night of the Iguana, The* 20
Nightingale, Benedict 17-19, 58, 99-100, 102, 113, 167, 172, 181, 187
*No Man's Land* 20
*No Sex, Please, We're British* 2
Noble, Adrian 86, 164-6, 168, 178
Nunn, Trevor 2, 11, 50, 51, 55, 58-9, 86

Oakes, Meredith 133
Oakes, Philip 139-40
O'Connor, Garry 12
*Oh! Calcutta!* 11
Okri, Ben 142
Oldman, Gary 184
*Oleanna* 34, 97-8, 99, 177, 186
Olivier, Laurence 2, 8, 52, 101, 159, 178, 188
Olivier, Richard 174
O'Neill, Eugene ix, 4, 21-5
*Orghast at Persepolis* 29
Ormerod, Nick 116
Orton, Joe 6
Osborne, Charles 27-8
Osborne, John 6, 17-18, 25, 117, 159, 171, 172

Osborne, Nigel 10, 12
*Our Country's Good* 181, 184
Owen, Michael 173

Pacino, Al 80-1
Paige, Deborah 96
Paige, Elaine 186, 188
Palin, Michael 116
Parry, Jann 62, 140, 142
Parry, Nina 178
Pasco, Richard 154
Paterson, Bill 46-7
Pearce, Garth 125
Pearce, Joanne 165, 168
Pearman, Michael 94
*Peer Gynt* 150-1
Pennington, Michael 169, 170
Pernak, Adam 181
*Persians, The* 131, 132
Peter, John 17-18, 19, 167, 187
Peters, Bernadette 35
*Phantom of the Opera, The* 51, 56
Piaf, 188
*Piano, The* 194
*Picture of Dorian Gray, The* 18, 185
Pimlott, Steven 55, 92
Pinnock, Winsome 181, 183
Pinter, Harold 5, 6, 16, 98, 145, 155, 171, 174, 186
*Pirates of Penzance, The* 4
Planchon, Roger 22
*Pocket Dream, The* 6
Poke, Greville 11
Pollard, Eve 122
Polo, Richard 94
Porter, Peter 142
Porter, Roy 58-60

Postlethwaite, Pete 162
Potter, Dennis 71, 195
Powell, Enoch 26
Pratt, Desmond 161
*Pravda* 74
Prem, Tara 48
Preston, Peter 65
Prince, Hal 51, 55
Prince Charles, HRH 68, 70, 164-7, 169
Prowse, Philip 11, 133
Pryce, Jonathan 162
Pulbrook, Susan 94

*Queen and I, The* 181
Quick, Diana 32
Quinn, Patricia 170

*Racing Demon* 149, 152, 154
Ratcliffe, Michael 62-3
Rawlings-Jackson, Vanessa 101
*Real Inspector Hound, The* 58
*Recruiting Officer, The* 181, 184
Redgrave, Vanessa 99-101
Redhead, Brian 167
Redington, Michael 36-7
Rees-Mogg, William 70-1, 73
*Requiem, The* 50
*Reservoir Dogs* 67, 74
Rhymes, Rupert 162
Rice, Tim 4, 50, 55-6
Rich, Frank 122
Richard, Cliff 122
Richard, Emily 170
Richardson, Natasha 4, 94
Rickman, Alan 174
Rigg, Diana 5
Ristić, Ljubisa 24

*Road* 181, 184
Roberts, Alison 165
Robertson, Liz 10
Robertson, Toby 11
Robeson, Paul 29
Robson, Robert 80
Roche, Billy 152
Rodway, Norman 168
Rosen, Michael 33
Rosenfeld, Jyll 38, 40
Ross, Jonathan 31, 40
Rowe, Clive 26, 28-9
Rowland, Millie 2, 94
Rowland, Toby 2, 4, 94
Rudman, Michael 2
Rundall, Jeremy 11
Rushdie, Salman 45-6
Rushton, Willie 129
Russell, Ken 71
Russell, Willy 162, 163
Russell Beale, Simon 68, 85, 91, 169, 170
Russell Brown, John 41
Rutter, Barrie 192
Rylance, Mark 173, 185

*Sabotage* 78-9
Sacks, Mel 39
Sacks, Oliver 174
Sams, Jeremy 184
*Sarajevo* 43-5
Sartre, Jean-Paul 74
*Saved* 194
Scarfe, Gerald 55
Schmidt, Michael 160
Scofield, Paul 10, 175, 176
Scott, Bob 101
*Seagull, The* 22
Sellars, Peter 131
Serban, Andrei 75, 150
*Serious Money* 184
Sessions, John 174

Shaffer, Peter 5, 168
Sharp, Lesley 184
Shaw, Fiona 153, 174, 186, 188
*She Would If She Could* 181
Shepard, Sam 34, 96
Shepherd, Ben 90
Sher, Antony 90, 91, 162, 173, 186
Sherrin, Ned 2-3, 18, 129, 160, 174
Shirley, John 146
Short, Martin 35
Shorter, Eric 99
Shulman, Milton 6, 19, 28, 90, 111, 171-2, 196-7
Siberry, Michael 186
*Silence of the Lambs, The* 73
Silver, Jonathan 192
Simon, Josette 30
Simpson, Michael 11
Sinden, Donald 2
*Sisters Rosensweig, The* 35-6
Smith, John 153
Smith, Maggie 4, 94, 140, 143, 186, 188
*Soldiers, The* 133
Sondheim, Stephen 51, 57
*Sound of Music, The* 2
Spall, Timothy 174
Spencer, Charles 18, 19, 113, 167, 187
Spriggs, Elizabeth 88
Squires, Dougie 10, 133
Stafford-Clark, Max 21-2, 98, 116, 170, 180-4
Stapleton, Anna 78
*Starlight Express* 50, 55, 57, 95
*States of Shock* 96-7
Steadman, Alison 126

Steel, David 129
Stein, Gertrude 131-2
Stein, Peter 71, 131, 133, 134, 150
Stephens, Robert 67, 85, 91, 150, 165, 169, 170, 185
Steven, Stewart 172-4
Stevens, Marti 94
Stevenson, Juliet 3, 91
Stewart, Ellen 75
Steyn, Mark 56
Stigwood, Robert 4
Stoppard, Tom 5, 13, 58-60, 128, 155, 173, 180, 186
Storey, David 3
Storry, Malcolm 91
Stothard, Peter 68-70, 73
Strachan, Geoffrey 178
Streep, Meryl 52
Strehler, Giorgio 22
Strong, Mark 154
Stuart, Chris 10
*Suddenly Last Summer* 94
*Sunset Boulevard* 1, 49, 51-2, 121-2, 186
Sweeting, Elizabeth 11
Syms, Sylvia 160

*Tamburlaine* 173
Taylor, Elizabeth 151
Taylor, Paul 19, 113, 167, 182, 187
*Tectonic Plates* 79
*Tell Me On a Sunday* 56
*Ten Days that Shook the World* 178
Thacker, David 168
Thaw, John 149, 152-3, 186
*Thérèse Raquin* 189
Thomas, Sian 174
Thompson, Emma 6

Thompson, Peter 121
Thornber, Robin 160
*Three Birds Alighting on a Field* 184
Thwaite, Anthony 142
Tinker, Jack 2, 13, 15, 18-19, 52, 90, 121, 129, 151, 160
*Tiny Alice* 11
*Titus Andronicus* 71-2
Toksvig, Sandi 6
Toll, John 12
Tomalin, Claire 140
*Top Girls* 184
Topper, Jenny 194
Townsend, Sue 181
Toynbee, Polly 154-5
*Travesties* 173
*Treatment, The* 84
Treglown, Jeremy 32
Trelford, Donald x, 62-4, 103, 145
Trelford, Kate 145
Trewin, J C 88
Tripp, Jack 191
Tuck, Lucy x, 144
Turner, John 90
Tutin, Dorothy 169
*Tutor, The* 133
Tweedie, Jill 139
*Twelfth Night* 142, 146
Tynan, Kenneth ix, 19, 44, 62, 115, 145, 175-6, 178, 198

Uglow, Jennie 142

Velder, Raol 37-9
*Venetian Twins, The* 85, 165-6
*Venus Observed* 2
Vidale, Thea 129
*View from the Bridge, A* 11
Vinaver, Michel 21, 25
Vincent Wallace, Hazel 11
*Visit, The* 178

*Waiting for Godot* 6, 171
Wallace, Neil 76, 79
Walters, Julie 162
Wanamaker, Zoë 170
Wandor, Michelene 61
Wardle, Irving 19, 112, 113-4, 167, 176, 187
Warnaby, John 90
Warner, David 11, 88
Warner, Deborah 71
Warner, Marina 139
Warner, Francis 16
*Warp, The* 150
Warrington, Don 162
*Wars of the Roses, The* 47, 88-9, 150
Wasserstein, Wendy 34, 35-6
Watkins, Alan 144
Webb, Danny 184
Weldon, Duncan 4
Wells, Stanley 165
Wertenbaker, Timberlake 181, 184
Wesker, Arnold 6, 21, 159-60, 162
West, Timothy 170
*Wexford Trilogy, The* 152
*Which Witch* 17
White, Michael 3-5
Whitman, Walt 27
Widdicombe, Gillian x, 44, 63
Wilde, Oscar 18, 29
Williams, Nigel 11, 33, 46-7
Williams, Tennessee 20, 34
Williamson, Malcolm 55
Wilson, Richard 184
Wilson, Robert 84, 131-2, 134-5
Wilton, Penelope 18, 47, 186

Wing-Davey, Mark 32
*Winter's Tale, The* 165
Wirthner, Naomi 96
Withers, Googie 94
Wolf, Matt 105, 182
Wolfit, Donald 188
*Wonderful Tennessee*
    105-8
Wood, John 169

Wood, Michael 32
Wood, Stephen 151
Woodall, James 178
Woods, Vincent 185
Woof, Emily 129
Worsley, T C 12
Worth, Irene 11
Wright, Nicholas 61,
    178

Wright, Stephen
    32
Wyatt, Stephen 32

York, Peter 194, 197
Young, B A
    ('Freddie') 7, 11,
    12, 47
Young, Martin 32